HISTORICAL ANALYSIS IN ECONOMICS

It is becoming increasingly apparent that economic policy is failing to resolve important economic problems at both the regional and global levels. While part of the blame may be attributed to politicians, there is a growing awareness that much of the fault rests with the economic profession itself. It is from this perspective that the authors of *Historical Analysis in Economics* approach their subject.

The authors argue that in order to give realistic policy advice it is necessary to have a good understanding of what is happening in the real world, as well as a good technical understanding of theoretical models. In practice, however, there is a mismatch between the nature of economic theory and the nature of economic reality. While most significant real-world problems emerge from longrun dynamic processes in society, economics is an abstract and deductive science that employs a shortrun static approach. The authors stress that if economics is to address the real problems in society it must develop path-dependent theoretical models and also attempt to reconstruct the dynamic process of change through time. In response to this crisis in the discipline, the objective of this book is to draw attention to the practical limitations of economics, and to suggest that deductive economics be modified and adapted through a closer relationship with economic history. The failure to do so could, the editor claims, result in economics losing its place as the premier policy adviser to national governments and international organizations. The authors are a group of international scholars, who draw on first-hand experience in Europe, the US and Pacific Rim. In examining the limitations of economic theory and the role that history can play in overcoming those limitations, the book defines a new role for economic history within the profession of economics.

Graeme Donald Snooks is Coghlan Professor of Economic History at the Institute of Advanced Studies, Australian National University, Canberra. He has held lecturing and research posts at Flinders University and the Universities of Queensland and Western Australia. He has published widely on the economic history of England and Australasia.

Also by Graeme Donald Snooks

DEPRESSION AND RECOVERY
Western Australia, 1929–1939

DOMESDAY ECONOMY
a new approach to Anglo-Norman History
(*with J. McDonald*)

EXPLORING SOUTHEAST ASIA'S ECONOMIC PAST
(*edited with A.J.S. Reid and J.J. Pincus*)

LAND AND SEA
the role of shipping in Australasian economic development
(*edited with J.J. Pincus*)

ECONOMICS WITHOUT TIME
a science blind to the forces of historical change

HISTORICAL ANALYSIS IN ECONOMICS

Edited by
Graeme Donald Snooks

London and New York

First published 1993
by Routledge
11 New Fetter Lane, London EC4P 4EE

Simultaneously published in the USA and Canada

First published 1993
by Routledge
11 New Fetter Lane
Simultaneously published in the USA and Canada
by Routledge
a division of Routledge, Chapman and Hall, Inc.
29 West 35th Street, New York, NY 10001

Typeset in September by Leaper & Gard Ltd, Bristol, England.
Printed and bound in Great Britain by
Biddles Ltd, Guildford and King's Lynn.

British Library Cataloguing in Publication Data
A catalogue reference for this book is available from the British Library
ISBN 0–415–08825–9

Library of Congress Cataloging in Publication Data
Historical analysis in economics/edited by Graeme Donald Snooks.
p. cm.
Includes bibliographical references and index.
ISBN 0–415–08825–9
1. Economics–Methodology–Congresses. 2. Economic history–
–Congresses. 3. Historical school of economics–Congresses.
I. Snooks, G. D. (Graeme Donald)
HB131.H57 1993
330′.072–dc20 93–3368
CIP

Dedicated to the pioneering realists in political economy

William Petty (1623–1687)
Gregory King (1648–1712)
Charles Davenant (1656–1714)

CONTENTS

FIGURES

TABLES

CONTRIBUTORS

Paul A. David	Professor of Economics, and William Robertson Coe Professor of American Economic History, Stanford University
Lionel Frost	Lecturer in Economic History, La Trobe University
Leslie Hannah	Professor of Economic History, London School of Economics
Timothy J. Hatton	Reader in Economics, University of Essex
G.R. Hawke	Director of Institute of Policy Studies, and Professor of Economic History, Victoria University of Wellington
Paul Johnson	Lecturer in Economic History, London School of Economics
Stephen Nicholas	Associate Professor of Economic History, University of New South Wales
David Pope	Professorial Fellow in Economic History, Research School of Social Sciences, Australian National University
Graeme Donald Snooks	Coghlan Professor of Economic History, Research School of Social Sciences, Australian National University
Jeffrey G. Williamson	Laird Bell Professor of Economics, Department of Economics, Harvard University

PREFACE

It has become increasingly apparent over the past few decades that economic policy is failing to resolve important economic problems at both the regional and global levels. While it is standard practice for economists to blame policy failures on politicians, some in the economics profession believe that much of the fault lies within rather than without. To give realistic policy advice it is necessary to have a good understanding of what is happening in the real world, as well as a good technical understanding of theoretical models. Some of us are not convinced that the present state of economics provides an adequate basis for understanding reality. While most of the significant real-world problems emerge from longrun dynamic processes in society, economics is an abstract and deductive science that employs a shortrun static approach to these problems. There is, in other words, a mismatch between the nature of economic theory and the nature of economic reality. If economics is to develop a realistic longrun dynamic approach, it must not only develop path-dependent theoretical models but also attempt to reconstruct the process of change through time. The objective of this book, therefore, is to draw attention to the practical limitations of economics, and to suggest, not that deductive economics be abandoned, but that it be modified through a closer relationship with economic history. If economics does not change along these lines, its position as the premier policy adviser to national governments and international organizations will be challenged by those from other academic disciplines, particularly by the new 'dismal scientists' – the radical ecologists.

In order to provide a forum for these fundamentally important issues, I convened a conference in the Research School of Social Sciences at the Australian National University in July 1991, with participants – including economists, economic historians, policy advisers, and official policy makers – from the UK, USA, New Zealand, and Australia. The conference theme was 'The role of longrun analysis in economics'. We found that there was considerable agreement about the difficulties that economics experiences in understanding reality and in providing an adequate basis for successful policy making. The consensus was that there exists an urgent need for a longrun approach to economics, and that this can best be achieved through a rigorous approach to economic history. This book presents a selection of the papers, subsequently revised, that were presented at the Longrun Conference.

On behalf of the authors in this volume, I would like to thank the following participants at the Longrun Conference for their challenging comments, which were helpful in revising the chapters in this book, and in writing the introduction. They include, in addition to the authors, Mac Boot, Peter Burn, Selwyn Cornish, John Edwards, John Gagg, Bob Gregory, Marnie Haig-Muir, Diane Hutchinson, Bob Jackson, Michael Keating, Philippa Mein Smith, Deborah Oxley, Gus Sinclair, Simon Ville, and Sam Williamson.

One aspect of the editor's role in a volume such as this is to impose uniformity of presentation on his contributors. In particular, he has to ignore any pleas for individuality or special consideration – except his own, of course. I have played the tyrant on one matter in particular. Despite the preferences of the contributors for either two separate words or two hyphenated words to describe the object of our interest, I have imposed one word – 'longrun' – throughout. My reason for committing this 'heresy' (according to my wife who is a professional editor) is that the longrun (and hence shortrun) is an integrated concept and, as such, it should be described by a single word.

As usual, I have received considerable assistance in the preparation of this book from the staff in my Department at the ANU. In particular I thank Ann Howarth and Barbara Trewin for assistance in organizing the Longrun Conference; Barry Howarth for the copy-editing and for preparing the index; Barbara Trewin, Ann Howarth, and Jeannie Haxell for the formatting and word processing.

Finally, I am delighted that Alan Jarvis at Routledge thought this project would make a worthwhile book.

GDS
Sevenoaks
Canberra

1

WHAT CAN HISTORICAL ANALYSIS CONTRIBUTE TO THE SCIENCE OF ECONOMICS?

Graeme Donald Snooks

INTRODUCTION

The most telling observation about modern economics is that the dimension of real time has been lost. As an abstract, deductive, and mathematical science, economics has focused upon shortrun, comparative-static analysis of both a partial and general kind. Within this frame of reference, economics has been highly successful. Microeconomic theory in particular – largely because of a more manageable scope of enquiry – is a very powerful tool for examining equilibrium conditions and outcomes. This is not at issue. What is of concern here is that the range of real-world problems which can be successfully analysed in this way is both limited – unnecessarily so – and limiting. The concerns of modern economics are not trivial, although there is some truth in Joan Robinson's jibe about the importance of analysing the price of a cup of tea, but they do not include the really big issues confronting human society at the present, and which are likely to dominate our future. This is not meant to dismiss important shortrun problems such as inflation or unemployment – problems that economists currently are having difficulties resolving – just the context in which they are analysed. The big issue facing human society today is how to achieve a balance between population increase, economic growth, and the dwindling stock of unpolluted natural resources, without economic and social collapse. This is an issue about the dynamics of human society on both a regional and global scale – an issue that transcends shortrun equilibrium analysis. The problem for economics is that it has very little to say about longrun dynamic processes.

If the most important and pressing problems require a realistic analysis of the dynamics of human society, and if modern economics is unable to tell us much about this matter, then how seriously should society take this science? No doubt the answer to this question will vary according to one's perspective. The concern in this book is more with what is required to give economics greater conviction when forced to face up to the larger issues confronting mankind. The argument here is that we should not abandon what has been achieved by deductive economics, rather we should augment it with an historical analysis of both shortrun and longrun economic problems – problems that are an integral part of the dynamic processes of human society. In this way it may even be possible to construct more realistic path-dependent models.

In order to highlight the limitations of economic theory in handling dynamic processes, this chapter will outline the timeless approach to economic change. It will be suggested that these limitations can be overcome by adopting an historical approach to economics in order to reconstruct real-world economic processes. The chapters in Parts II and III illustrate the way in which this can be achieved.

THE TIMELESS APPROACH

The limitations of the timeless approach to economic analysis can best be exposed by focusing upon the fundamentally important subject of economic growth. It is a subject of considerable interest to the profession, both past and present, but one that has proved frustratingly elusive for the deductive theorist. While growth has long been of interest to policy-makers, the first systematic treatment of the issue can be found in the works of the classical economists, including Adam Smith, Malthus, and Ricardo. This interest was carried forward by Marx; Schumpeter; Harrod and Domar; the neoclassicists, including Swan, Solow *et al.*; and more recently by the 'new' growth theorists. Without wanting to prejudge the outcome of the 'new' growth theory, it seems fair to conclude that the most impressive work on growth theory was produced before the First World War. The growth analysis of the classical economists – together with the work of those who relied heavily upon this foundation, including Marx and Schumpeter – was a central feature of their wider analysis of the capitalist economic system, and the insights it contains depend to a considerable degree on historical knowledge. Growth theory since the First World War, however, has been a highly specialized and largely detached area of study undertaken within the broader framework of economic analysis, rather than as an integral part of a grand system, and certainly without reference to historical reality. These more recent theories focus on a very limited number of variables and, as such, are of little use in explaining real-world, or historical, growth *processes*. What they can do, however, is to analyse a certain *outcome*, such as 'steady state', regular cycles, or convergence to or divergence from an equilibrium growth path. They can achieve this because they have been constructed to do so. As the perceived economic problems have changed, new models that can provide these outcomes have been constructed and then abandoned. There is no general theory that can encompass these *ad hoc* partial theories. No single theory can either explain all past growth outcomes (let alone processes) or successfully predict future growth outcomes.

The classical model of growth

What can the various growth models tell us about reality? Is it really possible to explain a process involving real time by adopting a timeless approach to model building? In order to address these and similar questions, a brief survey of the main types of growth models has been undertaken. The intention is to isolate and discuss the main features of these growth models in a general rather than a mathematical way. There are many good technical surveys elsewhere.[1]

The growth models of the classical school were concerned to examine and explain the dynamic forces underlying the British economic system of the eighteenth century. This interest was stimulated by a desire to ensure, through appropriate policies, that the British population gained the greatest material benefit from these forces, not only for its own sake, but also to achieve the greatest general progress of human civilization.[2] In the generalized classical system – in which there is one sector, agriculture (although this can be expanded to include other sectors), three factors of production (land, labour, and capital), and three corresponding economic groups (landlords, workers, and capitalists) competing for shares of the social surplus – the various elements of production, exchange, distribution, and accumulation are integrated to explain not only how the economy operates at a point in time but how it changes through time.[3]

Central to the process of growth is the accumulation of capital, which is stimulated by that part of the social surplus – profits – that accrues to capital. Only capitalists invest their surplus, because workers expend their wages entirely on the means of subsistence, and landlords devote their rents entirely to unproductive consumption. During a growth phase, the sequence of causation is as follows: profits rise; funds are invested in capital equipment, possibly embodying a degree of technological change (resulting in a further division of labour); the demand schedule for labour (MP_L) shifts to the right; nominal wages rise; population increases; the margin of cultivation is extended; diminishing returns in agriculture are encountered; production costs rise; profits are reduced (rents increase); and the rate of capital accumulation and population growth decline until eventually the economy reaches the stationary state. Although the classical economists understood that technological change and trade would delay the tendency towards the stationary state by shifting the demand schedule of labour outward, they believed that the ultimate fate of the mature capitalist economy was stagnation.

The fundamental flaw in this model, which J.S. Mill was supporting as late as the mid-nineteenth century, is that it was based upon assumptions that were not closely related to reality during the Industrial Revolution. As is well known, the classical economists underestimated the role of both technological change and international trade in counteracting the move to a steady-state equilibrium. In part this was because they focused upon a pre-industrial economy, and in part because they did not understand (as many still do not) the dynamics of pre-industrial societies. Had they been better historians they would have realized that the British feudal and medieval economic systems had experienced rapid growth (in per capita terms) involving technological change and international trade, as well as diminishing transaction costs owing to organizational change over prolonged periods of time. Technical change overwhelmed any tendency toward diminishing returns in agriculture, and international trade and foreign investment provided expanding opportunities for continued growth.

The timeless approach of the classical economists distorted their view, not only of the future, but also of the past. Their view of the past was obscured by the limitations of their abstract model, particularly concerning their theory of distribution. We have already seen that the classical economists regarded growth as a function of the proportion of the social surplus that found its way into the hands of capitalists, because both landlords and labourers used their shares unproductively. As feudal societies were dominated by powerful landlords, they argued, very little of the social surplus could have been invested productively, and hence feudal societies must have been unenterprising and largely stationary. This conclusion is important not because it was correct, which it certainly was not,[4] but because it became the conventional wisdom in England about pre-modern societies that has been subscribed to by economist and non-economist alike. Indeed it is still the basis of the explanation employed by some eminent scholars today.[5]

Marx's model of growth was a variation on the classical theme. While Marx accepted the importance of capital accumulation and its relationship to the *rate* of profits (rather than just the *size* of profits as in the classical model), he saw a greater role for technological change, which he regarded as the main driving force of the capitalist system, and the interaction with the world economy. On the other hand, he rejected the classical relationship between wages and population expansion, and substituted arguments about the 'reserve army of labour' and changing labour-force participation rates. Despite these changes to the classical argument, the outcome of Marx's model was much the same. Although capitalists attempt to maintain profits through innovation, the growing capital intensity of production (owing to the labour-saving nature of innovation) reduces the profit rate, places increasing pressure on wage rates, increases unemployment, and finally causes the capitalist system to collapse after experiencing increasingly severe fluctuations. Despite the many insights that Marx's economic system provided, it distorted his view of the past, present, and future. His view of reality was obscured, as it was for the other classical economists, by the inflexible use of theory. In Marx's case this largely involved adherence to the principle of dialectical materialism, which was a philosophical/political, rather than an economic, explanation of social change. He was committed to the idea of destructive class conflict – rather than the classical idea of creative competition – and an economic system that would generate this conflict. It did not seem to occur to him that such a system was economically irrational. Ironically the centrally determined system that replaced capitalism in some countries, notably in Eastern Europe, under the inspiration, if not the direction, of Marx was economically irrational and, as a result, finally collapsed at the end of the 1980s.

The Schumpeterian growth model

Schumpeter's growth model, like that of the classicists, was part of his theory of the entire capitalist system. Indeed, his concern was with dynamic processes underlying society as a whole. In his own words:

> Economic development is so far simply the object of economic history, which in turn is merely part of universal history, only separated from the rest for purposes of exposition. Because of this fundamental dependence of the economic aspect of things on everything else, it is not possible to explain *economic* change by previous *economic* conditions alone. For the economic state of a people does not emerge simply from the preceding economic conditions, but only from the preceding total situation.[6]

Needless to say, this is in marked contrast to the more narrowly focused growth theory that has emerged since the First World War.

Schumpeter's analysis begins with a discussion of 'the circular flow of economic life' in which all economic activity is repetitive, and undergoing a predictable routine. He focused upon an economic system in longrun general equilibrium, in which all factors are fully employed and which are 'paid' their marginal products, whether in the market or the household sectors. Economic growth only occurs when this longrun equilibrium is disturbed. And it is innovation that causes this 'disturbance': innovation embodied in new plant and equipment. Innovation of product or process in this model generates supernormal profits for the leading entrepreneur, which in turn encourages other entrepreneurs to follow suit. The original innovation may also call forth a series, or 'cluster', of complementary innovations. Accordingly there is a burst of investment financed by credit expansion, which in turn produces an increase in employment and output. As investment increases, and if there are no further innovations, profit rates fall until they reach normal levels, and new investment ceases. Once more we are in equilibrium.

As Schumpeter explains, the innovation-led boom 'altered the data of the system, upset its equilibrium, and thus started an apparently irregular movement in the economic system which we conceive as a struggle towards a new equilibrium position'.[7] In this model the progression from one equilibrium position to another passes through a cyclical movement of boom and depression. Schumpeter argues:

> the boom ... creates out of itself an *objective situation*, which, even neglecting all accessory and fortuitous elements, makes an end of the boom, leads *easily* to a crisis, *necessarily* to a depression, and hence to a temporary position of relative steadiness and absence of development.[8]

The boom involves a disequilibrium in which there is 'overproduction', 'skewness', 'the appearance of disproportionality ... between quantities and prices of goods' and between new and old businesses and industries, and also speculation.[9]

The depression is an inevitable outcome of this disequilibrium and 'the driving impulse of the process of depression cannot theoretically stop until it has done its work, has really brought about the equilibrium position . . . Nor will this process be interrupted by a new boom before it has done its work in this sense' owing to the uncertainties about 'new data' which make the 'calculation of new combinations impossible'.[10]

Schumpeter's theoretical discussion of the growth process is clearly informed by observation of historical processes of change. In fact, it is probably the most successful and influential attempt to use an inductive–deductive approach in the history of economic analysis. This was due in part to Schumpeter's training, which was both theoretical (without being mathematical) and empirical, and in part to his genius for observing and interpreting real economic processes. He was, as will be explained in Chapter 3, a 'realist' rather than a 'gameplayer'. Accordingly, it is to Schumpeter rather than any other growth theorist that those who wish to reconstruct real-world growth processes turn.

Schumpeter's overall grasp of reality was superior to that of the classical economists and Marx. He was able to distinguish between the capitalist and the entrepreneur, as well as between invention and innovation; he saw the connection between innovation and the rate of profit; he could see how technological change could prevent the emergence of the steady state; and he was able to integrate a theory of cyclical fluctuations with a theory of growth. His model does not just provide a method for thinking about causal relationships, it provides an unparalleled basis for understanding and reconstructing real, or historical, processes of change.

Keynesian and neoclassical growth models

Modern growth theory, which has emerged largely since the Second World War, can be distinguished from earlier work by its more abstract, ahistorical, and disembodied nature. The initial work by R.F. Harrod (1939) and E.D. Domar (1946) was inspired by Keynes' *General Theory* (1936).[11] As is well known, the *General Theory* presented a macroeconomic model that attempted to show how it was possible for short-term equilibrium to occur at a less than the full-employment level of national income. As Keynes' analysis was comparatively static in nature, Harrod attempted to translate this system into dynamic terms. The attempt is to be applauded, but the results, inevitably, are disappointing. Unfortunately, Harrod, unlike Schumpeter, does not provide us with any insight concerning dynamic *processes*. To Harrod, dynamic analysis meant merely the analysis of secular changes in output, capital accumulation, employment, and inflation. While he recognized technology, along with these variables, as an important determinant of growth, and as capable of affecting the ratio of required capital to output (depending on whether it is 'neutral', 'capital-saving', or 'labour-saving') it is not treated endogenously. In comparison with Schumpeter's analysis, this model is rather one-dimensional.

Basically Harrod was interested in the possible tension between the conditions required for full employment and those required to achieve a 'steady state of growth'. He employed the Keynesian variables of income, investment, and saving, although he thought of them in growth-rate, rather than absolute, terms. Briefly, his argument was that if growth were to achieve a steady full-employment path, the actual rate of growth (which requires the rate of capital accumulation to equal the *ex post* ratio of saving to income) would have to equal both the rate of growth that would satisfy economically rational entrepreneurs (the 'warranted' rate, or what would now be called a rational expectations equilibrium), and the rate of growth that achieves full employment with no inflation (the 'natural' rate). Any divergence of the 'actual' rate of growth from the 'warranted' rate will, through the acceleration principle, cause a cumulative divergence of an economy's growth path towards an inflationary or deflationary state. Steady, or equilibrium, growth is only achieved if the actual rate of capital accumulation is the rate that keeps entrepreneurs happy and, therefore, is equal to the actual rate of saving. This is Harrod's famous 'knife-edge': a fame out of all proportion to its real-world significance. And further, if the 'warranted' rate of growth is not equal to the 'natural' (or potential) rate – which is determined by the underlying demographic, resource, and technological conditions – the actual equilibrium growth path will not be at the full-employment level. In this scenario the rate of capital accumulation that satisfies entrepreneurs is not equal to the rate that is required to produce full employment with no inflation. Harrod, in Keynesian spirit, thought that the 'warranted' rate would exceed the 'natural' rate, thereby generating permanent unemployment, owing to the inflexibility of the rate of interest produced by Keynes' liquidity trap.[12] He accordingly advocated Keynesian policies to equate the 'warranted' and 'natural' rates.

We need to ask: in what ways did Harrod, and Domar after him, contribute to the development of growth theory and, more importantly, our understanding of the dynamics of human society? The main positive contribution to growth theory was to show that simple abstract models could be constructed so as to provide theoretical *outcomes* equivalent to those in the contemporary world, at least when Harrod (but not Domar) wrote his first paper on this topic. It could also be claimed that this was the first growth model to be developed in mathematical form – the first to be truly modern. But the model is extremely inflexible and is only appropriate, in any sense, to real-world situations in which economic change is highly unstable, or to those in which continuing inflationary or deflationary tendencies exist. Clearly it is not a general model of growth, and it tells us little about reality and nothing about historical *processes* or the dynamics of human society. Even an economic technocrat like H.F. Hahn has said:

> It is also unwise to identify the steady state – say, the steady state rate of growth in output per head – with historical trends in the variable. That would require a good deal more argument than the theories provide. A steady-state equilibrium is simply an extension of stationary equilibrium.[13]

It is illuminating that he needed to warn other economists of this obvious danger of equating variables in the Harrod model with quantifiable aspects of reality. Despite the technical precision of this model, and the models that were to follow, it possesses none of the perceptive understanding of real-world processes that is the outstanding characteristic of Schumpeter's model of growth. In this important sense, the Keynesian growth models constituted a step backwards in the history of economic thought – if we consider the role of economics to analyse reality. The unsatisfactory treatment of technological change, which totally ignores the achievement of Schumpeter, is another retrograde development. Only in the 'new' growth models of the late 1980s has technological change, and then only indirectly, been treated endogenously. Perhaps the best that can be said for these models is that they provided a foundation on which modern growth theory is based, and which some *believe* may ultimately tell us something worthwhile about reality. But that outcome has yet to be demonstrated.

Changes in the real world quickly made the Harrod–Domar model obsolete. The fear of Keynesians that either a deflationary or inflationary gap would emerge in the generation after the Second World War was unfounded. Indeed, during the 1950s and 1960s, Western economies experienced unparalleled rates of growth without significant levels of either inflation or unemployment.[14] While economists thought that this was largely due to the new Keynesian full-employment policies, economic historians, who are more accustomed to the complexities of reality, had strong reservations – reservations that have been amply borne out by the inability of economic policy to prevent the emergence of high rates of *both* inflation and unemployment from the mid-1970s. Despite their confusion regarding the underlying causes of the 'golden age', it was clear to economists that the 'predictions' of the Harrod–Domar model were incorrect. Accordingly, growth theorists such as Trevor Swan at the Australian National University, and Robert Solow at the Massachusetts Institute of Technology, developed so-called neoclassical models in which the equilibrium capital–output ratio adjusts to market forces in order to equate the 'warranted' and 'natural' rates of growth through the interest rate so as to produce a full-employment equilibrium growth path.[15] Swan elegantly demonstrated this neoclassical solution through his well-known growth rate–output/capital ratio diagram.

The Swan–Solow attempt to extend the Harrod model to achieve an equation of the 'warranted' and 'natural' growth paths led, in Schumpeterian fashion, to a vast 'cluster' of journal articles on neoclassical growth models. In the first place, there were attempts to clarify and correct the Swan–Solow solution, based upon the mistaken notion that Harrod regarded the actual growth path as an equilibrium path, by Kaldor (1955), Robinson (1965), Pasinetti (1962), Modigliani and Samuelson (1966), and Meade and Hahn (1966). There were also attempts to extend the simple one-sector model at first to include two sectors – consumption and investment – by Uzawa (1961), Solow (1962), Inada (1963), and Takayama (1963); and then to include many sectors by Morishima (1964) and Hahn and Matthews (1964).[16] This massive expenditure of intellectual resources on growth models merely provided a technical account of the conditions under which highly abstract and simplified models, involving a limited number of variables such as output, labour, and capital (in various combinations and forms), generate equilibrium growth. While the degree of technical sophistication of these models was far greater than that of Harrod and Domar, they suffered from the same limitations. These models tell us little about reality and they experience the same inflexibility (or lack of generality) as the Keynesian growth models, in that they are only 'relevant' to periods when the real-world economy is on a full-employment equilibrium path. The neoclassical model was unable to predict, and appeared totally impotent in the face of, the stagflation that emerged after 1974. And, even though technological change was more clearly specified by growth theorists, it was not treated endogenously, but rather grafted awkwardly on to the body of these growth models.

Therefore, while both Keynesian and neoclassical growth theories were capable of being adjusted to generate different *outcomes* – of both divergence from and convergence to an equilibrium growth path – they tell us nothing about real *processes*, nothing about the dynamics of human society. In fact, even one of the participants in the development of this theory has said:

> Neoclassical growth theory is not a theory of history. In a sense [i.e. in its focus upon longrun equilibria] it is not even a theory of growth. Its aim is to supply an element in an eventual understanding of certain important elements in growth and to provide a way of organising one's thoughts on these matters.[17]

He goes on to say that the theory provides 'a good base camp, for sallies into the study of particular economies'. This, of course, is a matter of faith rather than fact. I know of no empirical study of historical growth *processes* that has employed either the Keynesian or neoclassical growth model as an analytical device. It is possible, however, to nominate an outstanding study that is based upon Schumpeter's work.[18]

It is true, however, that growth theory appears to have stimulated an interest in measuring growth and its sources, usually referred to as growth accounting. But this empirical work, true to the theory, is interested not in processes but in outcomes, and it tells us little about the way in which economies change over time. Interestingly, there has been little interaction, despite the claim to the contrary by some 'new' growth theorists,[19] between growth accounting and growth theory. Most theorists have been dismissive of the empirical results on the grounds that they contradict the theory! In this sense, and only this sense, are the 'new' growth theorists the heirs of the classical economists.

The 'new' growth models

The late 1980s saw a revival of interest in growth models, possibly because of the problems Western economies had been experiencing over the previous decade in achieving desired rates of growth, together with the theoretical advances that had been made in the fields of technological change and dynamic general equilibrium models. This renewed interest in growth models can be traced back to a paper in 1986 by Paul Romer,[20] which attempted to demonstrate that investment undertaken in an economic system experiencing increasing returns to scale will not necessarily reduce the marginal product of capital to the discount rate. Accordingly, the incentive to invest could exist 'indefinitely', enabling sustained growth in per capita income over the 'longrun'. This approach cuts across the central stagnation thesis, based upon the idea of diminishing returns in growth theory since the time of the classical economists. Rather than follow the idea of diminishing returns back to the classical model, Romer briefly traces the idea of increasing returns back to Adam Smith's pin factory. In fact his starting point was not the important issues in the history of economic thought, but rather papers by Arrow (1962) and Uzawa (1965) on learning by doing and intangible human capital, together with other papers in the 1970s and 1980s on increasing returns. In other words, the 'new' growth theory is not grounded in earlier work on this subject.

If the 'new' theory is little concerned with its theoretical predecessors, what about their concern with reality? Romer claims that there is empirical support for the idea of increasing returns to scale leading to growth rates that increase over time, and for large countries to grow faster than small countries. To support this contention he presents three sets of data. First, he claims that the empirical results of growth accounting provide a rough indication that the increase in output is the result of something more than the increase in inputs, and that this in turn suggests that increasing returns to scale exist. Other 'new' growth theorists, however, have rejected the results of growth accounting because they *believe* that they underestimate the true role of technological change.[21] They may be correct (as suggested elsewhere[22]) but they do not say why their intuition is better than the empirical results. Secondly, he compares the growth rates of developed and undeveloped countries and concludes that while there is convergence within country groups, there is divergence between these country groups, which is further evidence of increasing returns.

Thirdly, he briefly looks at growth-rate data for the USA over the period 1800 to 1980,[23] and concludes that growth rates have increased over time, thereby providing additional evidence of increasing returns. Actually, what these data appear to show is that growth rates fluctuated widely even after being subjected to smoothing, and the only reason that the twentieth-century growth rate appears higher than that in the nineteenth century is the excessive weight given to the impact of the Second World War and the 'golden age' of the 1950s and 1960s – these three decades were historically abnormal, were largely a response to the 'historical squeezing' caused by the long years of depression and war,[24] and may never occur again in such a combination. These data are not good evidence of increasing growth rates, as the long period of slow growth and stagnation since the mid-1970s suggests.

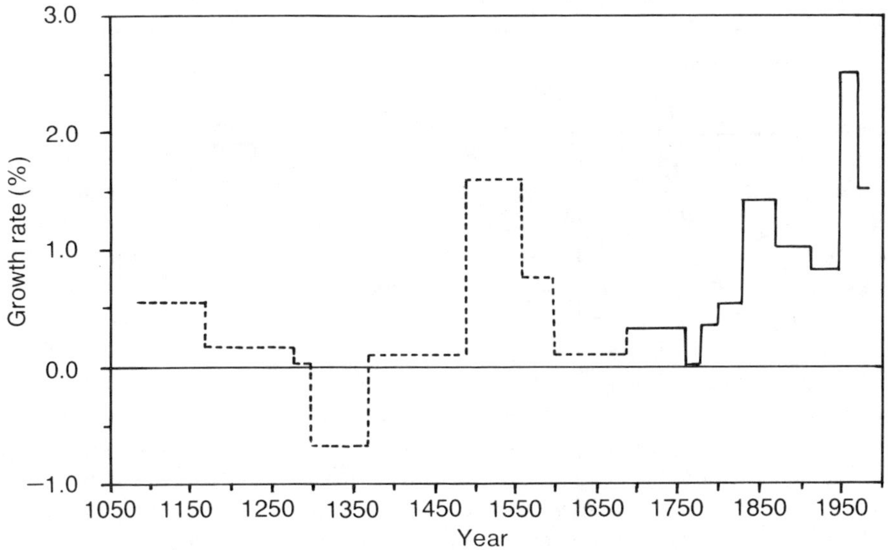

Figure 1.1 Growth rates of the English economy, 1086–1989
Source: G.D. Snooks, *Economics Without Time: A Science Blind to the Forces of Historical Change*, London, Macmillan, 1993.

Romer also mistakenly assumes that growth is a modern invention: 'A general pattern of historically unprecedented growth for the world economy is evident, starting in the last part of the 1800s and continuing to the present.'[25] Evidence of modest increasing returns – with the sum of the partial elasticities amounting to 1.15 – has been observed for England as early as the eleventh century, and rapid rates of growth of real per capita income have been experienced in Europe during the last millennium.[26] As can be seen from Figure 1.1, growth rates were as high as 0.6 per cent per annum in the eleventh century and 1.6 per cent per annum in the sixteenth century. In other words growth has been a normal feature of human society for at least the last one thousand years, but it has not been continuous, nor has it occurred at an increasing rate as the economy has grown in size. Rather it has proceeded by long upswings followed by long downswings – what I have called great waves of economic change – with each lasting for between 150 and 300 years.[27] And within these great waves of change, returns to scale, and hence growth scales, have fluctuated markedly. We just happen to be in a long, but fluctuating, upswing that began with the Industrial Revolution and could well end with the growing pressure of population and pollution on world resources. It is possible that we are on the crest of the modern great wave of economic change. Hence growth in the real world is far more complex than Romer recognizes. Like many economists before him, he employs a form of casual historical empiricism to rationalize theoretical preconceptions. No attempt is made to understand the dynamic historical forces that are transforming human society. Instead the 'new' growth theorists merely deal with the ripples that pass briefly across the surface of these great waves of economic change.

Whatever the inspiration of the 'new' growth theory, it focuses not upon physical capital but on 'knowledge capital', because 'the public good aspects of knowledge as information naturally create increasing returns to scale in many contexts'.[28] In doing so they are attempting to model – even if indirectly through 'knowledge capital' – technological change endogenously. This objective has led them to an investigation of investment in human capital and in the research and development of new technologies. This involves, in their words, 'a rigorous accounting of the resources used up in creating new knowledge, and . . . explicit consideration of the profit motive that drives private investment in R & D'.[29] These are issues with which Schumpeter was concerned at the beginning of the century, although his work was not their inspiration.

The 'new' growth theory of the late 1980s may be on the right track. It is concerned with the motivation – profits – that drive the system (finally modern growth theory has caught up with the classical economists!); with the integration of technological change and trade into growth models (moving on from the classical economists to Schumpeter); and with the analysis of the neglected role of human capital in growth theory. Nevertheless, these models are still highly abstract, overly simplified, unrealistic, and they have yet to deal with economic processes. Also the policy conclusions they draw are hardly novel. For example, Grossman and Helpman claim:

> The advances in growth theory enable us to address rigorously many issues that have long been central to international economics. For example, to what extent and in what ways might international trade serve as an 'engine of growth'? Do international exchanges naturally enhance the growth performance of individual trading countries? And what economic policies are especially conducive to high levels of welfare in a growing, open economy?[30]

There is a large literature on these issues in analytical economic history, of which those economists seem unaware.[31] Typically, they are willing to draw policy conclusions directly from their unrealistic theoretical models, without testing them empirically, or consulting the available historical results.

Of what value is growth theory?

For over two hundred years economists have attempted to model the changes that they have casually observed taking place around them. But what have they achieved? Does growth theory provide any insights to help us understand real growth processes in the past, present, and future? And does it suggest any policy prescriptions, beyond those provided by other means (such as historical investigations), that will assist individual nations and the international economy to maximize human welfare? To provide a positive answer to the first of these questions about real growth processes, it is necessary to test growth theory using historical data. Of the theories surveyed in this chapter the most useful in reconstructing historical growth processes is the least abstract – that by Joseph Schumpeter. Schumpeter was concerned with dynamic processes, and like the classical economists he saw growth as a process that embraced the entire economy and society. In contrast the Keynesian, neoclassical, and 'new' growth models, provide very limited insights regarding real-world processes, precisely because they are so highly simplified and abstract, and because of the very strong conditions that they impose. Also, as we have seen, they are concerned not with *processes* but with *outcomes*.

This raises a more general issue. Deductive theory may be useful in examining particular economic issues at a point in time, but it has little success in examining the way economies change over time. By attempting to explain a particular phenomenon, such as the price level for a particular commodity, at a single point in time, it is possible to abstract from the complex interactions between economic and non-economic forces and institutions, and here economic theory comes into its own. Economic growth and development, however, is a very complex interactive process involving the entire society with all its institutions and value systems undergoing changes that are non-marginal. Such a multi-dimensional process cannot be satisfactorily encompassed by the *ceteris paribus* world of deductive theory. Schumpeter is one of the few growth economists to formally recognize the complexity of real processes of change. In the opening sentences of *Economic Development* he says: 'The social process is really one indivisible whole. Out of its great stream the classifying hand of the investigator artificially extracts economic facts.' Not surprisingly his theory possesses a richness that is missing in the more abstract work of economists who have followed him. Modern deductive economics assumes away both the richness and the complexity that is required to explain the process in which they claim to be interested. In the event they have cast away the pearls that are worth more than their tribe.

Clearly the strength of economics is not in examining change, rather it lies in analysing specific economic phenomena at a point in time and, possibly, in comparing the results with a similar examination at another point in time. These economic phenomena include the operation of markets; the distribution of resources, goods, and income; and the working of the system of production. But it is not a very effective tool when used as the basis of growth accounting over longish periods. The reason is that the *ceteris paribus* nature of production function theory holds constant some of the important determinants of growth, such as institutional development involving changes in markets and in the resulting transaction costs. It is the variables that deductive economics assumes away – real time, the longrun, economic *processes* (rather than just *outcomes*), and institutional and 'cultural' change – that is the subject of economic history, as will be shown in Parts II and III of this book. On the other hand, it is doubtful that formal deductive models will ever be able to satisfactorily examine change in human society particularly over the very longrun.

On this issue, it is not clear what the 'new' growth theory regards as the 'longrun'. It would appear to have very little to do with real time as is made clear by the ahistorical claim of two of its advocates that, under conditions of increasing returns to scale, 'the incentive to accumulate capital may persist *indefinitely*, and longrun growth in per capita income can be *sustained*'.[32] There is no historical example of investment and growth occurring 'indefinitely'. They seem to be misled by the widespread view that growth began with the Industrial Revolution and has proceeded more or less continuously, indeed exponentially, ever since. In fact, as has been suggested above, growth can be considered a normal condition of competitive societies, but it has proceeded through a number of great waves of change rather than in a sustained fashion. Growth has been persistent throughout the very longrun, but it has never been 'indefinitely sustained'. It is these great waves together with variations in returns to scale and growth rates for shorter periods that we need to explain.

Finally, it is important to consider whether growth theory can provide policy prescriptions that are more useful than those that emerge from a careful observation, and analysis, of the historical growth process. Classical theory, for example, warned against government intervention in order to protect vested and non-progressive interests (particularly landlords), and championed free trade; Malthus also warned of the problems of population increase and of welfare policies that would encourage reproduction; Marx told of increasing unemployment and immiseration of the working class as capitalists attempted to maintain profit rates, which would ultimately cause the collapse of capitalism; Schumpeter re-emphasized the classical lesson about the importance of competition which, in this case, was required to provide an appropriate environment for the innovating entrepreneur, and he told us about the importance of the process of depression in preparing the way for a new phase of expansion; Harrod emphasized the need for Keynesian policies to avoid a growing deflation; the neoclassicists emphasized the importance of market forces in achieving a full employment equilibrium growth path; and the 'new' growth theorists have so far emphasized the importance of trade, innovation, and selective government intervention to maximize the welfare of countries producing export goods and investing in research and development. Of these policy prescriptions, the most original and helpful are those suggested by Schumpeter and the classical economists. The remaining suggestions do not appear to go beyond anything that either static economic theory (in reference to Harrod) or analytical economic history (in reference to the 'new' growth theorists) has told us. A more realistic approach to economic policy is demonstrated in Chapter 4.

THE HISTORICAL APPROACH

The historical approach, which goes some distance towards overcoming the limitations of deductive theory, can be *illustrated* by a brief overview of the historical research of a representative selection of international scholars. Naturally, the small sample of historical analysis reported in this book is meant only to be illustrative of the general methodological issues raised in Chapters 1 to 4. It should not be viewed as attempting to provide an alternative basis for economic analysis. Indeed, all authors represented here are concerned not to reject deductive economics (as did the historicists of the late nineteenth century), but to employ it in their historical research, and to work for a closer relationship between economics and economic history in teaching, research, and policy advice.

Nevertheless, the historical approach represented here deals with many of the important matters that deductive economics assumes away, including real time, the historical longrun, economic *processes* (rather than just *outcomes*), together with institutional and cultural change. In Part I an attempt has been made to show: how and why modern economics has emerged as an abstract, deductive, and mathematical science; the limitations of this approach in reconstructing reality and as a basis for policy; and how those limitations might be overcome by a closer relationship between theory and history. Parts II and III provide examples of research currently being undertaken by a number of well-known economic historians. The emphasis throughout is not on the methods employed, but on the role of historical analysis in economics.

The role of historical analysis

There is a growing perception, within and without the profession, that economics is experiencing significant difficulties in analysing real-world problems.[33] We cannot, therefore, respond, as Professor Hahn has suggested recently, by ignoring the nature of what we do as economists (or as historians).[34] We must be prepared to question our approach to reality if we are having trouble seeing it clearly, and to change our approach if necessary. We cannot afford to assume – the economist's disease – that we are always on the right track. A critical, but constructive, approach to what we do as economists is taken in the three chapters of Part I. They provide a sober assessment of the state of the profession and suggest ways forward.

Path-dependence

In Chapter 2, Paul David considers the way in which economic historians might play a role in increasing the real-world relevance of economics by transforming it into a truly historical social science. He begins with two observations: first, that economics is an ahistorical social science within a long intellectual tradition that can trace its origins back to Socrates; and secondly, that 'there are surface signs that a fundamental reconsideration of economics is now underway'. For those who are persuaded by the reality of path-dependence, particularly of a more deterministic kind, these two observations will sit uncomfortably together. David, however, is both aware of and undeterred by this problem, and seems to revel in the obvious irony.

In the wake of F.J. Teggart, David traces the intellectual origins of the ahistoricism of modern economics from Socrates, through the teleological approach of Aristotle which focused upon the 'natural' or 'normal' to the exclusion of the 'accidental'; through Pascal's abstraction from the 'abnormal' in the study of human affairs; through the insistence of eighteenth-century humanists that human actions are the outcome of natural laws determining human progress; to the nineteenth-century emphasis on evolution and progress which precludes discrete events. Economists of the eighteenth and nineteenth centuries, who are alleged to have inherited this intellectual tradition, excluded historical events, employed the mathematical technique of infinitesimal calculus, and adopted a concept of the longrun divorced from its historical context.

David's second observation concerns the changes he detects at the frontier of economics. These include the more frequent acknowledgement by theorists of the presence of positive feedback and multiple equilibria; and the willingness of economists in several fields (such as international trade and finance, location theory, industrial organization, 'new' growth theory, macroeconomics, and time-series analysis) to consider the role of 'transient influences' or 'events' in determining the particular equilibrium solution that emerges in their analysis.

In his optimism, David is willing to nominate both the probable implications of theorists adopting a path-dependent approach, and of the role that economic historians can play. Although his chapter speaks eloquently for itself, I will briefly summarize his position on these matters. David sees more attention in the future being given by theorists to the actual role and motivation of economic agents, because they have been alerted to the possibility of feedback effects; to non-linear, feedback systems (which have something in common with the earlier stages-of-development models), because of the realization that sudden shifts in economic structure can occur; and to the varying impact of economic agents on performance, because of the changing nature of the economic system over time. He is also optimistic that the central position of the theorist in economics will change because of a growing realization that, owing to the complexities of the real world, it is not possible to obtain appropriate solutions to economic problems on *a priori* grounds alone.

Hence, according to David, there is a role in economics for the economic historian, and that role is to provide detailed, persuasive, empirical examples, or case studies, to assist in the building of non-equilibrium dynamic models in economics, and to show the relevance of path-dependence. These examples, he suggests, might include the way institutional and organizational forms have evolved, and the longrun interactions between population and environmental resources.

The loss of time

In Chapter 3, I have attempted to show how modern economics came to be without time – how time came to be the lost dimension of economics. The story in my chapter provides some similarities and a number of contrasts to that by David. We are both concerned about the ahistorical nature of contemporary economics and we are working towards a closer relationship between theory and history; but I provide a more pragmatic interpretation of the emergence of an abstract, deductive economics, I am less confident that theorists will relinquish their position on centre stage, and I see a more independent role for economic historians.

There are four main themes in my chapter. The first is that the past 300 years have seen the transformation of economics from a practical and empirical art that was primarily concerned with the urgent problems of the day (mainly how to pay for wars), to an abstract, deductive and mathematical science that is largely driven by abstract ideas. In contrast to David, I see deductive economics, not as a function of an identifiable intellectual tradition – there are always competing traditions, one of which will be compatible with a particular discipline – but rather as a pragmatic response by self-interested individuals attempting to maximize their career opportunities. Time lost, therefore, is a story about the economist as economic man – a story about the triumph of the 'gameplayer' over the 'realist'. The major steps in this transformation included the single-minded deductive approach of Ricardo which replaced real time with analytical time, the deductive–mathematical method of the marginalists, and the shift of focus from the longrun to the shortrun during the Keynesian revolution.

The second theme is that this transformation has not been without its critics who, ultimately, may have an impact on what economists do. Ricardo and, later, the neoclassicists were attacked by the historicists (including Cliffe Leslie, Syme, and Ingram) in the late nineteenth century. The historicists rejected both the central assumption of economics – *homo economicus* – and the deductive approach that had been erected upon it. Taking their lead from the earlier German historical school, they announced their intention to displace deductive theory with a set of generalizations arrived at inductively from a study of historical processes. Not surprisingly, they failed – cooperation would have been a better strategy – but their legacy has lingered on in the form of a type of economic history that is suspicious, even contemptuous, of deductive theory and economic rationality. The other set of critics are from beyond the boundaries of the social sciences, and may eventually pose a greater threat to the profession of economics. The new 'dismal' scientists are the radical ecologists, who are dismissive of economics and appear intent upon displacing economists as the premier advisers to national governments and international organizations.

Thirdly, I see economic history as going further than merely contributing to a revised set of theoretical models by providing evidence – case studies – about real processes. This role, which was suggested by Paul David, is similar to the 'helpmate' role that some neoclassical economists have suggested in the past, of supplying time-series data to test their deductive models. Economic history has, I argue, a more independent role to play in reconstructing dynamic processes in order to examine the big issues facing human society, such as the dynamic interaction between population, growth, and natural resources. These issues are currently beyond the scope of deductive theory.

Finally, my interpretation of the transformation of economics over the last 300 years suggests that the internal dynamics of the profession, which has led to the dominant role of the theorist, will make it difficult to bring back real time. Why should theorists give up their central role when they have such a clear advantage in terms of numbers? Just as ideas did not account for the rise of the theorist, so they will not cause his demise. Only an exogenous shock will achieve this – possibly through a change in client demand resulting from the political success of the radical ecologists.

A basis for policy

Chapter 4, entitled 'Getting your hands dirty: economic history and policy advice', provides a rare example of the reflections of a well-known economic historian on the process of advising governments. It provides a fascinating case study. The economic historian is Gary Hawke and the case study is policy advice in New Zealand.

Arising from Hawke's experience as a policy adviser are a number of issues that illustrate aspects of the discussion in Chapters 2 and 3. The first of these issues concerns the importance of economic theory as a device for thinking about policy problems. Theory, according to Hawke, helps to sort out cause and effect, to emphasize the problems of scarcity and opportunity cost, and to place non-economic attitudes about markets, higher cultural values, human nature, etc., in a more realistic light. Most useful in this respect, he tells us, are the basic concepts, rather than the highly technical theory.

Secondly, Hawke stresses the limitations of theory for the policy adviser. Theory is 'an apparatus for thinking', not a description of reality. While this is well known in other contexts, it is honoured more in the breach than in the observance. The usual procedure in economics of drawing policy implications from complex models, with little or no empirical application, is seen as simplistic. A knowledge of the real-world context is also required. As Hawke says in a nicely understated way: 'The empirical setting, the context to which policy analysis refers, is not merely a minor consideration.' Here, then, is the role of economic history in policy advice: to provide a knowledge of institutional and structural change. As Hawke says: 'Longrun analysis is important, and economic history is the best way of developing it.'

Finally, Hawke suggests that economic history should play an important part in the education of economists, not just as a basis of policy, but in order to enable economists to develop their intellectual capacities to the full. Intellectual capacity

– but well informed by theory and history – is what is most needed in policy discussion, we are told.

Urbanization and the development process

We now turn to a number of examples of historical analysis, which illustrate the general methodological issues discussed in Part I. The two chapters in Part II are concerned with urbanization and economic development. Chapter 5, by Tim Hatton and Jeffrey Williamson, is a quantitative economic examination of the role of the urban–rural wage gap in the general process of economic growth; while Chapter 6 by Lionel Frost is a comparative case-study examination of the way in which cities grow. Both argue that their historical work is relevant to the urban growth process in today's Third World countries, and that non-historical economic studies are not sufficient on their own either to adequately deal with complex real-world issues or to develop useful policy. Both are unhappy with the shortrun comparative-static approach of economics, and both stress the importance of reconstructing dynamic processes.

The rural–urban wage gap and growth

Hatton and Williamson focus in Chapter 5 upon a central issue in modern economic growth – namely the existence of the urban–rural wage gap in the *process* of economic development. They approach this issue by considering three questions: Is the observed wage gap real or merely a statistical illusion? If it is real, is it an equilibrium wage gap (i.e. the result of 'sticky' industrial wages, urban unemployment, or flexible farm wages)? As the evidence suggests that equilibrium models cannot fully explain the wage gap, is it the result of disequilibrium forces and, if so, how do these forces change over time? By answering these questions they are able to conclude that the wage gap is not a sign of market failure, but of economic success.

In terms of this book's focus, the most interesting aspects of the Hatton–Williamson chapter are: first, their use of history to deal with issues – such as the real size of the wage gap – that cannot be resolved by theory alone; and secondly, their demonstration of the limitation of the economists' comparative-static method, and their development of a more realistic dynamic approach. Some discussion of these two matters is required.

Does a wage gap really exist? Hatton and Williamson employ historical techniques to bring the raw wage-rate data for city and country employment to a comparable basis, and to consider differences in costs of living and compensating differentials. While these considerations reduce the urban–rural wage gap, they do not eliminate it. Hence, in an attempt to explain what, they are convinced, is a real wage gap in developing countries, they employ existing equilibrium analysis in conjunction with time-series data from some eight countries. In the process they demonstrate the limitations of the economists' method. While they find evidence that labour supply responses generated 'equilibrating wage gaps' in the longrun, they suggest that this merely begs the further question as to what were the disequilibrating forces on the demand side that produced the wage gap. In other words, what really drives the wage gap? This leads them to consider the dynamics of the economic system that produces the wage gap, by specifying and testing appropriate empirical models against the historical record. Hatton and Williamson attempt, in other words, to go further than existing shortrun comparative-static analysis can take us. They place this issue in a longrun dynamic context. This is the role of history.

The conclusions that arise from their dynamic analysis are particularly interesting because they conflict with the expectations of economic theorists. In the first place they find 'that while wage gaps clearly signal disequilibrium they do not necessarily signal market failure'; and, again, 'wage gaps should be viewed as an indicator of *success*, not failure' as they increase the rate of industrialization in Third World countries. Secondly, Hatton and Williamson do not find the terms 'labour market integration' and 'segmentation' very useful, because they 'mask the dynamics of disequilibrating shock and equilibrium adjustment'. They stress the need to examine these shocks and responses over time. In this they have more in common with Schumpeterian analysis than with the remainder of modern growth theory.

Urban growth: models and case studies

Lionel Frost is concerned, in Chapter 6, with the way cities grow, and with the implications of this for the economic development of today's Third World. He begins by detailing the contrasting interpretations about Third World urbanization. The 'pessimists' view urban growth in the Third World as being out of control. As this 'overurbanization' is in danger of choking off existing economic development, some favour government intervention in order to halt the growth of these mega-cities. On the other hand, the 'optimists', generally orthodox economists, predict that intervention is unnecessary, as the rate of growth of cities will decline as the costs exceed the benefits.

In order to resolve this difference of opinion, which is based upon deductive reasoning, Frost claims that we need to consult the historical record. This is necessary in order to develop appropriate policies. He approves of Williamson's recent historical work on urbanization, and announces his intention to 'extend Williamson's comparative approach further, by examining *general* processes of city growth as revealed by cases scattered widely across time and space . . . drawn from the Pacific Rim, a region for which diversity is the signal general characteristic'. Indeed, the non-quantitative comparative approach adopted by Frost complements the econometric comparative approach of Williamson. Case studies, according to Frost, are important, because they show that existing economic models may or may not be appropriate owing to the existence of either facilitating or complicating institutional and political structures. In these case studies he focuses upon the ways in which costs of congestion in a growing city threaten to choke off economic development, and how these problems have been resolved or have defied resolution. These are useful lessons from history that can, indeed should, be applied to Third World countries. It is in this way, according to Frost, that history matters.

Longrun issues in labour, business, and banking

Part III includes four chapters that examine a number of longrun issues which are central to the growth of nations: longrun structural changes involving the increasing retirement rates of older British workers; longrun institutional change; the 'cultural' determinants of economic performance; and the role of banking in economic fluctuations. Each of these studies demonstrates the need to integrate historical analysis into the science of economics.

Structural change and retirement

In Chapter 7, Paul Johnson reminds us that the 'structure of the labour force in the developed countries has been transformed over the last hundred years by two fundamental behavioural changes – the increasing labour force participation of married women and the even earlier withdrawal of older workers'. While married female participation has received a great deal of attention, 'longrun trends in the employment and retirement of older workers have attracted little attention from historians in Britain'. His surprise at the latter omission is justified as, during the hundred years down to 1981, labour force participation of men over 65 years declined from 75 to 10 per cent. Had the 1881 participation rate of older men applied in 1981, then the male workforce in that year would have been 14 per cent larger. Similar trends occurred in other European countries.

In his pioneering British study, Johnson undertakes a careful and exhaustive study of census data between 1881 and 1981 on the participation rates of older males and females. His data analysis includes time-series participation rates, participation/age profiles for selected census years (1911, 1951, and 1981) and for selected birth cohorts (1872–76, 1907–11, and 1932–36), participation by economic sector, and occupational concentration/age profiles for census years. While this data analysis throws light upon a number of detailed historical issues, its main purpose is to offer an explanation for the changing retirement pattern of British workers over the past century, and thereby contribute to the important policy debate on this issue. Johnson considers a number of hypotheses – including changes in health, financial circumstances, and structural matters – and comes to the conclusion that the 'almost continuous longrun decline in participation rates . . . has been shown to a large extent to be a result of structural change in the economy'. This conclusion was reached by empirically rejecting all alternative hypotheses. It is of interest that the changing participation rates for older workers cannot be explained directly, as it is possible to do for the increasing market participation of married women after the Second World War,[35] by employing regression analysis.

Of particular interest is Johnson's conclusion about the need to take the longrun dynamics of the economy into account when framing policies concerning retirement. He writes:

> The OECD has expressed concern that 'countries will face growing fiscal burdens as expenditures increase and the working-age population shrinks or remains constant in size', and has suggested that efforts be made to reverse the longrun decline in labour force participation at higher ages . . . But before trends can be reversed they have to be understood, and explanations for the retirement trends of older people are not self-evident.

This is a very important point, particularly when the behavioural trends are a response to fundamental changes in the economy's structure. Far more harm than good can be done in attempting to reverse such a longrun trend. Clearly, it is essential to understand the dynamics of society before meddling with the outcomes of that process. Is it little wonder that policy based upon shortrun comparative-static analysis has such a high failure rate. All policy advisers should, as Gary Hawke argues, be informed by history as well as theory. Indeed the study of economic history should be a compulsory part of the training of all would-be policy advisers.

Longrun institutional and cultural change

If your time horizon is short, and if your concept of time is analytical rather than real, then institutional change is unimportant. But if you are, as social scientists should be, concerned with the real world and how it changes over time, then institutional change must be taken into account. The question then becomes: what role do institutions play in economic growth, and do they have a life of their own? In my opinion, longrun economic growth (and even shortrun fluctuations, as shown in Chapter 10) is a function of institutional change, as well as the sources favoured by economists, such as changes in technology, economies of scale, and the quality of the factors of production. While institutional change can be shown to be important in modern growth (as in Chapters 8 and 9), it played an even greater role in pre-modern growth with the change from feudalism to mercantile capitalism.[36] But while both technological and institutional change facilitate growth, neither is the ultimate source of economic change, neither evolves as a result of endogenous forces. Rather they change in response to exogenous economic forces, which include the interaction of economic agents with the changing supply of natural resources and other factors of production. Neither technological change nor institutional change, therefore, has a life of its own. This is a personal opinion and other authors in this book may have different views on this issue. I do not speak for them.

Stephen Nicholas' object in Chapter 8, on the new business history, is to analyse longrun institutional change. Why? Because: 'Institutional evolution . . .

can lead to economic growth or to stagnation and economic decline.' Growth occurs, he tells us, when institutional change captures the efficiency gains resulting from a reduction both in uncertainty and in the costs of transacting. This is why, to Nicholas, history matters.

Nicholas draws upon his recent research into the application of agency theory to a number of historical cases involving institutional change. He begins by developing a theory of contracts model, which 'depicts economic institutions as nexuses of explicit or implicit contracts for transacting in goods or services'. Within this framework, markets, firms (hierarchy), or the various intermediate stages (including subcontracting, franchises, licences, and longrun contracts), provide the range of economic institutions for 'structuring exchange contracts'. He stresses that the contractural arrangements are not independent of their institutional – and presumably their general economic – setting. The creation of an institutional 'culture' in which trust and cooperation allow the substitution of non-specific contracts for more costly formal contracts is emphasized.

Nicholas effectively applies this contracts model to the Hudson Bay Company in the seventeenth and eighteenth centuries, and to a sample of contractural arrangements entered into by twenty-one British firms with overseas agents in the period 1870 to 1939. In this way he is able to show how transaction costs were reduced in the longrun by changing the contracts between overseas agents and head office, and in shifting their business from agency to sales branches, and finally to production plants. He concludes: 'In all cases studied, contractural arrangements were analysed within their historical context. History matters, especially the creation of a "corporate culture" or collective memory within firms, which attenuates opportunism ... The integration of history and the theory of contracts promises to provide new insights into institutional change in the longrun.'

Leslie Hannah, in Chapter 9 on the cultural determinants of economic performance, is concerned to elucidate an issue that has attracted much attention in the discussion of economic performance both through time and through space: the role played by 'cultural' matters. He begins by considering the Wiener hypothesis that British culture harboured strong anti-industrial, anti-enterprise, and/or anti-business attitudes during the period 1850 to 1980, and that those attitudes, which were reinforced by the educational system together with literary values, adversely affected British business performance. Wiener argues that public schools and universities directed young men away from business careers and towards more 'gentlemanly' callings. But, as Hannah points out, other empirically-based studies show that between 1905 and 1971 public school 'men' dominated the boardrooms of leading businesses. It was the social elite that presided over British business at the time of its relative decline.

Hannah was curious to discover if there had been any change of business leadership during the 1980s and, if so, why. To Hannah's surprise, the social and educational backgrounds of the chairmen of the top fifty British companies changed significantly between 1979 and 1989: the contribution of public schools halved; there was a modest increase in the proportion (from 62 to 72 per cent) of chairmen with university degrees; the influence of Oxbridge declined; there was a significant increase in the proportion of graduates seeking business careers; and the quality of these people, in terms of matriculation and university scores, increased markedly. Given the age of those at the top of British business in 1989, the origins of these changes are to be found in the years following the Second World War (if not before). Hannah sees this as part of a pervasive social and cultural change that took place in Britain during the 1950s, 60s, and 70s:

> These were the decades of widening educational opportunity, but also ... of profound changes in attitudes both within and towards business. As the major continental European countries began perceptibly to overtake British living standards in the 1960s, social and cultural changes accelerated, stimulated by the increased contemporary perception of the national, industrial, and personal importance of business success.

In concluding, Hannah claims that the world of British business is 'substantially more meritocratic than it was a generation ago'; that it possesses more and better human capital, both of which will 'greatly strengthen the capability of British business to further improve their strategic performances in the increasingly competitive markets they now face'; and that, while cultural forces are important, they should not be seen as 'unchanging and unchangeable'. He elaborates the latter point thus: 'Even a conservative society like Britain's can undertake substantial reappraisal of itself and change dysfunctional cultural traits after observing that they are damaging to its longrun economic health.' Critics may claim, however, that this calls into question the primacy of 'cultural' forces. Nevertheless, the force of Hannah's argument is that any economic analysis of the present is incomplete without a knowledge of 'cultural' dynamics.

The final chapter, by David Pope, is also concerned with the role of institutions in the process of economic change, namely the shorter-term impact of financial deregulation on the Australian economy towards the end of the nineteenth and twentieth centuries. Implicit in this chapter is a story about the interaction between the Australian banking system and its regulators, and of its impact upon economic performance.

Pope's study is interesting because it involves a comparison between two episodes of deregulation in Australia, about a century apart, which were followed by similar displays of excessive lending on insufficient security for speculative purposes. In both periods some end-of-boom features (in the early 1890s and early 1990s) were similar – exposure of widespread corrupt political and bureaucratic practices, the bankruptcy of large speculators, and the difficulties of financial institutions. The obvious contrast between these periods, however, was that the extensive banking crisis of 1893 was not repeated in the early 1990s, largely because of government backing of the contemporary financial system, and the (not mentioned) fact that the banks that would have collapsed are state instrumentalities and are being bailed out by the taxpayer.

Pope deals with these issues as they relate to the banking system. He compares and contrasts both the processes of deregulation in the 1980s and in the second half of the nineteenth century, together with the shortrun responses of the banking system to deregulation in both periods. He concludes, in effect, that had policy-makers and other participants in the events of the 1980s understood what had happened in the 1880s, they may have acted more prudently. But the lessons of the more distant past had been forgotten. According to Pope, a longrun approach to economics could have some very important economic (and social) payoffs.

Pope's analysis, however, should not be interpreted in terms of downturns being caused by financial excesses. It is interesting to note, parenthetically, that financial crisis was conspicuously absent in Australia at the onset of the Great Depression. The historical record suggests that financial excesses were a response to the same fundamental economic forces that were driving the real economy towards the close of the long booms in the second halves of both centuries. But, certainly, they reinforced and complicated the downturns that were taking place in the real economy. The lessons of the past, had they been learned (perhaps they had in the 1920s), might have modified the excesses in the 1980s, not only in the financial sector, but in sectors throughout the economy. In both the 1880s and 1980s there were hoards of speculators who, recklessly riding illusory waves of greed, were the demanding customers of the banking system. But the latter had no collective memory of the former.

CONCLUSION

What can historical analysis contribute to the science of economics? The following chapters provide eloquent answers to this question. They provide insight into longrun, real-world dynamic processes that are influencing the present and will continue to influence the future. They demonstrate the role of institutions in influencing economic outcomes. And they show that a knowledge of past crises and their causes could help prevent some of the worst excesses in the future. Ultimately this could lead to the emergence of more realistic path-dependent models and to a better understanding of the dynamic processes that are, and have always been, transforming economic society.

Historical analysis, therefore, can extend the range and influence of economics by providing economists and policy advisers with a better understanding of the real world and its urgent problems. But if we are to learn from the past, time's lessons must be institutionalized by requiring all aspiring financiers, accountants, actuaries, professionally trained businessmen and women, economic advisors, and official policy-makers to include economic history – and not just of the recent past, as there already exists a collective memory of this – in their studies. The authors in this book, therefore, urge a closer, more fruitful relationship between theory and history in economics in particular, and the social sciences in general. This should occur in teaching, research, and policy advice.

Part I

THE ROLE OF HISTORY IN ECONOMICS

2

HISTORICAL ECONOMICS IN THE LONGRUN: SOME IMPLICATIONS OF PATH-DEPENDENCE

Paul A. David

INTRODUCING 'HISTORICAL ECONOMICS'

'Historical economists'[1] have convinced themselves that there have been circumstances – important circumstances – in which 'history really mattered', and that the future of economics as an intellectually exciting and productive discipline lies in its becoming a properly *historical* social science; a social science, that is, in which the 'path-dependence' of economic outcomes resulting from (some, and certainly not all) market and non-market resource allocation processes is established empirically.

In an historically oriented discipline of economics the standard modes of analysis would afford investigators a thorough understanding of the reasons why particular sequences of events in the past are capable of exerting persisting effects upon current conditions; of how adventitious, seemingly transient actions may become so magnified as to exercise a controlling (and sometimes pernicious) influence over matters of far greater economic and social significance. Hence, 'historical economics' is not, and cannot be, the application of 'modern economics in the service of history' – *pace* Donald McCloskey[2] – for the simple reason that so much of modern economics remains essentially *ahistorical.* Rather, it is the discipline into which modern economics should, and may, with luck and effort, eventually evolve. When the transformation has progressed farther in that direction than it has at present, the kind of training to which neophyte graduate students in economics are subjected will be more useful than it now is as a source of insights into both past and current economic affairs.[3]

The present writer has attempted on previous occasions[4] to convey a strong sense of how 'history matters' in economic affairs, by presenting applied studies focused on the behaviour of stochastic systems whose outcomes are *path-dependent.* The story of the QWERTY typewriter keyboard was the most frivolous and, at the same time the most evocative of these tales. A path-dependent process is 'non-ergodic': systems possessing this property cannot shake off the effects of past events, and do not have a limiting, invariant probability distribution that is continuous over the entire state space. In the case of deterministic systems the property of path-dependence manifests itself most immediately through the outcome's 'extreme sensitivity to initial conditions'.

In several of my recent essays that have a more explicitly theoretical cast,[5] attention has been drawn to the happy circumstance that those who share similar hopes and visionary delusions can read some favourable signs for the future of our discipline in the latest fashions among economic model builders. More and more frequently theorists are acknowledging the existence of local or global *positive feedback* effects – and consequent multiple equilibria, arising from a variety of mechanisms at the microeconomic level. Rather than shunning models with multiple equilibria on account of their indeterminacy, economists working on central problems across a surprisingly broad range of specialties – in international trade and finance, location theory, industrial organization, so-called 'new' growth theory, macroeconomics, and time-series analysis, and still others[6] – increasingly seem content to leave open a door through which transient influences, including minor perturbations specific to an historical context, can play a critical part in 'selecting' the particular equilibrium solution that emerges.

In this chapter my intention is to venture further than to conduct an appreciative review of these long hoped-for, and wonderfully encouraging developments that have been taking place on the frontiers of our subject. Make no mistake. This does not imply that an analytical review of the relevant literature would be a trivial exercise. Many underlying sources of positive feedback processes in the economy are being elucidated as a consequence of the renewed interest among theoretical and empirical researchers in the implications of economies of scale, scope and coordination, of Marshallian externalities and local network externalities, of endogenous technical progress through learning-by-doing and learning-by-using, of habituation phenomena affecting tastes and behaviours, and of adaptive cognitive processes (such as Bayesian information processing) affecting the formation of expectations.[7]

Moreover, it would be important even during this early stage of exploration to try to discern whether there may be some deep, unifying elements in the variety of new departures. That challenge, however, will not be taken up here. Suffice it to say that all of the foregoing mechanisms may be seen to create various forms of 'sunk costs', and irreversibilities in the reactions of agents, through which transient conditions and even seemingly extraneous events in the past leave persisting effects on the evolution of the economic system.

Now, it is rather remarkable that economists seem able to perceive these mechanisms everywhere around them, whereas only a short while ago – and certainly throughout most of my professional lifetime – they were very difficult, if not impossible, to see. But, rather than entering into speculation about the comparative prevalence of positive feedbacks in various aspects of economic life during the past, the present, and the future – which are questions that will be satisfactorily answerable only after much careful empirical study – it will be more useful here to consider the way in which programs of theoretical and empirical research, and approaches to policy studies in economics eventually would be reoriented by a widening acceptance within the profession of the notion that path-dependence is an important feature of many resource allocation processes.

Before proceeding, however, some reference should be made to the fact that modern economics itself has a complicated history that has 'mattered', perhaps more than we are comfortable acknowledging. Indeed, our altered ability to discern positive feedback mechanisms at work in the world around us may have as much to do with the internal social dynamics of our science, and the external intellectual environment formed by developments in other disciplines, as it does with the technological and institutional and transactional phenomena we are observing.

LONGRUN ANALYSIS AND THE AHISTORICIST PATH IN ECONOMICS

The dominant ahistorical formulation of much of modern economic theory has its roots in the bedrock of Western philosophical and scientific traditions formed long before Adam Smith. Clinging tenaciously to those traditions has caused economic analysis to become elaborated along lines that fail to address some fundamental problems concerning causation, as perceptive contributors to the canon have felt obliged to notice on more than one occasion – before pressing onwards. Indeed, although economists since Smith have recurringly been tempted by other, more historically oriented paths of analysis that offered themselves for exploration, even 'the best minds' have been drawn back quickly into extending the well-beaten track along which the main body of the profession was advancing.

From the pen of the famous historian J.B. Bury, who wrote early this century, flowed the oft-cited injunction to look backwards for an understanding of our present condition: 'to comprehend the significance of the present we must be acquainted with the history of the past'.[8] The procedure of explaining or elucidating a given present by stating its antecedents in time is what constitutes the core 'historical method'. Thus, the historical method involves the recognition of three terms: an existent present, a point of departure or beginning, and a series of occurrences connecting the origin with the present. The formula is identical with the genealogical method of the Greek philosophers and represents the perpetuation of the first means employed in the attempt to deal with the succession of events and changes in the course of time.[9] Generation upon generation of young economists have been carefully schooled to *not* think this way about their subject.

The ahistorical method familiar in much of modern economic theory, and mirrored in the other social sciences, is, by this standard of comparison, more recent in its origins. Even so, the latter far antedate the introduction of formal mathematics into our discipline, and owe their beginnings to lines of thought in Western science that stretch back (well before Adam Smith) to Pascal, Descartes, and farther, all the way to the teleological reasoning of Aristotle. Those scientific traditions, in effect, emerged as a more sophisticated alternative to the older, primitive genealogical method of 'historical explanation', and it was their eventual extension to the domain of social systems that ultimately accommodated the intensive mathematization of the latter's subject matter.

Frederick J. Teggart, whose unduly neglected work *Theory of History* appeared from Yale University Press in 1925, was fully aware of the long road leading to the separation evident in his day between history and social science.[10] He was nevertheless critical of both the ahistoricism of the social sciences and the anti-analytical cave into which traditional historians had withdrawn to celebrate the elements of individuality, uniqueness, and contingency which they took to be the essence of history. According to Teggart:

> The contrast between the acceptance of the 'present' as a situation, emerging as a result of antecedent actions, and the 'present' as a condition of things, resulting from the operation of changes in the past, reveals the source of all the difficulties and differences of opinion which have arisen in dealing with history as a subject of study and investigation.[11]

In the 1920s history as an academic subject was concerning itself with situations and happenings, with actions and motives, not with the problem of change or with the processes through which institutions, arts, and ideas have undergone modification in the course of time. As a consequence, the end-object of academic history had become the production of narratives which embodied, for each generation, the 'human interest' of the past; not in producing statements as to 'how things work' in human society. But matters were little better on the other side of the contrast. Just as the individualist historians concentrated attention upon events while ignoring the study of processes of change, so Teggart found, 'the study of evolution has concentrated attention upon processes of change to the exclusion of events'.[12]

The routes leading to this state of separation had their origins in Socratic philosophy. Socrates, by introducing the logical method of definition, discovered a new order of existence – which, unlike the pre-Socratics, did not take external nature as its point of departure, and instead was subject to teleological laws. In Aristotle's view, teleology was the true mode of approach to the study of nature:

> The explanation of a thing is reached only when we are able to view it in the light of a purpose. All movement is directed toward some end, and becomes intelligible only when this end has been discovered and defined.[13]

If this has the look and feel of modern functionalist sociology and neoclassical general equilibrium theory about it, you should not be surprised; we in the social sciences have been running in some very old grooves.

Aristotle had the further idea that only what took place of itself, or contained the principle of change in itself, was natural. In opposition to what is natural, he recognized that which is accidental, or which comes by chance and not 'by nature' – that is to say, the emergence of results which were not intended. From this it follows that the aim of scientific inquiry is to determine what is natural or normal. This doctrine had a determining influence on modern conceptions of the purpose or aim of science. For Teggart it represented 'the greatest single obstacle to the unification of the studies of "history" and "evolution"'.[14]

In the seventeenth century, Blaise Pascal advanced the same argument for abstracting from the 'abnormal' in the study of human affairs, by using the analogy between the study of society and the study of human physiology: if we are to arrive at a knowledge of the true workings of the human organism, it is evident that we must ignore the peculiarity, abnormalities, and accidental characteristic of any particular specimen examined. The humanists of the eighteenth century, following Pascal, assumed that the scientific study of change must have as its aim the determination of the natural or normal course of development of social groups, abstraction being made from the accidental interferences or hindrances occasioned by historical 'events'. Further, as a consequence of the adoption of René Descartes' conception of the method of science, it was assumed that progressive change is natural or normal, that it is always slow and gradual, and that it leads toward a condition of perfection. It was assumed further that the laws of nature represent the orderly provision which nature has made for the attainment of her purposes or ends.[15]

In the eighteenth century, the belief that all occurrences, including human actions, are subject to strict 'laws of nature' pervaded all disciplines, including the 'moral' or psychological and social, as well as the 'natural' sciences. The deterministic conception of the universe as a vast 'machine', which had culminated in Newton's mechanics, remained combined with the theological idea of an harmonious 'order of nature', in which every thing or being has a definite, ideal function to fulfill 'in the wisely planned economy of the cosmos'.[16]

These ideas of natural law, as Teggart notices, were fully developed in the work of Adam Smith, one of whose contemporaries in the Scottish philosophical school understood him to be seeking to illustrate 'the provisions made by nature for a gradual and progressive augmentation in the means of natural wealth, and to demonstrate that the most effective plan for advancing a people to greatness is to maintain that order of things which nature has pointed out'.[17]

Although references to history and analysis were mingled on almost every page of the *Wealth of Nations*, in Smith's scheme historical events are conceived merely as interferences with the 'natural order'. In his 'Account of the Life and Writings of Adam Smith', the late eighteenth-century Scottish philosopher, Dugald Stewart, summarized the method of abstracting from 'events' to discern the underlying deterministic structure:

> in most cases, it is of more importance to ascertain the progress that is most simple, than the progress that is most agreeable to fact, for . . . it is certainly true, that the real progress is not always the most natural. It may have been determined by particular accidents, which are not likely again to occur, and which cannot be considered as forming any part of that general provision which nature has made for the improvement of the race.[18]

A point of view was thus arrived at, more or less coincidently with the origins of the modern discipline of economics, which regarded historical 'events' as unimportant and irrelevant for the purposes of scientific inquiry in the investigation of 'progress'. By the early nineteenth century the idea was already crystallizing among economic theoreticians that they should abstract from the particularities of historical contexts, and concern themselves mainly with elucidating the 'natural' tendencies that would become manifest in some imagined longrun equilibrium. Augustin Cournot, whose *Researches into the Mathematical Principles of the Theory of Wealth* first appeared, in French, in 1838, expressed this methodological commitment in the following way:

> To lay the foundations of the theory of exchangeable values, we shall not accompany most speculative writers back to the cradle of the human race; we shall undertake to explain neither the origin of property nor that of exchange or division of labour. All this doubtless belongs to the history of mankind, but it has no influence on a theory which could only become applicable at a very advanced state of civilization, at a period when (to use the language of mathematicians) the influence of the *initial* conditions is entirely gone.[19]

The irony in this is that the concept of 'the longrun', rather than invoking an appreciation for the historically imposed constraint upon the evolution of particular economies, came to be applied in a timeless, ahistorical manner. It was that imagined state which would be attained when economic agents had accomplished all adjustments in endogenous variables, and therefore both initial conditions, and intervening events in the past would have ceased to matter. Longrun analysis *per se* cannot be a 'cure' for ahistoricism. Thinking about the longrun does not necessarily make one an historian. What matters is *how* you think about it; or, to put the point differently, whether you admit the possibilities that the dynamical process at work may be a non-ergodic one which gives rise to what has been referred to elsewhere as 'strong history'.[20]

Despite the modern connotations of the term 'evolutionary economics' as being something vaguely heterodox and sympathetically oriented towards cumulative historical processes, the advance of evolutionary biology in the course of the nineteenth century actually served further to reinforce the estrangement that had occurred between the 'scientific' study of societal change and the 'historical method'. As Teggart and, more recently, Niles Eldredge point out, it had this effect by concentrating attention upon cumulative processes involving continuous, and imperceptible modifications, to the exclusion of any role for the succession of discrete 'events' such as those with which academic historians had come to be preoccupied.[21]

The foundations of the theory of 'evolution' were intimately connected with the eighteenth-century idea of 'progress': nature has established a plan or 'natural order', in accordance with which 'natural operations' are always constant, uniform and regular. A fundamental aspect of this view is that, under all conditions, change is slow, gradual, and continuous, and proceeds always by infinitely slight gradations. Thus, zoologists like Buffon and Lamarck applied the doctrine of continuity in their approach to the conceptual relationships among the organisms in their classificatory schemes, and to the sequential relationships of time series obtained from geology. The assumption that change is invariably slow and continuous implied for Lamarck (writing in 1802) that it was possible to neglect the element of time: 'For Nature, time is nothing. It is never a difficulty, she always has it at her disposal'.[22] Thus, the dictum that 'Nature never makes leaps' came to be accepted as assurance that there never have been discrete 'events' in the history of the forms of life.

Charles Darwin took over and insistently urged acceptance of the continuity principle, which had the effect eventually of giving greater currency and weight to the dictum 'Natura non facit saltum'. Alfred Marshall embraced 'the biological analogy' to the extent of making this dictum the epigraph of his *Principles of Economics* (1890), thereby reaffirming the removal of consideration of events also from the agenda of economists – and, incidentally, lending support to the application of the mathematical technique of the infinitesimal calculus for the analysis of economic change. Yet, that was not a step Darwin was compelled to take because the geological evidence was particularly compelling in support of Charles Lyell's views about the continuous and universal operation of biological change. Quite the contrary, for there were, in fact, serious discontinuities in the fossil record.[23] Rather, it served Darwin's purpose to afford the least possible rhetorical advantage to proponents of the 'old belief' in Creation, against which he was inveighing. We, and the other social sciences, have been the legatees of that too-durable conceptual pre-commitment, undertaken for extraneous and adventitious reasons that, perhaps, seemed worthy in the transient heat of debate.

HISTORICAL ECONOMICS IN THE LONGRUN – SOME IMPLICATIONS

Depending upon how you feel about path-dependence, the foregoing digression into the history of thought could be either heartening or horribly discouraging. It certainly will have suggested to some, in a paradoxically self-referential manner, that analyses of 'lock-in' phenomena associated with path-dependence might be taken as warning us to remain sceptical – or at least only guardedly optimistic – about the surface signs that a fundamental reconsideration of economics is now under way. Admitting that much does not say that the intellectual path we have (collectively) trod must have been 'the best way' for economic knowledge to advance. We know – if only from the commonplace instance of QWERTY – that non-ergodic systems can settle into 'basins of attraction' that are suboptimal; but also that perturbations and shifts in the underlying parameters can push such systems into the neighborhood of other, quite different attractors. Therefore, I believe it is thoroughly justifiable to insist that an understanding of the kind of self-reinforcing dynamics that generates a multiplicity of stable equilibrium configurations in physical and social systems also points to reasons for entertaining the possibility that we are, indeed, witnessing a significant intellectual 'regime change'. Several considerations may be briefly mentioned in this connection with this hopeful prospect of an eventual collective escape from the trap of ahistorical economic analysis.

First, over the past two decades physicists and philosophers of physics have come to accord more and more emphasis to causation in physical theories, and to the importance of distinguishing the mathematical derivation of an effect from the causal process that generates the effect.[24] Physicists today seem to want to know at some level of generality not only what happens, but *why* it happens. Now, even a complete and 'realistic' derivation of equilibrium relationships does not, in itself, provide an account of the process by which an effect will be generated. It may indicate those factors that figure importantly in any such process, but the need to describe a causal sequence remains. Thus, a sophisticated appreciation of the role of historical narrative has supplanted the older conception of explanation in physics, which simply subsumed a particular event under a 'covering law', or general regularity.

Economist theorists, too, have begun to worry more than they used to do about causation, a condition that became particularly evident in the disaffection with the artificiality of the 'tatonnement' process imagined in the theory of competitive general equilibrium.[25] Causes are 'events' or changes in the pre-existing state that produce other changes, which we label 'effects'. If there is no perceptible change in a system, then, *ipso facto*, there can be no perceptible causation. Robin Cowan and Mario Rizzo recently have called attention to one of the profound consequences of the mainstream theoreticians' view that one could proceed as if there never have been 'events' in the history of the economic systems. They write:

> The elimination of change and, consequently, of causation is characteristic of much current neo-classical thinking. Part of the implicit research program is to 'demonstrate' that what appears to be internal change really is not. Both actual change and the potential for change are illusory, because the economic system is always in equilibrium ... The neo-classical response to a putative disequilibrium phenomenon (which would have agents encountering unpredicted changes and so altering their beliefs) is to show that by including a formerly ignored market (often the market for information) in the analysis, the phenomenon is an equilibrium after all.[26]

This inattention to causal explanation involving sequential actions, and to the disequilibrium foundations that must underlie any predictively useful theories of economic equilibrium,[27] has impoverished modern economic theory and contributed to the disjuncture between theoretical and empirical programmes of research. Efforts within the profession, finding external encouragement if such is needed, must move us towards acknowledging the possible path-dependence of outcomes. For example, in the standard Edgeworth–Bowley box analysis of exchange, it is trivial to show in general that if one permits Pareto-improving trades to occur at non-equilibrium prices, exactly where on the contract curve one will end up is not completely determined by the preferences of the agents and their initial commodity endowments. The actual equilibrium configuration of prices and quantities that is eventually attained will have been determined also by the details of the intervening sequence of (non-equilibrium) transactions. Only by ignoring such conditions can the popular algorithms now used in solving 'computable general equilibrium' (CGE) models pretend to provide an answer to the question: 'what will be *the* outcome if consumers have these preferences, producers produce according to these (convex) technological constraints, and the economic system starts with this distribution of commodity endowments?'

Secondly, there has been a great weakening in the reinforcement that economists who pay attention to the natural sciences can derive for persisting in focusing on the investigation of linear, or linearized systems – in which equilibria, when they exist, typically will be unique. During the past decade natural scientists and engineers have been turning increasingly to problems in the analysis of complex dynamical systems of the 'self-reinforcing' or 'autocatalytic' type – notably in chemical kinetics, in statistical mechanics and associated branches of physics, in theoretical biology, and in ecology.[28] As fascinating as these phenomena are, economists should not expect to find paradigms ready-made for their use in dynamic Ising models of ferromagnetism, or in the oscillating chemical reaction model of Belousov–Zhabotinskii, or in the theory of 'solitons' (non-dissipative wave phenomena), or the 'strange attractor' models that generate the Lorenz 'butterfly' effects that have become emblematic of deterministic chaos. Our positive feedback systems, unlike these physical systems, contain volitional agents whose actions reflect intentions based upon expectations, and we therefore will have to fashion our own paradigms. But, undoubtedly, there will continue to be 'spillovers' from the natural sciences, especially in conceptual approaches and research techniques.

Therefore, a third favourable external consideration to be noted is simply one of the impacts of 'the computer revolution' on quantitative research. Advances in computational power and programmes available for studying, and displaying graphically, the properties of complex, non-linear dynamical systems – advances which are being induced in large measure by developments in other sciences – are steadily reducing the attractiveness of striving to formulate mathematical economic models with unique real roots, the qualitative properties of which can be uncovered by purely analytical methods.[29]

In short, there has been an alteration of the general climate of thought, which is according new significance to details of historical sequence – a development associated with the growth of interest in non-linear dynamics across many disciplines and the consequent emergence of the so-called 'sciences of complexity'.[30] This intellectual ferment may be eroding the basis of the former stability of the ahistorical path on which our particular discipline has remained trapped (all too self-contentedly, it should be said) for well over a century. But equally, if not more decisive will be the attainment of 'critical mass' among the subset working on problems of positive feedback within the discipline of economics.

In the enthusiasm for the novel it is often too easy to lose perspective and appreciation for the familiar. Therefore, I must make it clear that I believe that any satisfactory development of 'historical economics' will eventually have to integrate heterodox insights with the knowledge previously gained about (linear) systems in which random disturbances are always 'averaged away', and convergence to the unique equilibrium solution is assured. After all, there are many aspects of economic life where the interactions among agents (through markets and via other channels of social exchange) do not seem to be dominated by perceptible positive feedback effects. Decreasing and constant returns activities, like situations too fleeting to permit the acquisition of habit, or too thoroughly explored and disclosed to offer significant scope for experiential learning, are *not* likely to generate the multiplicity of equilibria required for such strong forms of history as system bifurcations and 'lock-ins' by adventitious occurrences.

So, it will continue to be important work to empirically identify those resource allocation processes that are well explained in terms of linear models informed by conventional 'convergence' theories, leading to historical narratives of a simpler form in which the influence of initial conditions – arising from sunk costs of a non-durable sort – is quite transient, and thus compatible with longrun *ergodic* behaviour. Eventually, in such circumstances, the system under consideration will shake itself free from the grip of its past, and the relevant empirical question concerning the influence of history becomes 'Just how long is the longrun?'

It is time to describe what conditions would be like on the new path, towards which that imagined critical mass of 'historically oriented economists' will be attracting their colleagues. We can proceed by reviewing some of the more general implications that flow from the adoption of the path-dependence approach to the study of economic phenomena:

1. Because transient situations and 'events' leave a persisting influence (hysteresis), the details of timing and circumstance which are the very stuff of narrative history cannot be ignored or treated simply as rhetorical devices; economic models that failed to specify what happens away from the equilibrium position(s) would not be taken seriously. Consequently, a lot more empirical attention would have to be devoted to characterizing the reactions of agents to unpredicted changes in their environment.
2. At certain junctures, individual human actors of unheroic stature can indeed affect the longrun course of history, and so, under conditions of positive feedback, the personality of inner-directed entrepreneurs, and the ideological convictions of public policy-makers turn out to possess far stronger potential leverage affecting ultimate outcomes than they otherwise might be presumed to hold; greater attention would therefore be paid to the heterogeneity of beliefs, and to the degree to which agents were 'inner-directed', rather than

'other-directed', in their expressed preferences. In systems where positive feedback dominates, it is the inner-directed agents who exercise a disproportionate influence upon the motion of the system, because those who are other-directed tend eventually to adapt to the views of those around them.[31]

3 Sudden shifts in structure, corresponding to the new evolutionary biologists' notions of 'punctuated equilibria', can be explained analytically in non-linear, positive feedback systems. This may open a way for the formulation of dynamic models that are compatible with 'stage theories' of development, whereas stage theories formerly have had a bad name in economics because they merely offered a choice between simple taxonomies and tautologies.

4 Analysis of stochastic processes that are non-ergodic and display the property of converging to one out of a multiplicity of stable attractors shows that comparatively weak 'shocks' occurring early in the dynamic path can effectively 'select' the final outcome.[32] Later on, however, when the system has slipped into one or another basin of attraction, it acquires sufficient momentum that economically costly actions are required to redirect its motion. This implies that effective public intervention in social and economic affairs is more a matter of achieving optimal timing than has been admitted by ahistorical modern welfare analysis.[33] 'Windows' tend to open only briefly for taking fiscally and administratively feasible actions that could tip the system's evolution in one direction rather than another. The study of history, along with that of underlying structural conditions that define the location of 'basins of attraction' and the 'watershed lines' (separatrixes) between them, would therefore be an integral part of policy analysis, inasmuch as it would help to anticipate and identify such propitious moments for action.

5 Another implication to add to this list concerns predictability. 'Complexity', as a property of dynamic stochastic systems, implies that the domain of empirical relevance for the theory of rational expectations is quite severely circumscribed, as a suitably complicated statistical paper by Mordecai Kurz has recently shown.[34] The nub of the problem is that there are some dynamic structures that can never generate a time series long enough for the agents involved to be able to use it to form consistent probability estimates about future possible states of the world. If we would understand the behaviour of historical actors who were obliged to make choices in conditions of Knightian uncertainty, more attention will have to be devoted to learning about the cognitive models they call upon when interpreting their society's visions of its past and forming expectations about its future. Even for economists, then, '*mentalité* matters'.

6 Finally, perhaps the most heretical implication of all is that the central task allotted to economic theorists would need to be redefined. Acceptance of the idea that mechanisms of resource allocation and the structures of material life resemble biological mechanisms, in that they have evolved historically through a sequence of discrete adaptations, would seem to warrant this

conclusion. Francis Crick argues that it is virtually impossible for a theorist, 'by thought alone, to arrive at the correct solution to a set of biological problems', because the mechanisms that constitute 'Nature's solution to the problem', having evolved by natural selection, are usually too accidental and too intricate. 'If one has little hope of arriving, unaided, at the correct theory,' suggests Crick, 'then it is more useful to suggest which class of theories are *un*likely to be true, using some general argument about what is known of the nature of the system.'[35] This is one respect in which economics – many of the most profound contributions to which can be, and in some instances already have been formulated as 'impossibility' propositions – might well model itself on biology rather than physics. To underscore this point one can do no better here than repeat Crick's observations on the subject, with some suitable interpolations:

> Physicists [and economic theorists who mimic them?] are all too apt to look for the wrong sorts of generalizations, to concoct theoretical models that are too neat, too powerful, and too clean. Not surprisingly, these seldom fit well with the data. To produce a really good biological [economic?] theory one must try to see through the clutter produced by evolution to the basic mechanisms lying beneath them, realizing that they are likely to be overlaid by other, secondary mechanisms. What seems to physicists to be a hopelessly complicated process may have been what nature [historical evolution of technologies, institutions, and cultures] found simplest, because nature [those evolutionary processes] could only [or largely] build upon what was already there.[36]

CONCLUSION

Ultimately, the success or failure of non-equilibrium dynamic model-building in economics, and the recognition or rejection of path-dependence as a property of resource allocation processes that must be confronted by mainstream practitioners of economics, will depend on the production of detailed, persuasive empirical examples. Connecting the new models with reality is required, especially if what we are now witnessing is to become more than just another pretty 'theory bubble' that will soon burst and leave behind little of any substance.

Economic historians should be prepared to accept some special responsibility in this regard, for such convincing applications are most likely to be found in the realms most familiar to them: the evolution of institutions and organizational forms, of technologies, and the long-term interactions between population and environmental resources.

3

THE LOST DIMENSION: LIMITATIONS OF A TIMELESS ECONOMICS

Graeme Donald Snooks

INTRODUCTION

The outstanding success story of the social sciences, particularly during the post–Second World War period, has been the rise of the discipline of economics. Not only does economics possess the most comprehensive and mathematically elegant body of theory outside the 'hard' natural sciences, but also its graduates have come to dominate most public and many private institutions, and have captured the high ground of policy advice given to national governments and international organizations. It is a success that has been formally recognized by the Nobel Prize Committee – the only such recognition given to the social sciences. There are those, however, who question the basis of this success. Economists have been challenged by two outspoken groups – the historicists, who are convinced that the rejection of history by economics amounts to the rejection of economic reality; and the environmentalists who, since the 1960s and particularly the 1980s, claim that the reality rejected by economists is the ecological system of which the economy is only a part, albeit an increasingly destructive part.[1] The environmentalists have mounted a serious challenge which, if successful, could break the dominating policy influence of economists. Yet this need not be so. If economics finally heeds the historicist criticism, which stretches back to the 1870s in the Anglo-Saxon world, the resulting increase in realistic content – including an enhanced awareness of the ecological context – should increase its relevance to real-world problems and strengthen its political influence.

The only justification for any discipline in the social sciences, apart from its educational value, is whether it assists practical men and women, together with policy-makers, to understand the reality of human society. For economists, that reality is the process by which human beings attempt to satisfy their material needs and desires.[2] Accordingly, the tools of analysis – the deductive theory – should not be confused with the reality that is being pursued. There is a subtle tendency, despite the protestation of some economists, for such confusion to arise. It is this tendency – a result of the short-cut to success by economics – which threatens to undermine the position that the discipline has achieved. In these circumstances there is good reason for economists to pause and reflect upon what they are doing and why. In this spirit this chapter draws attention to the increasingly fragile grasp of economics on reality, and suggests how that reality can be regained. This is meant to be an exercise of constructive criticism from within the profession. There are those from without who are determined to displace economics entirely with a prescriptive discipline based upon the natural sciences.

Briefly, the argument in this chapter is that the emergence of economics as a deductively-based discipline, particularly during the last one hundred years or so, has led to the downgrading of the importance of applied economics in general and economic history in particular. Over this time, the discipline has been transformed from the practical empirical art of political economy to the abstract deductive science of economics. While this methodological transformation was necessary for the development of the discipline, it brought with it significant costs, particularly the loss of applied and historical skills which are essential to the exploration of reality. These costs resulted from the tempting short-cut taken by the discipline in its rush to the forefront of the social sciences. Had a balance been maintained by the profession between abstract deductive theory on the one hand, and applied historical analysis on the other, its position today would have been more secure. Unfortunately, economics has developed in an unbalanced fashion during the last century, and the theorists, rather than the realists, have come to dominate the profession. As a result, economics has increasingly come to reflect intellectual fashion rather than the reality that alone can justify its influential position in modern society.

It is further argued that economic history, broadly defined to encompass all human time down to the present, is the laboratory of economics.[3] Experimental economics, which has recently attracted greater interest in the profession, is not a substitute for economic history because its scope of enquiry is limited to issues of motivation and static neoclassical market models, and these only in the present. As history is the only method of exploring the full scope of reality directly,[4] the loss of skills of historical analysis by the discipline – the loss of real time – has led to a receding reality in economics. The implications are critically important. It is argued that the loss of historical, or longrun, perspective is a major reason for the growing irrelevance of a large proportion of economic theory and for the failure of economic policy in Western economics during the 1980s – a failure that has led to, or at least exacerbated, high rates of unemployment and/or inflation, dangerously large deficits on current account, unprecedentedly high interest rates, excessive speculation, a heavy dependence upon overseas capital and technology, excessive speculation, and the growing failure of key financial institutions.[5]

By advancing these claims, I am not advocating the rejection of deductive economics. To the contrary, deductive economics has an essential role to play, not only in suggesting possible economic relationships that may exist in reality, but also as an aid to historical analysis. Rather my argument is for a more balanced approach to economic studies, an approach that will emerge from a *rapprochement* between theory and history. Theory, history, and statistical method must become equally important foundations for the teaching and practice (particularly regarding policy) of economics. Theory must be refined by history, just as history must be informed by theory.[6] Economics began as a practical empirical art and, although it has acquired important and powerful tools of analysis, it cannot afford to lose itself in the world of abstract ideas, where it is in very real danger of becoming a branch of metaphysics and hence being irrelevant to the practical world of mankind. This is not a trivial academic matter, rather it is a matter of the greatest importance and urgency. The warning bells, in terms of persuasive public criticism from historicists and environmentalists, have been sounding for some time.

ECONOMICS AND TIME

Over the last three centuries, the practical art of political economy has been transformed into the abstract science of economics. A radical change occurred not only in the name by which the profession recognizes itself, but also in its objectives, methods, status, and influence. It will be argued that, while the discipline of economics gained intellectual rigour and precision during those three hundred years, it did so at the expense of an increasingly fragile grasp upon reality. The essence of this receding reality was, and is, a rejection of historical experience. It is the purpose of this chapter to explore the process by which, in the profession of economics, time was lost.

Then and now

A stark contrast is provided by a comparison of the economics profession at the time of its emergence as a 'modern' social science, in the late seventeenth and early eighteenth centuries, with its position in the late twentieth century. In the time of Petty, Davenant, King, Law, Cantillon, and Steuart, the newly emergent discipline of political economy attempted to emulate the natural sciences by developing generalizations or principles based upon the application of logical thought to the empirical results obtained from a systematic observation of reality. In other words, it attempted to adopt a 'Newtonian experimental, inductive method of enquiry'.[7] The empirical data employed by the early political economists included both historical observation and relatively sophisticated estimates of national income – the so-called Political Arithmetic of Petty, Davenant, and King. This evidence was collected and reworked in order to resolve urgent economic problems and to propose corrective action. In the process, *ad hoc* generalizations that could explain what was happening in the real world were developed. At this early stage, however, the political economists were unable, or thought it undesirable, to follow Newton's lead in expressing these generalizations in mathematical form.

By the early eighteenth century, therefore, the new profession of political economy had produced a body of literature – in which the principal actors were motivated by self-interest – that attempted to explain and predict the working of aspects of the English economy: aspects that had urgent policy implications. While this literature presented itself as objective and 'scientifically' based, it had yet to break free from a moral and philosophical framework. In the beginning the 'discipline' of political economy was a pragmatic, shapeless mixture of *ad hoc* inductive generalization, current empirical data, and historical information, all of which was overlaid with moral and philosophical judgements. The later specialist areas of theory, statistical analysis, and economic history had yet to emerge from this primeval chaos.

At the end of the twentieth century the discipline of economics had been much changed by the intervening three hundred years. Indeed, the pioneering political economists would have found it difficult to recognize the discipline as the one they had brought to life. Although considerable emphasis is still given to the policy orientation of the discipline, a large proportion of economists spend most of their careers acting as if the important issues are intellectual rather than practical. The correlation between the content of leading economic journals and learned conferences on the one hand, and urgent economic problems on the other, does not appear to be very high – a fact that has not gone unnoticed by interested observers, such as financial journalists and concerned economists.[8] It is quite clear that the agenda for much of the content of academic journals is determined from within rather than without the profession. Economic theory feeds upon itself at least as much as upon real-world problems. In many cases either no pretence is made to provide solutions to real-world problems, or the 'solutions' provided merely concern artificial problems.

A major difference between 'then and now' is that the previously undifferentiated field of economic studies has become divided into a number of broad fields between which there is little communication. The economics profession now consists of three main subgroups: the theorist, the applied economist (who is led by the econometrician), and the economic historian. Of these sub-groups the most prestigious within the profession is the theorist, followed by the econometrician and other applied economists, and last, and certainly least, by the economic historian. In each of these divisions the elite groups tend to be those most skilled in technical abilities such as mathematics in theory, statistical methods in applied economics, and theoretical and quantitative techniques in economic history. Accordingly, in each area the emphasis has been upon the sophistication of technique rather than upon the understanding of reality. The fundamental weakness of the profession is the refusal to integrate these broad divisions into an effective attempt to understand reality. It would appear that the internal dynamics of the profession are centrifugal in nature, and it will need a new external and urgent force to fashion the various parts into a new and more effective structure.

The really fundamental contrast, however, concerns the discipline's methodology. The historical–inductive method of the early political economists has yielded to the ahistorical–deductive method – a method that is highly technical and mathematical – of modern economists. No longer are the principles of economics drawn from systematic observation of past events – the exploration of reality – but rather from a process of logical deduction based upon intuitive, or even arbitrary, assumptions. Modern economic theory, therefore, is an intellectual game rather than the generalized explanation of an observed reality; it is determined more by the world of ideas than by the world of human affairs. No doubt the pioneers of political economy would be perplexed by the course taken by economic theory.

Ironically, the increasing precision and abstract nature of economics has been accompanied by the profession's growing status and influence. The less it is understood by the layman, the more it is respected. Prior to the mid-seventeenth century, the economic policy and intervention of governments were determined by the practical experience and the historical intuition of the ruling elite and their agents. The past was the only guide to the present. And the economy was run as if it were the personal estate of the ruler.[9] With the continued emergence of markets and the growing complexity of economic activity throughout the medieval and early modern period, the English economy could no longer be treated simply as a large estate. Greater economic management skills, together with a better understanding of underlying economic processes, were required. The emergence of political economy, which is usually examined only from the supply side,[10] must be seen as a response to these changing requirements. Political economists such as Petty, King, Ricardo and Malthus, together with policy advisers influenced by the new science, gained a debating advantage over their lay colleagues. In part this was due to the greater clarity with which they saw economic processes, and in part to the intimidating technical armoury they possessed. To compete with the economically literate, other policy advisers had to become familiar with the basic principles of political economy. Thus the 'profession' grew and, at the same time, became increasingly remote from the uninitiated. Indeed, the more intellectually rigorous economic theory became, the more it attracted intelligent and ambitious students who wished to pursue academic careers, or careers in business and public service.

The largely incorrect association of professional economic advice with economic prosperity also played an important part in the discipline's development. As economists became more involved in advising decision-makers in government and business, they became closely identified with the rise and fall of economic prosperity. When the economy was buoyant and those who held political power were prosperous, the status of economists rose and their ranks increased. Of course the acclaim given to economists is out of all proportion to their real role in creating and sustaining periods of boom. Similarly, economists have had to suffer a disproportionate share of the blame for recessions and depressions, and during these periods their status and influence has declined – the 1980s were not unique. But the profession appears to gain more during the booms than it loses during the recessions. Institutional progress in the profession, therefore, appears to resemble the ratchet effect.

Our comparison of origins and present outcomes suggests that the nature and influence of the economics profession has changed radically over the past three hundred years. In the beginning economics was an historical, philosophical, and moral enquiry, whereas it is now self-consciously ahistorical, aphilosophical, amoral, abstract, and mathematical. It has been transformed from a discipline intent upon exploring reality in order to solve urgent economic problems, to one in which the world of ideas is more important than the world of human affairs.

From realism to abstraction

The history of economic thought is a well-worked area of intellectual endeavour. My interest is not in recounting the contribution made by the great economists over the last three hundred years,[11] but rather to trace out the shift in professional preoccupation in economics from the exploration of reality to the playing of abstract games. There are a number of dimensions in this transformation, which include:

1. the methodological shift from induction to deduction;
2. the declining status and influence of applied economics and economic history;
3. a changing focus from longrun to shortrun, together with a shift in emphasis from dynamic to static analyses.

The attempt by the early political economists to apply the prevailing scientific method – the Newtonian empirical–inductive approach – to exploring economic reality with a view to changing it for the better, was only partially successful. Although they attempted to achieve a degree of objectivity in their work, they were unable, or thought it undesirable, to break free from the prevailing philosophical and moral climate of the time.[12] And in contrast to their colleagues in physics, they did not express their inductively-based generalizations in mathematical form, nor did they develop integrated models of the prevailing economic system. The task of developing sophisticated theory through the process of induction proved, for reasons to be discussed later, to be too difficult.

The first major steps in the long process of methodological transition were taken independently by the French Physiocrats and Adam Smith in the second half of the eighteenth century. Their contributions involved attempts to discover and model the basic underlying processes in an economy. The Physiocrats, the chief of whom were Quesnay and Mirabeau, attempted to model the economy in a quantitatively precise way to show the circular flow of incomes and expenditures between the three economic groups of landlords, farmers, and 'unproductive' (that is, non-agricultural) workers. Although it was a rather simple and unrealistic model, which did not have many imitators, it was an early example of an abstract form of analysis arrived at by a mixture of observation and deduction.[13]

Adam Smith in the *Wealth of Nations* (1776) also attempted to explore the underlying economic processes, in his case by developing a model (based upon division of labour and capital accumulation) to explain the process of growth that he saw as being a natural outcome of the English economy in the late eighteenth century. Using as his central assumption the now familiar idea that economic agents acted consistently in their own self-interest, Smith developed simple models by employing historical observation together with inductive and deductive thought. To persuade others that these simple abstract theories (which are really quite imprecise) were capable of revealing the underlying mechanism of economic change, Smith marshalled historical and comparative data to 'illustrate' their relevance.[14] His purpose in isolating a model of the English economic system was to propose advice that would maximize the rate of economic growth – namely to work within the parameters of the system rather than to divert and frustrate it. Although Smith built upon the work of his predecessors, who attempted to analyse the English economic system that they saw as being held together by the self-interest of economic agents – writers such as Law, Cantillon, and Steuart – he established an approach to the subject that set economics on its modern course.

Although Adam Smith's work provided a sound foundation for future developments in economics, it also initiated an historical sleight of hand. It has already been noted that he attempted to demonstrate the relevance of his theories by *illustrating* them with historical examples. I say 'sleight of hand' because only those facts, events, processes, and interpretations of history that support a particular theory are paraded, while the rest of history, which may be unaccommodating, is ignored. It was for this use of history that Cunningham attacked Marshall in an article called 'The perversion of economic history' in the *Economic Journal* for 1892. And it is a misuse of history that is with us still.[15] This is an interesting phenomenon. Economists may apply the most rigorous econometric techniques to contemporary cross-sectional data when testing their theories, but when they attempt to provide them with greater universality by appealing to longer periods of time, they invariably abandon their rigour in favour of more impressionistic techniques. It is almost as if they believe that history is not worthy of serious study and can be plundered in a haphazard manner.

The first assault on real time: Ricardo and the neoclassicists

Although Adam Smith employed deductive reasoning, albeit not very precisely, it was David Ricardo who completely divorced economic model building from the experience of the past. Ricardo stripped economics of everything he considered superfluous to the economic problem under consideration, including history, sociology, philosophy, and the institutional setting. He did this by abandoning the inductive–deductive approach employed by earlier political economists in favour of a consistently deductive approach based upon the central assumption of economic rationality. As a recent commentator has said: 'His ingenious mind, essentially that of a brilliant theoretician never displayed any significant interest in the past.'[16] The resulting theory, which addressed central issues of the day, was ahistorical and abstract to the degree that it could have been (but was not) expressed in mathematical form. Much of it focused upon microeconomic issues concerning the theory of value and the functional distribution of income. It is important to realize that the abstract, ahistorical, and aphilosophical nature of Ricardo's work was unique – and was perceived to be unique – in the early nineteenth century; Malthus, for example, commented that: 'The principal cause of error, and of the differences which prevail at present among the scientific writers in political economy, appears to me to be a precipitate attempt to simplify and generalize.'[17] Yet while this approach was unique in Ricardo's time, it was to become the standard approach in the discipline with the development of the new neoclassical economics in the last quarter of the same century. While Malthus criticized the methodology of Ricardo, the later reaction to his own work varied. Some, such as Cliffe Leslie and Foxwell, saw him as using the historical method of induction, while others, such as Ingram, felt that Malthus had begun deductively and only in subsequent editions had added a large amount of 'illustrative' historical material.[18] The latter view is more balanced.

With the simultaneous but independent development of the marginal theory of value by W.S. Jevons in England,[19] Carl Menger in Austria, and Léon Walras in Lausanne in the 1870s, economics took on an international character. The new microeconomics – the marginal revolution – that emerged in the closing decades of the nineteenth century was a response not only to the changing economic system in Europe which generated a demand for a more systematic and sophisticated body of economic principles, but also to the general intellectual climate that was becoming increasingly scientific.[20] What is important here for our purposes is not the nature of the theoretical contribution in microeconomics, but the nature of its methodological underpinning. It is generally recognised that this period marked the watershed between political economy and economics – between, in other words, the art and the science of the discipline. In this process of transformation, economics – or more to the point neoclassical economics – became more abstract, deductive and highly simplified, and, in the process, it became less realistic. Mathematical elegance replaced the clumsiness of a science clothed in words. But the new economics was less accessible to the uninitiated than classical economics, not only because it was more abstract and mathematical, but also because it appeared little concerned with macroeconomic issues.

Marshall gave the impression of bringing intellectual balance back into neoclassical economics.[21] Not only was he able to elegantly reconcile the combatants in the game of value theory by employing the effective demand–supply model, but Marshall also gave the impression to the uninitiated that he had placed neoclassical economics back into historical context and into the language of the educated layman. Yet his achievement was more apparent than real. Although Marshall apparently intended to place his analysis of the 'present' in 'an evolutionary, hence historical, theory of economic change', this grand design did not get very far.[22] His rhetoric and his practice did not coincide. The historical chapters in the *Principles* (1890) are – unlike his theoretical work – vague, imprecise, and tautological, and constitute an impressionistic appeal to the past. One scholar has referred to it as 'little more than historical theory'.[23] In this, Marshall is typical of economists who generally take an unprofessional approach to history. Basically, he was making a half-hearted gesture to the intellectual expectations of the time. Marshall used history merely to rationalize his theory, to give it a veneer of universality and, possibly, to placate his more aggressive 'historicist' opponents such as William Cunningham. History was used, therefore, for personal rather than professional ends. The initiated, however, were not deceived. The younger generation of economics students were attracted by the abstract and mathematical rigour of Marshall's theory, and recognized his fundamental opposition to the operational use of history in economics. They were required to do little history in their courses, and even that focused narrowly on the previous few decades: two-thirds of the new Cambridge economics degree was reserved for theory, with only one-third for applied economics, political science, and 'recent' economic history.[24] In a revealing autobiographical sketch in 1917, for example, Marshall recalled his first encounter with economics after an earlier training in mathematics: 'they [his mentors] told me that I needed to study Political Economy. I followed their advice, and regarded myself as a wanderer in the land of dry facts; looking forward to a speedy return to the luxuriance of pure thought'.[25] He also said: 'I don't much believe in the possibility of direct induction', and admitted that he only used history for 'illustrative' purposes.[26] This was the real example that Marshall provided for those that came after him: the real core of economics was pure thought, and empirical–historical material was only useful in so far as it illustrated the supremacy of pure thought. Marshall's fiercest opponent, Cunningham, saw this clearly, and did not like what he saw. In his famous 1892 article mentioned earlier, Cunningham attacked Marshall for attempting to support his deductively based theory by an impressionistic appeal to the past. This approach, which can be traced back to Adam Smith and beyond, 'perverted' economic history because it extracted only those facts, events, processes, or interpretations that supported a predetermined point of view, ignoring all that contradicted it.

This is not to say that Marshall and his followers were uninterested in practical problems or in influencing the affairs of men by their abstract ideas. But in their work the problems and policies arose largely from abstract theory and an intuitive grasp of the world around them, rather than from a detailed empirical examination of reality. Although the neoclassicists adopted mathematical methods to facilitate the development of deductive theory, they (with the exception of Jevons) had little time for statistical techniques which could have been used to apply to their theory of the real world.[27] One might expect a considerable degree of overlap between abstract and real problems while economists keep a close check on the world around them, however, it is highly probable, as the balance of interests shifts from empirical to theoretical matters, that problems and policies will become subordinated to intellectual priorities. This appears to have happened over the last one hundred years. Accordingly, Cunningham's charge about the perversion of economic history can be extended to the perversion of policy-making, with theory dictating the issues rather than the reverse.

The counter attack: the historical school

There were those who reacted against the abstract, deductive form of economics created by Ricardo and extended by the neoclassicists. The most forceful amongst these were adherents of the historical school of economics, who accused the Ricardians and neoclassicists of being dangerously abstract and unrealistic. History, they argued, provided a far sounder basis for deriving economic principles. As is well known, this empirical–inductive school of thought had its origins in Germany as a reaction against the British deductive school,[28] largely because of German unwillingness to accept the policy implications – particularly concerning free trade – of the British profession. It is an interesting fact that the German historical school not only rejected the abstract deductive approach of Ricardo and his followers, but in the later nineteenth century also sought methodological inspiration in the biological rather than the physical sciences. Accordingly, they emphasized the evolution of economies and were concerned with the organic unity of the process of change. More recently, a cliometric historian has explored the different insights that economics might have provided had it adopted the methodology of the biological sciences.[29]

The historical school in Britain, which resisted the deductive nature of orthodox economics and the central assumption of economic rationality, derived inspiration from the German reaction against deductive theory. The two leading proponents of the British historical school in the 1870s were Irish scholars – T.E. Cliffe Leslie, a political economist, and J.K. Ingram, an historian.[30] They claimed that all economic thought was relative to time and place and hence was not universal. Their influence was greater than it might have been at another time, because it was generally recognized at this stage that the economics of the classical school was more relevant to a pre-industrial society than to the mature capitalist economy that Britain had become. The influence of classical economics, therefore, began to recede; indeed it probably would not have lasted so long but for the amazing intellectual influence of J.S. Mill, a disciple of Ricardo, who attempted to make the master's work more realistic by the use of historical and contemporary illustration.[31] For a decade or so, the historical school was a serious contender for the vacant title, at least in terms of providing a new basis for economic policy, if not in providing an alternative body of economic theory.[32] It was more acceptable to the majority of the profession than the brash new neoclassical school, because very few economists of the time had the necessary mathematical training, whereas most had had extensive exposure to history. Indeed, at both Oxford and Cambridge during this period, economics was taught as part of the history programme.[33] The American institutional school, the most lasting memorial of which was the National Bureau of Economic Research (NBER) established in 1920, was also influenced in its anti-deductive approach (which included D. Dewey, J.M. Clark, and W. Mitchell) by the German historical school.

Yet the influence of the historical school was not to last. As N.S.B. Gras commented in 1920, 'The historical method, as applied to economic studies, seems in large part to have failed at the hands of both the younger and older group of historical economists.'[34] Despite the eventual and resounding victory of the neoclassicists, supporters of the historical school did linger on at the London School of Economics until the late 1920s under the protective influence of Beatrice and Sidney Webb. The leading lights at LSE in this period, all of whom were appointed because of their anti-neoclassical sympathies, included W.A.S. Hewins, Edwin Cannan, and R.H. Tawney. It was not until the appointment of John Hicks in 1926, Lionel Robbins in 1929, and F.A. von Hayek in 1931 that neoclassical economics gained the ascendency.[35] This marked the end of the English historical school as an effective academic force. Its only intellectual heirs are the economic and social historians in Britain who have faithfully carried on the anti-deductive and anti-economic rationality attitudes of the founding fathers of Cunningham and Ashley – but not the desire to generalize from the particular attitudes that characterized the historical school – down to the present time. None of those historians, however, has even been able to attract the attention of orthodox economists, let alone cut them to the quick as Cunningham was able to do to Marshall one hundred years ago. Instead, they have been left to snipe ineffectively at the flanks of analytical economic historians who employ orthodox economic theory and quantitative techniques in their work.

It is important to understand why the historical school failed in its bid to provide an alternative body of economic principles to the classical and neoclassical schools. Clearly the explanation is complex, but it seems to me to involve the following interrelated elements. In the first place, it had promised more than it could deliver; the historical school failed to produce an alternative structure of inductive thought that could stand alongside that of the rapidly developing deductive school.[36] The intellectual task of exploring the economic processes underlying historical reality was far more difficult than the construction of simple deductive mathematical models. Secondly, it is difficult in an inductive school to obtain agreement about a body of generalized ideas. There are a number of reasons for this. On the one hand, it is well known that inductive inferences cannot be drawn precisely from the premises, but only with some degrees of probability, because there is no logical necessity for the unobserved to continue the pattern discerned in the observed. Different scholars, therefore, can, and do, make different inferences based upon the same number and type of observations. On the other hand, as different scholars may have access to different numbers and types of observations, they may arrive at different inferences even if they could agree on those occasions that the type and number of observations were the same. Thirdly, the deductive school in the late nineteenth and early twentieth centuries enjoyed a growing reputation both in academia, because it was able to provide a manageable intellectual challenge for 'bright' university students, and in the political and commercial spheres, because it provided the tools required to tackle practical microeconomic problems in the largely buoyant late Victorian–Edwardian economy. Fourthly, Marshall's attempt – deliberate or not – to disguise the degree of abstraction of his neoclassical synthesis, and to give it an historical veneer, probably helped to deflect some of the force of the historical school's attack, and to make it more palatable to a wider audience. Fifthly, the success of Marshall at Cambridge in 1903 in finally breaking free of history's apron strings, and in establishing a separate economics tripos, meant that students could be given larger doses of history-free economics, they could be nurtured away from the glowering presence of hell-fire historicists such as the Rev. William Cunningham, and they could be warned of the 'dangerous fallacy' of the historical school.[37] Sixthly, J.N. Keynes' *Scope and Method* was considered by the neoclassical school to be the last word on the relative merits of the deductive and inductive approaches.

Finally, the historical school failed because it refused to employ the simple models of its arch-rival. The historical school made the fatal error of competing, rather than cooperating, with neoclassical economics. Its decline and eventual extinction should be seen in these terms. There is a lesson here: if the profession of economic studies is to reach its full potential, theory and history must be regarded by the great majority of its practitioners as complementary rather than competing activities. Neither partner will prosper for long without the other. When economic history rejects economic theory – as in the case of British economic and social history – it loses its identity and runs the risk of being absorbed by general history. Similarly, theory without history (that is, reality) runs the risk of losing the confidence of those who pay the piper, and hence of having a continuing influence in the world.

Rolling back real time

With the demise of its opposition, the neoclassical school grew rapidly in influence. In the first few decades of the twentieth century, Marshall's *Principles* provided a stimulating intellectual basis for research and teaching in economics. Although those involved in developing economics claimed to be concerned with urgent economic problems, their preoccupation – if we ignore 'deviants' such as Joseph Schumpeter who focused upon the process of macroeconomic change – was with microeconomic issues. In the event, their work became even more abstract, ahistorical and, as unemployment emerged as a major problem after the First World War, distant from the concerns of policy-makers. The point at which the intelligent layman could profitably read the work of economists had long since passed. During these years, Marshallian economics was amplified and extended in England (by Pigou, Dennis Robertson, Keynes, and Joan Robinson), in Europe (by Walras, Böhm-Bawerk, Wicksell, etc.), and in the USA (by J.B.

Clark) in order to analyse general equilibrium, welfare, capital and interest, and money, interest, and prices. Whatever the indirect practical impact of their work, clearly they were preoccupied with pure theory.

While large-scale unemployment in Britain, together with the precarious state of the international economy in the interwar period, led neoclassical economists to take macroeconomic issues more seriously than before, the emphasis on abstraction became more intensive and extensive in the profession. Although the remarkable theoretical contribution made by J.M. Keynes in the *General Theory*, for example, was in response to the fact of the Great Depression, it was based not upon a closer examination of historical processes, but on intuition about current economic institutions and circumstances. In a revealing statement Keynes said:

> It is astonishing what foolish things one can temporarily believe if one thinks too long alone, particularly in economics (along with the other moral sciences), where it is often impossible to bring one's ideas to conclusive test either formal or experimental.[38]

Here he discounts the use of history as a method of testing 'one's ideas', possibly in part because he was convinced by his father's dismissal of the methodology of the historical school,[39] but more fundamentally because he was aware from his earliest academic work of the problem of induction.[40] Keynes instead appeals to the intuition of fellow theorists rather than the results of either applied economics or economic history, which was left to others – those lesser mortals who were prepared to get their hands dirty testing some of Keynes' propositions (such as the consumption function, the multiplier, and the trade-off between inflation and unemployment) using historical data. Keynes himself was quite content to move directly from abstract theory to advising governments of various nations without empirically testing his theory. Indeed, there is good evidence to suggest that he developed the policy before the theory.

Ironically, the *General Theory* not only directly stimulated empirical work, it also encouraged the official collection of macroeconomic data that, in conjunction with the development of econometrics from about the same time,[41] led to the emergence, largely in the USA, of a new industry of applied research in the neoclassical as well as the Keynesian traditions. The importance of the contribution of this applied work to the development of theory is often underrated, particularly in Britain (and there, particularly at Cambridge, Keynes' *alma mater*). As G.J. Stigler points out in his review of *The New Palgrave: a Dictionary of Economics*:[42]

> Many empirical findings of economics have histories that are at least as interesting and important as most theoretical developments. The history of the estimates of the consumption function, and the effect these estimates had on professional thinking, is one example. The estimates of the Cobb–Douglas production function, and the growing sophistication of the estimation procedures, is a second example. The influence of measurements of price levels on monetary analysis is a third example.

He concludes by saying that 'The decision to exclude empirical studies is a serious blemish.' He could also have mentioned the empirical–historical work underlying the Phillips curve and trade-cycle analysis. It is significant that a major multi-volume compendium of economics that attempts to encompass the achievements of the profession, both past and present, can overlook the theoretical contribution of the large body of significant empirical work undertaken since the Great Depression. Economics, particularly in England, is still firmly in the hands of anti-empiricists. One of the main reasons for the lack of integration of applied work into the body of economic theory is the separate development of the basic techniques used in both. Economic theorists adopted mathematical methods as early as the 1870s (although they did not become widespread until after the 1930s) in order to develop their deductive models, but neglected applied statistical techniques. These applied techniques – which were introduced in the early years of the twentieth century, were used more widely after 1931 when the Econometrics Society was established, but only became common after the mid-1940s – would have provided some systematic information about the real world. But the two traditions have always remained separate, possibly because, from the beginning, mathematics has been associated with deduction, while statistics, and later econometrics, was associated with induction – the method of the historical school.

If the economics profession, on important occasions such as the publication of *The New Palgrave*, can overlook the contribution to theory of its applied economics branch, what role does it see for economic history? Of the two thousand entries in *Palgrave* only a handful are devoted to topics and scholars in economic history,[43] and one of these topics is a six-page entry on economic history itself. Conspicuously absent is any discussion of historical method or the historical treatment of contemporary issues. How does this compare with the position when Palgrave published the first edition of his *Dictionary of Political Economy* (1894–99)? The first edition is strongly influenced by the historical approach to economics, both in general and in the way in which individual subjects are treated. It is interesting that Palgrave's preface to the first edition of Volume 1 treats the historical school and the deductive school equally: 'The development of the historical school has opened out new and fertile fields, while the wants of those who follow the mathematical method of study have also to be considered.' And in the important entry on the 'method of political economy', induction and deduction are treated as equally important pillars of positive economics, while it is concluded that 'each method may learn from the results of the other'.[44] Also in the first edition there are a large number of historical subjects,[45] some of which were on the medieval period,[46] and also most contemporary issues (such as prices, insurance, banking, currency, import duties, etc.) were placed in an historical context. The contrast, therefore, between the first edition of 1894–99 (or indeed the second edition of 1923–26) and the third edition of 1987, could not be more stark. History and historical method, which permeate the first edition, are almost totally absent less than one hundred years later. There can be no doubt that the economics profession currently does not see a very important role for economic history.

Despite this neglect by the economics profession of applied work in general and economic history in particular, there is an important place for these activities. As Stigler has suggested, empirical work can and should provide a testing ground for deductive theories, the results of which may lead to the abandonment of some theories and the effective modification of others. This is, in fact, a restricted form of induction – restricted by the parameters of the deductive theory that stimulated the empirical work. What I mean is that the applied economist tends to see reality through the eyes of the theorist, and seeks out only those variables suggested by the theoretical models. Is it surprising, therefore, that to the economist, both theoretical and applied, the world takes on the appearance of the profession's abstract models? This problem is sometimes compounded by those I will call economists' historians, who also adopt the tunnel vision of economists when dealing with the past and who deal in 'stylized facts' that look very similar to the backward predictions of simple economic models.[47] In these circumstances theory is not just a tool, however much the more perceptive economists may protest, but is a surrogate 'description' of 'reality'. This is precisely where analytical economic history can play an invaluable role. By reconstructing reality, the economic historian can demonstrate the limitations of this narrow focus, and possibly could assist in the revision of theory.

Swimming against this tide of unrealistic abstraction was development economics which emerged after the Second World War and the consequent collapse of colonialism in Asia and, later, Africa. The critical issue facing newly independent Third World nations was how to achieve rapid and sustained economic development and growth. For strategic reasons, First World countries were also vitally interested in this issue. Not surprisingly, as this was a dynamic real-world issue of considerable complexity, the existing simple, static economic theory was found wanting. Some economists made an eclectic attempt to marshal existing economic theory that dealt with growth in the works of Smith, Malthus, Mill, Marx, Schumpeter, Harrod and Domar, and Hansen, together with partial theories concerning population growth, technological change, international trade, development strategies, foreign investment and aid, taxation, savings, and the role of government.[48] But it provided little insight or assistance concerning this complex real-world problem. Accordingly, orthodox economics lost interest in this issue, and economic development programmes either disappeared from the subject offerings of economics departments, or were left in the hands of those economists who either were emotionally committed to the issue or who did not have the technical skills to make a career out of theory or econometrics, or the subject was left to economic historians (such as Rostow[49]) who became interested in applying their craft to important real-world problems. The high-fliers in economics, however, turned this defeat into a victory of sorts by subsequently placing development economics in the same category as economic history – the 'soft' social sciences – and hence not worthy of serious consideration. But the real-world problem, unlike mainstream economists, refused to go away.

Despite the embarrassing failure of growth and development theorists, the mid- to late-1960s saw the high tide of the economics profession in terms of its status, influence, and relative size in the academies. Economists claimed, and were given, much of the credit for the prosperity of the 1950s and 1960s – a period that has since become known in Western economies as the 'golden age'. In this period of unparalleled prosperity economists felt they had the theoretical key to unlock all the mysteries of the present and future. As they had no need to explore reality, they had no need of history. Many forgot that economics was only a way of thinking, a method for solving problems, a tool box for understanding reality. Accordingly, the focus of the profession in this period was not on making theory more effective as a tool of analysis, but on making it more precise. This was the high point of the arrogance of the economics profession. But the economic circumstances that made it possible were not to last, as history – had economists bothered to consult it – could have told them.

With the emergence in Western economies, after 1973, of major economic problems – slower, even negative rates of growth, and high rates of both unemployment and inflation – the status and influence of orthodox economists declined. This made it possible for dissenting members of the profession to make themselves heard. Some, like Milton Friedman, revived neoclassical theory (such as the quantity theory) and reshaped it to fit the circumstances of modern Western economies. Others, such as the 'new classical macroeconomists', attempted to resolve the conflict in the neoclassical synthesis by assuming that markets were highly competitive, and cleared instantly. In doing so they also revived an earlier attitude to the adverse effects of government intervention in economic activity. Hence the outcome of our era of greater economic uncertainty is a greater diversity of analytical and policy views than has been experienced since the Great Depression. All this must be confusing to the politician and businessman seeking economic guidance, to say nothing of the educated lay person. What remains unchanged, however, is the major emphasis placed by the profession on highly abstract, mathematical, and ahistorical models. Even with the obvious failure of economic policy in the late 1980s to prevent deteriorating economic conditions, the need to take real time into account has not been seriously considered.

The fall of applied economics: the triumph of gameplayer over realist

The history of economic thought is dominated, therefore, by a shift in methodological focus from induction to deduction. In the process the status of applied economist and economic historian has progressively declined, while that of the theorist has increased. As a result, according to the conventional wisdom, 'the best students were encouraged to concentrate their research efforts on abstract and theoretical, rather than practical and empirical, problems'.[50] While I agree that students were encouraged to focus upon theoretical rather than applied topics, the notion that these were the 'best' students requires further examination. No doubt they were the 'best' at theory, but were they the 'best' at understanding reality? I will suggest in this section that the changing focus in methodology encouraged a new entrant into the profession of economics, the 'gameplayer'; and that this new entrant eventually displaced, at least from the 'top' of the academic discipline, the former inhabitant, the 'realist'. While a healthy discipline in the social sciences requires a balance between these two extreme types of thinkers, the economics profession, especially in England, has come to be dominated by the 'gameplayer': applied economics has been left to those who are not regarded as being of the first rank, and economic history has been abandoned entirely to those who clearly have no head for theory at all (such as Cunningham, Ashley, Clapham, and their followers). This is the pervading myth of economics.

The gameplayer is a relatively late-comer to the profession. As we have seen, economics was created by realists in the seventeenth century, realists such as Petty, Davenant, and King, who were concerned to understand their economy and to resolve urgent problems. The realists held centre stage until the early nineteenth century, when Ricardo's highly abstract and simplified economic models moved the realists noticeably towards the wings and gave the profession a premonition of things to come. The attack on the realists began in earnest in the closing decades of the nineteenth century and came from the neoclassicists. Although Marshall attempted to play down the hostilities, it was clear by the turn of the century that the gameplayers were dominating centre stage and that the realists had been forced to the fringes of the drama. From then on, pure theory was equated with intellectual excellence and, among potential entrants, the gameplayers – who became known as the 'best' students – were encouraged at the expense of those who had a preference for, and were skilled at, exploring reality. The only challenge to the gameplayers came, ironically enough considering the non-empirical nature of his work, with the publication of Keynes' *General Theory* in the mid-1930s. This seemed to herald a revival in applied economics but, in fact, much of this was due to the upsurge in econometrics that also began at that time. The Keynesian focus on simple macroeconomic variables, however, provided a convenient basis for the new econometric work. The response of the gameplayers was not to concede the central stage to these new players, but to marginalize their influence by giving them their piece of the action to one side of the main show, through separate departments (or subgroups in existing departments) of econometrics. Untainted by these highly technical empiricists, the gameplayers have been able to continue their austere play down to the present.

To clarify the distinction between the extreme personality types that I have called 'gameplayer' and 'realist', I shall outline their characteristics in greater detail. In pure form, the gameplayer is a person who views life as a series of manageable problems – rather than a complex and possibly unknowable reality –

that may be difficult in a technical sense but which are capable of solution. The best gameplayers enjoy, and are good at, working out the connections between variables in technical games and models, and feel uncomfortable when attempting to see patterns in reality through observation. Nobel Prize Laureate Robert M. Solow quite candidly says: 'Most of the economists I know, including myself, don't have any talent for direct observation, nor, by the way, do we have any methods for dealing with it, which is not a reason not to deal with it.'[51] They are good at mathematical exercises not only because they possess the necessary skills, but also because they are able to take the limited objectives of mathematical games seriously. Gameplayers tend to show early promise owing to a lack of complexity of mathematical problems, at least in comparison with the complexity of reality which requires considerable experience and maturity of thought, as well as 'intelligence', to resolve.

The talents of gameplayers are obvious. At all stages of life they demonstrate an ability to solve mathematical and logical problems, and to play 'intellectual' games. At school they are regarded as 'bright', and at university they are seen as the 'best' students. This type of personality also receives more general recognition than other intellectual types from the public. Although the general population may not excel at gameplaying, it is something they enjoy (crosswords, quizzes, computer games, chess, etc.) and they can recognize and appreciate the abilities required to excel at it. To the public, the talented gameplayer is the archetypal intellectual. It is not surprising then that the gameplayer receives due recognition for his/her skills.

The Realists, in pure form, view life as a complex mystery which they attempt to understand, but will not be unduly perturbed if this proves impossible. Indeed, it is precisely the intellectual difficulties and risk of failure that attract the best of this personality type. Intellectual games, however, are not of interest to the realists because they appear to have little purpose in themselves, or because they tell them nothing directly about reality. Reinforcing their set of preferences is their lack of comparative advantage in playing games. Their comparative advantage is in discerning complex relationships in reality or, in other words, discovering order in the chaos of the real world. In contrast to their opposite number, the realists generally take longer to reach their full potential, largely because of the experience and maturity required to do so. And it is the continued accumulation of experience that enables them to produce their best work beyond middle age. Recognition of their powers comes more slowly, if at all, not only for this reason but also because there is no popular parallel with which the public can identify. The road to realism is long and hard.

How do we account for the growing dominance of the gameplayer in economics, or indeed in social sciences generally? This is a complex matter and involves forces on both the demand and supply sides. On the demand side, as we have seen, the growing sophistication of industrialized economies has generated a need for highly trained economic technicians with an array of theoretical, mathematical, and technical skills. This has attracted the gameplayer and repelled the realist. On the supply side, the main issues appear to include: technical efficiency; professional practicality; and self-interest. Simple abstract models based upon deductive thought provide an easy and effective way to understand the likely relationship between important forces in society. Once expressed in mathematical form, any particular set of relationships can be manipulated with relative ease both in the mind and on the computer. It allows greater and more rapid development, because it is a more efficient way of constructing a body of generalization about the way reality might work. In contrast, as we have seen, the process of attempting to construct economic principles by induction is far more difficult because, owing to the inherent lack of precision, it is not possible to do so in mathematical form. The precision of deductive thought is both its great strength and its fundamental weakness.

Professional practicality plays a part. As suggested earlier, it is very difficult to reach agreement regarding generalizations drawn from historical observation. Inferences cannot be made with a high degree of precision as they can using deductive methods, and the inferences are likely to change as historical knowledge increases. Deductive methods overcome these problems and increase the probability of constructing a generally accepted set of economic principles. This encourages the gameplayers at the expense of the realists.

Fittingly, self-interest plays an important role. Mathematical model building, once the basic techniques have been mastered, is relatively easy, and it can be used to produce academic articles quickly. As one is compelled to assume that academic economists are economically rational, they will adopt those research techniques that maximize their research output, because the 'glittering prizes' – academic jobs, promotion, research funds, awards – go to those with the most publications in the leading journals. How many economic historians, for example, have been awarded the Nobel Prize for economics? In their turn the successful gameplayers consciously select like-minded students who are called, quite misleadingly, the 'best' students. What is not made clear, or probably even consciously realized, is that what these students are 'best' at is gameplaying. Because academic gameplayers do not have a comparative advantage in the exploration of reality, they have little interest in applied areas in general and economic history in particular. Hence they use their institutional power advantage to discourage and even exclude the non-gameplayers.

From the longrun to the shortrun

The longrun perspective

For most (about 80 per cent) of the last three centuries, economics has been cast comfortably in a longrun framework. Adam Smith, for example, saw his analysis of the late eighteenth-century British economy as part of a longer process of transition of the economic system through the economic stages of hunting, pasturage, farming, and commerce. He was concerned to set the process of change in real rather than analytical time. Marx, of course, adopted a similar approach, but for different purposes. It was Ricardo who took economics out of real time and placed it in analytical time. Yet even Ricardo, despite his emphasis on microeconomics (the theory of value and the theory of distribution), was concerned with the analysis of longrun economic forces – he emphasized population growth, capital accumulation, and technological change, and was concerned with the dynamics of the growth process.

The two contenders who vied for primacy following the demise of the classical school – the neoclassical and historical schools – had very different approaches to time. Obviously the historical school took real time very seriously, and attempted (at least in the Germanic version) to place their analysis within a variant of Smith's historical stages thesis. As their concern was with dynamic *processes* they had little time for analytical time. By way of contrast the neoclassical school dispensed with real time as Ricardo had done, but in addition they abandoned interest in the dynamics of growth even in an analytical framework. But the neoclassicists were concerned with macroeconomic equilibrium in the longrun. And even this limited vision of the longrun led to an awareness, at least, that in the real world economic changes of whatever origin took time to work themselves out. This in turn was a sufficient, although probably not a necessary, reason to take an interest in longer-term changes in the economy. Marshall, more than any other neoclassical economist of his time, demonstrated a degree of curiosity about history mainly because of the intellectual expectations of his age. But he was not able to integrate his comparative–static microeconomics into a framework of this type. Of course there were isolated economists, such as Joseph Schumpeter, who continued the classical interest in the dynamic process of economic change, but they had little or no influence on the development path of the profession.

The second assault on real time: Keynes and the shortrun

The neoclassical dominance continued, as is well known, until the appearance of Keynes' *General Theory* in 1936. At a single stroke Keynes shifted the attention of economists interested in macroeconomic issues from the longrun to the shortrun. By the 1950s and 1960s every economics undergraduate could quote (generally incorrectly) Keynes' dismissive reference to the neoclassical concept of equilibrium as being 'the longrun in which we are all dead'. Indeed, Keynes' analysis was static as well as shortrun in nature, as he was little concerned with issues of growth. This, as is discussed in Chapter 1, was left to Harrod and Domar, and later the new neoclassicists, but even their approach to growth was highly abstract and unrealistic. While there was a burst of interest in growth models in the 1950s and 1960s, and again in the late 1980s and early 1990s, they were not concerned with dynamic processes, but rather with longrun equilibria (which in this sense were not even theories of growth).[52] The prevailing focus in orthodox economics was basically Keynesian until the mid-1950s, and then a neoclassical synthesis of pre-Keynesian and Keynesian economics until the mid-1970s when it was challenged by both the 'new classical economics' with its timeless emphasis, and by the brief flowering of monetarist economics, which did bring with it a longer-run approach. This Keynesian-inspired emphasis upon the shortrun, therefore, was an important event in the growing dismissal by orthodox economics of economic history. If economists need only focus upon shortrun analysis, there is little point in even glancing back beyond the last year or so, because economic circumstances will have changed and therefore be irrelevant. The *General Theory*, together with Ricardo's *Principles*, delivered the two most important blows against the use of real time in economics.

At the same time applied econometrics, which in the interwar period had been concerned to model the process of economic change in a realistic manner, also became less realistic and more 'artificial' in its approach to the economy. As Mary Morgan says: 'Dynamic [econometric] models sank under the tidal wave of largely static Keynesian models, general equilibrium theories, and Cowles simultaneous equations systems.'[53] The nature of econometrics changed after the 1940s in a manner similar to the way economics had been changing since the advent of neoclassical economics. Morgan concludes:

> applied econometrics seemed to enter a less creative phase. Data were taken less seriously as a source of ideas and information for econometric models, and the theory-development role of applied econometrics was downgraded relative to the theory-testing role ... Econometric models came to be regarded as the passive extensions of economic theory into the real world, as the 'statistical complement of pure economics' rather than as representatives of a 'synthetic economics' in which theoretical knowledge and information from the real world are combined.

In the 1930s the mathematical theory and statistical model building in econometrics relied more closely upon reality. The resulting dynamic disequilibrium models, which were more detailed and complex, attempted to explain causal sequences and to show the impact of policy on these processes. By the 'golden age' of the 1950s and 1960s, econometric theory and model-building had developed a momentum of its own by casting off its associations with reality. These models focused not upon dynamic disequilibrium but upon static equilibrium, in the same way that general economic theory did.[54] They were no longer concerned with the explanation of real time. And the issues that were examined, together with the policy prescriptions that emerged, were inspired by theoretical rather than empirical considerations. The leading edge of applied economics had, by the 1960s, succumbed to the same unbalanced development path of theoretical economics. This, of course, was only partly due to the influence of Keynes – the intellectual dynamics were the same here as in economics – but the influence of Keynes certainly accelerated the transformation.

As great as Keynes' contribution was to the advancement of economic theory, he did the profession a great disservice by greatly accelerating its move away from reality. His legacy is with us today. Most economists see little point in gaining any empirical knowledge of the economy with which they claim to be concerned. For example, Colander and Klamer (1987), by surveying graduate students in economics, made the disturbing discovery that only 3 per cent regarded knowledge of the economy as 'very important', and as many as 68 per cent regarded it as 'unimportant'. No doubt an even higher percentage would regard economic history, stretching back over the last one hundred or so years, as being even more 'unimportant'. This attitude obviously reflects that of their teachers. This was confirmed by a survey undertaken in 1988 by the American Economic Association and published in the *American Economic Review* (May 1990). When asked to rank the 'relative importance now given to various branches of economics', the response of the three groups surveyed (faculty members, recent PhDs, and undergraduates) was, according to the reporter, as follows: 'Economic theory leads the way followed in order by econometrics, empirical economics, and application; institutions, and literature are at the bottom of the list.'[55] Although economic history is not mentioned here (an interesting oversight) it was bracketed with 'institutions' in the questionnaire. Even economists who protest that they do see a role for economic history are quick to qualify their expression of support by saying, 'but of course we wouldn't want you to teach anything before the Second World War, and we would prefer if you focused upon the period since deregulation of the banking system in the early 1980s'. To this way of thinking the period since the Second World War is the longrun, and anything before that is the *very* longrun and obviously totally irrelevant to current problems. The essential point, of course, has been missed. There are two reasons for taking a longrun view: first, as economic change, particularly in terms of institutions and even systems, is accelerating, it is necessary to examine even longer periods of time in the past in order to encompass the magnitude of likely future change. Secondly, we begin to understand how an economy is likely to react to future shocks by examining how it has reacted to past shocks, taking into consideration any structural changes that have occurred in the past and may occur in the future.

THE CRITICS OF ECONOMICS

Deductive economics has been strongly criticized by two groups of scholars in the past one hundred years – the historicists in the late nineteenth century and the ecologists one hundred years later. The attack of the historicists has already been noted, but here we need to consider in more detail the origin and nature of their criticism. While some of the historicist criticism has been uninformed, much of it has found its mark and has never been responded to satisfactorily by economists.[56] The most militant and effective attacks made by historicists were launched in the period from the early 1870s to the mid-1920s, and were responded to rather ineffectively by the leading economists of the day, such as J.S. Mill, Alfred Marshall, Arthur Pigou, and J.M. Keynes. Since that time historicist criticism has been less authoritative and less effective. Indeed, over the last half-century it has gone completely unnoticed by orthodox economists, who have only bothered to contest the attacks of radical economists of various types – Marxists, neo-Ricardians, and post-Keynesians – mainly during the late 1960s and the 1970s. Unfortunately, since the Second World War, historicist criticism has degenerated into a surprisingly bitter and misinformed attack by historians with little or no training in theory and statistics on the work of quantitative and analytical economic historians (or cliometricians). This is the legacy of the historical school, whose more extravagant (indeed silly) statements have been embraced, while their sensible criticisms have been ignored, by many of those in the British tradition of economic and social history. In their turn the cliometricians have reserved their criticism for the historians rather than the economists who they have attempted to emulate.

The first major Anglo-Saxon attack upon deductive economics, as we have seen, was launched in the 1870s by two scholars at Dublin University, Cliffe Leslie and Ingram. While Leslie did much of the ground-work for this attack, it was Ingram who, with a more effective militant style, brought the claims of the historical school to the serious attention of political economists in England.

Leslie's ideas were formulated in the 1860s, largely under the influence of the historical jurisprudence of Sir Henry Maine, and the German historical school of economics. They first emerged in print in 1870,[57] but reached their fullest expression in his 1876 manifesto, an article entitled 'On the philosophical method of political economy'.[58] Leslie rejected the deductive method of Ricardo as 'illusory exposition based upon simplistic primitive assumptions' in favour of the inductive and historical method employed (occasionally) by Adam Smith, because, he claimed, economic generalization was relative to the 'different states of society' and modern man was motivated by more than 'the desire of wealth'. 'Our whole national economy is a historical structure, and in no other manner to be explained or accounted for.'[59] And he concludes by claiming:

> The abstract and à [*sic*] priori method yields no explanation of the laws determining either the nature, the amount, or the distribution of wealth, and ... the philosophical method must be historical, and must trace the conversion between the economical and the other phases of national history.

Leslie's critique of deductive economics received a widespread and sympathetic hearing even from J.S. Mill, and some even believed that the historical approach would become the dominant school of thought in economics. While Leslie was unable to deflect the deductive school from its ascendent path, he did draw attention to the possibility that deductive theory may not be universally applicable in time and space, and, even more importantly, that as the present has emerged out of the past it can only be fully comprehended by an analysis of those forces responsible for its emergence.

Yet it was the fiery rhetoric of Ingram, who was less original than Leslie, that attracted most attention to the historical school. In 1878 Ingram presented a presidential address to the Economics and Statistics Section of the British Association for the Advancement of Science, in which he made an uncompromising attack upon deductive economics. This address was aimed at 'a reform of economic studies' and at 'launching this great question on the field of general English discussion'. On this significant occasion, Ingram drew attention to the crisis in English political economy which, he claimed, owed much to the heretical deductive method 'introduced' by Ricardo. In full flight, Ingram accused the deductive school of 'error', 'pretension', 'vicious abstraction', 'metaphysical habit of mind', 'speculative imagination', and of generating a body of thought consisting of 'hasty generalizations from insufficient and ordinary premises'. And in concluding his provocative address he stated his position more simply and clearly than Leslie was able to do:

> (1) That the study of the economic phenomena of society ought to be systematically combined with that of the other aspects of social existence; (2) That the excessive tendency to abstraction and to unreal simplifications should be checked; (3) That the a priori deductive method should be changed for the historical; (4) That economic laws and the practical prescriptions founded on those laws should be conceived and expressed in a less absolute form. These are, in my opinion, the great reforms which are required both in the conduct of economic research, and in the exposition of its conclusions.[60]

It was on the matter of deductive method and economic rationality that Ingram was most eloquent. He described the deductive heresy of Ricardo's 'vicious abstraction' and argues:

> Now in matters of human life especially, we have only to carry abstraction far enough in order to lose all hold on realities, and present things quite other than they in fact are; and, if we use these abstractions in the premises of our reasonings, we shall arrive at conclusions, either positively false, or useless for any practical purpose.[61]

Warming to this theme, he claimed that economists employing the deductive method 'wander away from any relation to fact, and lose themselves in a region of nebulous metaphysics'; and, he continued, 'It is a characteristic feature of the metaphysical habit of mind . . . to mistake creations of the speculative imagination for objective realities.'[62] The only corrective, Ingram claimed, is the inductive or historical or 'realistic' method, particularly as a basis for economic policy.

Ingram's widely read attack of 1878, which was followed up by his popular *History of Political Economy*, was influential among political economists during the 1880s, at least until Marshall succeeded in developing a set of principles to replace those obsolete principles of the classical school. While this radical and militant critique did not, as we have seen, displace the deductive method in economics, it did draw attention to a fundamentally important problem that is likely to emerge in any excessively deductive social science – the temptation to regard theoretical conclusions as a substitute for reality and, therefore, as an adequate and proper basis for formulating economic policy. One hundred years later this fundamental criticism has yet to be taken seriously by economists.

The English historicists influenced the emerging British tradition in economic and social history through their impact upon W.J. Ashley, William Cunningham, and J.H. Clapham. The clash between the militant Rev. Cunningham and Alfred Marshall in the early 1890s, on the one hand,[63] and Clapham and Arthur Pigou in the early 1920s, on the other, is well known.[64] These clashes were not, however, decisive, and each party withdrew assuming victory and taking with him a feeling that little was to be gained from further interaction. As a result economics and economic history pursued separate and increasingly divergent paths in Britain and the USA, although not in Australia.[65]

Historicist criticism, which for five decades had caused leading economists in the Anglo-Saxon world to think hard about the value of their endeavour, had run its course by the mid1920s. Nevertheless, during this period it raised issues of the utmost importance that have never been countered by economists: the lack of reality or speculative nature of deductive economics; the risks involved in drawing policy prescriptions from theory that has not been applied to reality; the neglect of historical processes that are involved in the present and will be involved in the future; the misuse of history in the attempt to give theory the appearance of universality; and the limited application of certain theory in time and space. It has been possible, until recently, for economists to neglect these issues, because their role as premier policy adviser to governments has not been challenged. For about four decades after the collapse of historicist criticism, deductive economics encountered few natural enemies. During this time it developed without interference. That has changed. Since the late 1960s intruders from beyond the boundaries of the social sciences have finally dared, or bothered, to enter the economist's domain. This new challenge emerged from ecologists such as Paul Ehrlich and from scientists in the Club of Rome. These critical voices have been joined by an amazing upsurge in environmentalist groups which are beginning to have considerable political influence. It remains to be seen what impact this new criticism will have on the role of economists as policy advisers.[66]

CONCLUSION: WHAT IS THE FUTURE FOR ECONOMICS?

The current focus in economics is still directed at highly abstract, mathematical, and ahistorical theoretical structures. There has been no noticeable attempt in universities for economists to work more closely with economic historians, or for economic history to become an essential part of the education of economists. Even in the face of overwhelming evidence that economic policy has failed to prevent economic stagnation, inflation, and unemployment, the need to take historical reality into account has not been seriously considered. The failure of policy is blamed on politicians, rather than upon the profession's rejection of historical reality. It is doubtful, however, that politicians see this problem in the same light and, as a result, the role of economists as premier policy adviser will undoubtedly be seriously challenged. Already we have seen how successful the environmental scientists have been in attracting the attention of governments throughout the Western world. The fate of the economics profession may well depend upon the ability of economists to provide more realistic policy advice, and this can only be achieved if economists place their activities back within the context of real time.

The purpose of this study is to say that: it's time to take time into account. Analytical economic history ranging from the present into the remote past of 1000 to 3000 years ago can contribute not only to economic generalization but can, with a degree of precision sometimes equal to that of applied economics, give realistic content to economic theory. Given the unbalanced development of the economics profession, which has accelerated since the time of Pigou, it is essential to bring back real time. This will not be achieved by acquiescing in the superiority of economics and general history as Clapham did, nor by militantly rejecting deductive economics as Cunningham and the earlier historical economists did, but by forcefully demonstrating to economists that without rigorous economic history their house may fall before the onslaught of the environmentalists. The objective is not to displace deductive economics, but to become an equal partner with it in building a more balanced, realistic, and viable profession of economic science that can take a major part in building a secure future for mankind. This must be the future of economics.

4

GETTING YOUR HANDS DIRTY: ECONOMIC HISTORY AND POLICY ADVICE

G.R. Hawke

INTRODUCTION

'Getting your hands dirty?' was the response of a colleague to my first venture into the field of policy advice. Other responses were less polite, but I was led to consider the comparative advantage of economic historians in such activities. Reflecting on this in 1984, I concluded that the comparative advantage was substantial, but that the flow was not all one-way.[1] Commenting on policy issues is advantageous for an economic historian too. There is a danger of committing an anachronism but it is small relative to the benefits of wider experience – extinction of any lingering belief that those responsible for policy decisions have some source of wisdom denied to mere academics or journalistic commentators, awareness of the power of custom and of what were novel ideas in a much earlier time, understanding of the force of personality and the kind of dynamics that can exist in any decision-making group. I was aware that not too much can be claimed. I do not think it is possible to identify any skill in policy analysis which can be gained only through economic history. Equally, the processes of university administration, viewed with an adequate detachment, can give an economic historian an opportunity to learn at least most of what is available from participation in policy advice.

Since 1984, I have had much more experience of policy advice, but my conclusions have not been changed substantially. (I appreciate some irony in that, since I have become much more conscious of the power of personalities relative to ideas as I shall explain later.) My additional experience has been in three parts. In 1985, I became a member of the New Zealand Planning Council, which I have chaired since 1986 (probably to extinction). Since 1987, I have directed the Victoria University of Wellington's Institute of Policy Studies, and in 1988 I convened a Cabinet Social Equity Committee Working Group on Post-compulsory Education and Training.

It will be apparent from this that I am talking from the viewpoint of an observer of policy formation more than that of a participant in policy formulation. 'Policy advice' can mean many things. Anybody can tell a government what it is sensible for it to do – with varying levels of credibility and persuasiveness. As New Zealand's government departments have been required to define their outputs more precisely, policy advice has loomed larger in their concerns. Many people have a vision of cabinets engaged in searching consideration of an issue which they find of compelling importance, and formulating a clear and coherent response (usually defined as one which the advocate favours). In fact, cabinets mostly take yes or no decisions on a series of issues defined by departmental advisers, and 'policy advice' includes the formulation of those issues. It is only in the third of my areas of involvement that I have been close to policy advice in that sense.

The New Zealand Planning Council is a quango with a statutory mandate to 'monitor and report on New Zealand's social, economic, cultural and environmental development'. It has some parallels with the Australian Economic Policy Advisory Council, but has been more distant from politicians. It grew, in the later 1970s, from two major motivations: a sense that government gave too little consideration to medium-term issues because of its preoccupation with immediate problems, and a desire for greater integration of social and economic policies. In recent years, governments in New Zealand have been persuaded of the importance of the medium term – the *Budgets* of the last few years read more like Planning Council reports of the 1970s and early 1980s than like the *Budgets* of those years. Consequently, the distinguishing characteristic of the Planning Council has come to be more and more its insistence on looking at economic and social issues together. Furthermore, the government of 1984–90 wanted to get policy advice from a wider area of society than its predecessors, and its ministers wanted a greater degree of autonomy from public service advisers. The Planning Council therefore put less emphasis on reporting to government and more emphasis on its function of participating in public debate and explaining to groups in society the constraints which made it impossible for government simply to endorse their sectional views.

The Institute of Policy Studies is part of the university's attempts to bridge the gap between academic research and the concerns of policy-makers. Its aim is to promote study, research, and discussion of current issues of public policy, both foreign and domestic. It is to a large extent a 'paper corporation', familiar to academics throughout Australia and New Zealand in that it has few resources of its own. It essentially depends on securing funding from government departments and the private sector, working on a project by project basis, and the job of the Director is to locate overlaps between research which academics or others are interested in doing and which other people are willing to finance. (Its publications while I have been Director are listed in the Appendix to this chapter). Like everybody else, it attempts to foresee policy issues of the future, not so much to demonstrate wisdom as because academics do not work well to timetables. My predecessor and his advisers thought in 1983 that at some time in the not too distant future the issue of value-added tax would have to be addressed; by 1984, the government was wanting the results of the research before it was completed. In 1989–90, the Institute sponsored a long-range look by a Treasury official on secondment at what happens if one thinks in terms of redistribution instead of taxes and social welfare transfers.[2] A government statement in December 1990 announced the establishment of a Change Team (chaired by our principal researcher) and we are currently waiting for this year's *Budget* to see what has survived a closer scrutiny of administrative feasibility and the ravages of political acceptability.

The third experience on which I draw is chairing the Cabinet Social Equity Committee Working Group on Post-compulsory Education and Training. After the 1987 election, with the government committed to making social policy the key concern of its second term, Geoffrey Palmer, then Deputy Prime Minister, was appointed to chair the Cabinet Social Equity Committee (CSEC). He sought advice from ministers on priorities and envisaged working groups assisting the CSEC to develop policy in appropriate areas. Post-compulsory education and training was one such area. Palmer's intention was that CSEC itself should decide social policy. Each working group was to be a mixture of officials and consultants from outside the public service, and it was to formulate material into a form appropriate for a Cabinet committee to make decisions. CSEC initially took a great deal of interest in the membership of the Working Groups, but, inevitably, over time it had to leave departments to make appointments. CSEC continued to choose members from outside the public service, and it continued to approve the nomination of conveners. This was important, because a key difference between Working Groups and former interdepartmental committees was that the report of each Working Group was the responsibility of its convener. Departmental dissents and reservations were to be noted, but the Working Groups were not expected to seek consensus. The intention was to sharpen the advice on which ministers could base their decisions.

The process worked as intended, through reports, decisions, legislation, and implementation, only for a few Working Groups. Those in the education field, on early childhood and post-compulsory education, benefited from the process of change which had already been begun. The group on equal employment opportunities was promoted by a well-placed convener, support from women members of the government caucus, and pressure from many women for 'their share' of government intervention. Most Working Groups eventually disappeared back into interdepartment negotiation. (Some, such as that on regulation, nevertheless had significant results.) The successful groups dealt with well-defined problems, not with social policy as a whole. A coherent social policy could not come from a scatter-gun approach, which was the inevitable result when the chair of CSEC invited nomination of problems to be tackled.

The CSEC Working Group device was a kind of half-way house between departmental coordination and the imposition of outside authority. Making reports the responsibility of conveners was the key change, but the supply of conveners who were independent and yet sufficiently knowledgeable about departmental processes was always limited. Working Groups depended on the cooperation of departments, and my members were more departmental representatives than individuals. Indeed, the process can be seen as giving the office of the chair of the CSEC the responsibility which in some countries is that of the Prime Minister's Department. The experiment showed that the main difficulty in social policy was not bureaucratic inertia, but the difficulty of defining and resolving issues. The notion that ministers could decide an appropriate social policy without a process consisting of interdepartmental consultation was disproved.

ECONOMICS IS NOT SUFFICIENT FOR POLICY ADVICE

Many years ago, before we became sensitive to the way language reinforced barriers to gender equality, Solow wisely commented that, while he preferred applied economists to be familiar with high-level theory before they used low-level theorizing, it was the latter which had most practical utility:

> In physics so far as an outsider can judge, you have to master the simple theory in order to gain access to the fancy theory; and many spectacular practical achievements seem to have come from the fancy theory. In economics, things are different. I like a man to have mastered the fancy theory before I trust him with the simple theory. The practical utility of economics comes not primarily from its high-powered frontier, but from fairly low-powered reasoning. (I think this occurs not for any intrinsic reason, but because the data are not available to give precision to high-powered theory. And in addition it often turns out that the high-powered theory of today is the low-powered theory of tomorrow.)[3]

We have become more sceptical of whether parallels between physics and economics are useful, but Solow's comment does not depend on the references to physics. Measurement techniques have improved but remain important. This refers both to what we may loosely call primary measurement and statistical processing, 'loose' because our most basic data requires considerable processing. Recent revisions to New Zealand's balance of payments statistics show the limitations of some of our most basic information, which result from both difficulties in the collection of material by the Department of Statistics following the abolition of exchange control, and from conceptual issues about what constitutes an economic transaction between New Zealand and the rest of the world as national economies become more integrated.[4] I have ventured the speculation that we will see some revisions of New Zealand's growth data because deflation processes become inappropriate and biased when the relative size of different economic activities changes markedly, as happened in New Zealand in the 1980s. This is no more than an example of the index number problem.

I do not want to underestimate the importance of measurement. It can seem futile to debate whether a growth rate is half a per cent or 1 per cent, or perhaps the economy is flat, especially when we are forecasting what happened six months ago. But the answers may be important to many current plans. The implications may be even greater when we are concerned with the longer term, and they are familiar to economic historians. When scholars brought the perspective of modern economic development to the experience of the Industrial Revolution, there was a fundamental reassessment of the speed of economic adjustment. The result is now so familiar that it can be encapsulated in a numerical example.[5]

Consider an economy that can be divided into two parts. One is modernized and grows at 4 per cent per annum. The other is traditional and grows at 1 per cent per annum. Initially, the former composes only 10 per cent of the total. Because of its faster growth rate, its share of the total increases. But as a matter of arithmetic, after twenty years it constitutes only 17 per cent of the total. (And the growth rate of the economy has increased from 1.3 per cent to 1.5.) After fifty years, the modern sector is 32 per cent of the total and the aggregate growth rate is 2 per cent per annum. After seventy-five years, the modern and traditional sectors are of equal size and the growth rate is 2.5 per cent. And after a century, the modern sector constitutes two-thirds of the total and the growth rate is 3 per cent per annum.

That is delightfully simple, but the initial figures are not unrealistic, and it shows why economic change in Britain remained slow in the face of dramatic technical achievements in particular parts of the economy. (It is, however, an aid to understanding, not a finished explanation. In particular, it does not capture the way in which change was diffused. There was no 'traditional' part of the economy which remained unaffected by improved means of production.)

The result also presents problems to economic historians. Changes may be significant even when they are small, but they are necessarily harder to detect and even more difficult to measure with precision. Sometimes it appears that available figures are being asked to bear too much weight, and that the sources, which are sometimes little more than guesses, have too large a range of error to permit us to discriminate between alternative possibilities. The reason for this, however, is not excessive zeal by modern scholars, but the implication of the arithmetic example we have just discussed – rates of change which imply quite different courses for the economy are themselves close together – the difference between 1.3 and 1.5 is twenty years of unprecedented industrial growth.

So measurement is important. Nevertheless, I doubt whether Solow's emphasis on measurement was justified. The principal difference between social sciences and natural sciences is that the subjects of the former have a much greater capacity for learning. The understanding created by economists gets disseminated to those whose behaviour they study, and that behaviour is modified. I understand that this happens in the natural sciences too, but there can be little doubt that it is a faster and more fundamental process when people are the object of study. The targets we are trying to measure are moving more rapidly. They are moving more because of the measurements and thinking in which we are engaged.

This seems to me the principal reason for conceiving of economics as Keynes did in the 'Introduction to the series' in a number of Cambridge Economic Handbooks:

> The Theory of Economics does not furnish a body of settled conclusions immediately applicable to policy. It is a method rather than a doctrine, an apparatus of the mind, a technique of thinking, which helps its possessor to draw correct conclusions.[6]

Endorsements of this proposition are common, but its implications are deep. Newspapers and political speeches often contain claims that something must be wrong because it contradicts a conclusion of economic theory; the writer or speaker does not mean that there should be an enquiry into consistency of thinking or the reasons why correct application of a technique of thinking leads to a surprising conclusion. And this is not limited to ephemeral sources; it can be found in the literature of economic history and of economics itself.

The latter is most fundamental. If one really accepts that economic theory is an apparatus of thinking rather than a body of conclusions, there is not a great deal of sense in asking about its validity in any sense other than its internal consistency, except in a particular context. Hicks was concerned about the real world, and really believed Keynes' dictum that economics was simply a means of thinking. Blaug has recently criticized Hicks on the grounds that his view of economics deprives us of any ability to decide whether an argument is valid.[7] But it does no such thing if we think in terms of assessing an argument about a particular empirical setting. This might also explain the somewhat puzzled attitude of economists in general to the work of Hicks.[8]

I have deliberately passed lightly over the distinction between economic theory and economics; it was the 'Theory of Economics' about which Keynes wrote. 'Economics' is much wider. It is not going too far to call it a 'culture', a group of people sharing some fundamental beliefs and engaged in some common endeavours, although I have no doubt that anthropologists would object to such a loose use of a concept that is more central to their concerns than it is to mine. It seems to me that economists have become more unified in recent years. As has been noted by Wade Hands,[9] whereas economic methodologists, like philosophers in general, use '*ad hoc*' mostly in the sense of Popper – essentially evasive tactics – economic theorists have come to use it more in the sense of Lakatos – not consistent with the central thrusts of rationality and optimization. We still accept what Popper called 'situational logic', that in seeking to understand behaviour we assume that individuals make assessments of where they are and act according to their beliefs about how they are most likely to achieve some objective; tempting though it often is, to assume that people are irrational deprives us of any power of explanation. But economists, initially I think in the search for better micro foundations for macroeconomics, have reasserted the primacy of income maximization and prices as incentives. They are more ready to dismiss any deviation from this central core as *ad hoc*. There are gains and losses in this, but, although it makes sense to think of economics as a culture as well as an intellectual discipline, it remains important to distinguish between these topics of study. In particular, confusion is avoided if one distinguishes between assessing the validity of an argument and describing the process by which arguments are constructed.

I appreciate that this diminishes the extent to which economic theory is self-contained. But the term 'economic theory' does suggest some abstraction. If we must have a utilitarian justification for economic theory, I think we should not look for examples of how theorists can advise policy-makers (or business decision-makers), but rather to the value of theoretical studies as a learning device. Clarifying concepts and checking the consistency of logical argument is an important part of the education of the next generation, and economic theory needs no other utilitarian defence. Those who have followed recent debates over educational policy in either Australia or New Zealand will see further value in an argument which supports the mutual interdependence of teaching and research within universities.

The argument could be pursued along several trails. It does not imply that an economic theorist cannot be a good policy adviser – only that the individual must have skills and knowledge in addition to those of an economic theorist. It does not imply that we should not distinguish political compromises from economic analysis, but it does imply that we should admit the possibility that we need to distinguish between good policy analysis and analysis which has congenial conclusions even if congeniality is judged by the rigour with which standard economic theory is adopted. The 'policy implications' drawn from complex models, with or without application to a more or less arbitrary data set, often seem simple-minded to those concerned with policy advice (and incomprehensible to most concerned with policy decisions). The empirical setting, the context to which policy analysis refers, is not merely a minor consideration.

ECONOMICS IS USEFUL FOR POLICY

There seems little need to argue that economics is useful for policy formulation. Although there are obvious dangers of circularity in arguing that institutional change reveals optimal decision-making, the increased number of economists in government service is probably sufficient. The more interesting question is the relative importance of economics and other influences. I propose to explore this in relation to the change in economic policy in New Zealand after 1984.

The need for change was widely recognized. Most important, it was apparent to leading official economists. The election of a new government in July 1984, especially one which resulted from a snap election and had therefore given few hostages to particular interest groups, provided an opportunity for an unusually sharp change of direction.[10]

The centre-piece of economic policy became efficiency and equity. The traditional statement of the objectives of economic policy, in terms of economic growth, income distribution, minimization of inflation, balance of payments equilibrium, and full employment, was reconsidered. Fundamental objectives and means to those ends were more clearly distinguished. Emphasis on efficiency and equity was the result.

There are trade-offs between efficiency and equity. A modern civilized society cannot leave some of its members without an adequate standard of living; this necessarily creates some disincentives to providing for oneself. If we rely on an insurance-based medical scheme, we still have to provide for those who gamble on good health and lose, and even for those who deliberately invoke moral hazard and choose to take the risk of relying on public support. If we seek to provide income support for those aged who are unable to support themselves, we affect the incentives of others to save. These tensions are unavoidable, and guarantee that there must be continuing political debate about how the balance of advantage for society as a whole is moved by economic and social change.

The new policy environment deals with both efficiency and equity. There is room for debate about each of the two components. It might seem that efficiency is a more 'technical' and therefore less debatable topic, but, before one can determine whether one is securing maximum output from given resources, one must be sure of what is being produced. If broadcasting is simply provision of entertainment, then its efficient organization is different from what is required if 'public broadcasting' is distinct from 'commercial broadcasting' and is concerned with nation building as well as entertainment. One must also know the market for which output is being produced. Whether or not a producer or marketing board is to be preferred to competitive marketing on efficiency grounds depends critically on the nature of market being served. There are, therefore, debates about the meaning of efficiency, even when one puts aside simple misunderstandings which result when people interpret efficiency as being concerned with cost-minimization rather than with the ratio of benefits to costs. But there is no doubt that passions are higher when the meaning of equity is debated. In particular, as more weight was given to achieving incomes comparable to those available overseas, less was given to securing full employment. The combination of protection and investment in low-yielding projects which had been used in earlier years was no longer acceptable, but no alternative was found. As the government put more emphasis on social policy after it was re-elected in 1987, divisions within its ranks became deeper, culminating in December 1988 in the departure from Cabinet of the Minister of Finance who had directed the change in economic policy since 1984. For the rest of its life, until its electoral defeat in 1990, the government failed to reconcile the conflicting pressures it was under. Prime Minister Lange resigned in August 1989, but his successor, Palmer, was no more successful, and after 13 months he gave way to Moore. However, in the six weeks before an election, he could achieve little.

The problem was that the government could not cohere around a plausible view of the relationship between economic and social progress. Economic strategy had acquired a new coherence. It built on some earlier changes, especially the Closer Economic Relations (CER) agreement with Australia, but there was a change of emphasis of a magnitude not seen since 1938. The essential change was towards a determination to make the best possible use of New Zealand resources so as to minimize the difference in living standards in New Zealand and in those countries with which comparisons are usually made. There was no such coherence in strategy towards the social role of government.

There is a widespread impression that Treasury has been entirely responsible for these policy changes, and that they have been driven by a political agenda. While the argument to be developed in the subsequent sections of this chapter implies that we will be in a better position to evaluate the basis for these beliefs some time in the future when a historical perspective is available, I am prepared now to advance some contrary views.

I have already observed that Treasury officials were especially important. My additional point is that they were not alone and did not always prevail. There was a ready consensus that change was inevitable, shared by other officials, especially in the Reserve Bank and in the State Services Commission, even before Roderick Deane moved from the former to the latter. They were dealing with politicians who wanted to establish a place in history as a reforming administration. More important, Treasury's views did not always prevail in the policy process. Most fundamentally, Treasury was well aware of the tension between the fiscal situation and the other elements of policy being adopted. It wanted policy settings which would have reduced the share of the adjustment borne by the tradable goods sector. It could not persuade Cabinet that a faster pace could be forced on changes in the level and composition of government expenditure.

The more important question for this discussion is the source of the ideas underlying the economic and policy analysis. Treasury officials have political views, but they extend across a large part of the spectrum found in the community at large. There is a spread of attitudes within Treasury to defence expenditure and to social welfare expenditure, which we might use as indicators of political allegiance. What Treasury officials have in common, they share with other economists. What was important was a reassertion of the importance of prices and incentives. Public choice theory, agency theory, and analysis of transactions costs were important not so much for what was preoccupying writers in the journals, but for how people thought about the use of resources.

This then becomes a more general reflection. Of course, sophisticated economic thinking is important in the formulation of policy advice. It is not possible to engage in a discussion of tariff policy at the level needed for policy formulation without understanding the notion of 'producers' subsidy equivalent', which in turn requires an appreciation of general equilibrium effects, let alone such ideas as effective protection which was formalized only in the 1960s. It is even more obvious that to participate in policy debate, it is necessary to have some understanding of modern statistical techniques (and of their limitations).

And yet what is most required is familiarity with the underlying ideas. A firm grasp of the concept of income and of its limitations is a good starting point. Understanding the paradox of thrift is even better – the difference between *ex ante* and *ex post* is often fundamental, even if it is only understood as the difference between intentions and realizations, which is hardly at its core. Once it is recognized that the collective may have different interests from each of its parts, it is relatively easy to grasp the core of the prisoner's dilemma, and from there much modern organizational interest follows fairly readily. What is important, however, is that we should not be thinking of two prisoners and a district attorney (and getting anxious about the transmission of American thinking to a different institutional setting), but about the articulation of decision-making mechanisms. That requires real familiarity, and makes possible an instinctive recognition that time is important; the best way of handling a one-off negotiation may be very different from managing a continuing relationship.

This illustrates the way that fundamental economic ideas influence a wide range of thinking. The same point could be made with respect to the idea of investment. In a first-year undergraduate class, we readily think about how we can introduce the idea of reserving resources from current consumption in order to create the conditions in which we can reasonably expect greater contributions to consumption at a later date. We want to get on to exercises about accelerators and capacity utilization, and on to linkages with interest rates and the relationship between the financial sector and the real economy. We certainly do not want to get bogged down in Böhm-Bawerk and the notion of 'roundabout methods of production', even though we may want to introduce the idea of 'human capital'. And yet it is those extensions which are likely to be important in many policy contexts. As we hear our colleagues complain about the folly of filling in applications for research grants when they could be spending their time getting on with the research, we can sympathize, but not wholeheartedly, because as economists we are conscious of the parallel with any investment.

All of which merely adds detail to Solow's observation. And yet I wonder whether it gets to the heart of why economists are so often resented by those in the policy community with a different background. Fundamentally, what distinguishes economists is a concern with resource allocation. We cannot accept that any problem can be solved simply by providing more resources to deal with it, not at least without considering where those resources are to come from, and therefore checking that we are making a social gain by giving up what the resources currently produce. It is just a matter of ensuring that the analysis is complete, or at least adequate to justify an action. It shows the great strength of economics; because it is concerned with well-substantiated linkages between variables, it includes indirect effects as well as direct ones. It illustrates why economists are so irritating; they have few constraints on them because virtually nothing government does has no resource implications and therefore economists have something to contribute to all policy areas. Is it any wonder that critics from right and left of the political spectrum, from all areas of policy, from Defence to Social Welfare, and including Environment, Science, Health and Customs, let alone Education, think that Treasury should go back to being pure book-keepers and leave others with at least primacy in their own field?

But resource allocation is part of those fields. And resource allocation is closely linked with markets. 'Market' is a word which is often used with pejorative overtones. It is associated with aggression and self-interest, and contrasted with compassion and the higher values of civilization. Economists have an entirely different conception. For them, markets ensure that 'the law of the jungle' does not prevail and provide means by which resource allocation decisions are made rationally.

A market is an institution which means that people can trade so that both parties are better off. It provides security for people. In origin, a market was probably a place where it was known that certain rules would be maintained so that people would not be cheated or simply have their possessions stolen. From that starting point, modern commercial law developed, and markets are now often almost wholly abstract, but the key is still the same – a set of institutional structures which provide willing parties with an opportunity to exchange things to their mutual satisfaction with some recourse to outside bodies if they think they have been misled.

Markets were very important in material progress in earlier centuries. The security which people felt in being able to trade without having their possessions confiscated may have been one of the most important advantages of Western Europe in achieving economic growth, higher living standards, and greater personal freedom.[11]

Notice the importance of rules in this conception of markets. Government action sets the essential constraints which ensure that the actions of individual market participants do not conflict with wider aims. The rules around market activity have long proscribed slavery, trade in some commodities like drugs, and so on. They were extended in the nineteenth century to preclude some monopolistic practices. Economists do not usually concern themselves with issues of social control, but they know that reliance on markets is not a surrendering of social control. Once it has been decided that some social control is desirable, and that is often the most difficult decision, the choice is usually between direct and indirect social control. On the other hand, economists do not often concern themselves with wondering about why we accept a prohibition of slavery but seek to settle questions of minimum wages purely on their economic implications. Nor do we readily explore questions such as whether the readjustment of the rights of investors and creditors, which was the result of limited liability legislation in the nineteenth century, has any implications for current discussion of the relative rights of employees and shareholders.

But while we can ask, as I shall do later, for a breadth of interest among economists, my immediate concern is that we recognize the way in which economic thinking is important for policy debate. It is not in the advanced theory that the precise conditions under which decentralized transactions produce social optima are explored; it is in understanding the nature of markets and recognizing their social utility. Most people think of markets as an auction market dealing with fruit and vegetables. But they are vastly more varied than that. Many academics have told me they want nothing to do with buying and selling education as a commodity, and when I tell them that they are doing so, with government acting as agent for beneficiaries, they think I am being facetious or malicious. It is in overcoming such lack of understanding that economics contributes most to policy discussion. I suppose it could be argued that my concern is essentially a matter of semantics. Economists tend to think interchangeably of markets and resource allocation; it is the latter which is important and economics could do without the word 'markets'. But it is important that we do not allow echoes of nineteenth-century English prejudices against 'trade' to get in the way of sensible policy decisions about the allocation of resources. And we could do the same with many economic concepts. Most people think of competition in terms akin to the law of the jungle – for every winner there is a loser. The concepts of positive-sum game and of competition as a system of organization which enhances the total output to be distributed require some understanding such as is provided by familiarity with economic theory. We have sterile debates about competition versus cooperation instead of discussion about how we decide the areas in which we should emphasize each of competition and cooperation.

All of which seems to lead to the conclusion that economics is not only useful to policy analysis but that irritation with economists is readily explained as essentially a lack of understanding of the core of economics. But there are grounds for caution before we accept such a congenial conclusion. Economists and conservatives are inclined to rely on nineteenth-century individualism, and to see social policy as a safety-net. Sociologists see individuals as moulded by all kinds of social pressures, as members of many interacting communities, with their freedom of choice constrained by social forces. The gap is not as stark as that, because economists allow for individuals forming groups as they like, and sociologists talk readily enough about the autonomy of the individual. But it does seem to me to be important to try to establish some distinction between economic analysis and the political philosophy of individualism. The latter is a matter of political debate.

The economic perspective is only one way of looking at things. Perhaps we should not be concerned with worries about costs, the communal provision of some services such as access to housing being simply a sign of a civilized economy? I resist this argument; I don't think we should think of social policy as choosing between the views of economists and non-economists, saying that in some cases we are concerned with costs and that in other cases we are not. Just as markets are always a combination of governmental and non-governmental activity, so policy initiatives always involve the use of resources which could be made available for other government or private uses, while the objective of a policy initiative may be something like social cohesion, which is more familiar to other disciplines than to economics. Access to social services is very much an economic issue, although defining the services draws on other disciplines too. So just as 'public broadcasting' may be a different commodity from 'commercial broadcasting', public education may have attributes different from those of private educational services. Discerning these is simply part of the process of defining a particular market. But it is very hard to see where the line is between economic thinking and the political views of the individual.

There is another particular aspect of this question. Economics largely proceeds on the basis of examining the implications of individuals or coalitions pursuing their own interests. The interaction of private and public benefit is at the core of the discipline. It gives less attention to how individuals and groups assess their own interests. I recently heard the chairperson of a large commercial development organization comment on how he originally had no interest in the arts, but included artistic elements in a building because the relevant local authority offered an incentive in the form of extra floor space. As a result of that inducement he developed an interest in the arts, and provision for them is now included in the company's planning even in areas where the local authority offered no such inducement. It is a nice question whether the bonus scheme in question fits into a general policy stance of not preferring one activity over another. Should the arts receive special attention? There is less of a problem where one thinks of a market as a social framework for individual action. It then looks like a neat piece of tactical planning within a wider concept of strategic planning.

This is part of a much broader issue. As devices for enabling individuals and organizations to pursue self-interest within a general conception of the public interest, markets depend on their participants being well informed, whether about the value of the arts or anything else. Public goods are not the only barrier to relying on orthodox markets – opportunistic behaviour of various kinds has to be guarded against. Much current discussion about the 'information society' could be assimilated into a fuller discussion of choosing markets or other institutional arrangements for educational and social policy.

And the answer to the question posed at the beginning of this section? Economics was important to the change of policy after 1984. The essential problem, the gap between New Zealanders' aspirations and how they were using their resources, was widely perceived. It was an understanding of economics which provided a coherent argument. Familiarity with current economic thinking was important, but ability to deploy fundamental economic concepts across the whole spectrum of government activity was even more so. And it was the principal reason for the pre-eminence of Treasury.

WHAT ELSE IS NEEDED IS APPRECIATION OF CONTEXT

Most economic theory, then, whether or not it is supported by standard empirical testing, is valuable to the policy process because it shows the significance of links between variables which could easily be treated as independent. There was a time when the budget balance was discussed mostly in the context of aggregate demand. More recently, it has been regarded as important to link it also to the balance of savings and investment. Why is this? At one level, it is simply the result of discovering that interesting intellectual problems arise when one explores different linkages, and that is a sufficient reason for academic study. But there are other aspects too. The 'absorption' approach to the balance of payments has a lengthy history, and the intellectual issues have been around a long time. Greater significance has arisen from changes external to the intellectual development of a discipline. I suggest that two are of particular importance here.

One is that we are still exploring the implications of a general shift from fixed exchange rates to floating exchange rates. A great deal of our thinking is in terms of national governments and sovereign states, and it takes a long time to appreciate that savings and investment now have to be seen in an international rather than a national context. I do not think that it is any accident that historians are finding new interest in the formation of national states from the sixteenth century through the nineteenth century, or that the media is finding fascination in the current problems of Yugoslavia.

The second external influence is a broad social change. Demographic trends are taking us towards an ageing society. Intelligent policy discussion includes the implication that in future it will be more difficult to transfer income from those of working age to the retired. I have noticed this especially in Japan. There the inference has been drawn that it is wise to accumulate investments which can provide income support for the aged, especially investments in countries where the age structure is younger.

The discussion in Japan is more complex than this, as policy discussion always is. Other ideas are influential, including a simple fear of inflation and even some doubts over whether young people are not becoming too ready to enjoy a comfortable life rather than work as their parents did (which I suspect has been felt by every successive generation and would like to see investigated by a competent historian). Some people also welcome any argument which can be used to defend balance of payments surpluses against arguments that Japan should be more willing to help other countries where local products find it hard to compete against Japanese exports. But the argument is held sincerely, and it represents a genuine integration of social and economic policies which will become more influential elsewhere. It is a genuine integration, not the use of a call for more integration of social and economic policy which is really a disguised unargued plea for higher welfare expenditure and less concern with fiscal discipline.

Institutional setting is usually thought of at a more micro-level, and it may be very important. One might wonder, for example, why New Zealand seemed to be more attractive when a larger proportion of Japanese investment was portfolio rather than direct. The growth of Japan's investment in foreign securities was in part merely an aspect of internationalization of the financial environment, but it was also related to release from exchange and capital controls, which in turn was related to American pressure to free up Japanese markets. There was nothing peculiar to New Zealand in this. Nor was there in the background of an appreciating yen, and it is unlikely that there were significant mistakes in predicting exchange rate movements. Rather, there was still an element of regulation-generated capital outflows. Japanese life assurance institutions do not generally regard capital gains as available for distribution to policyholders, and were reluctant to generate uncertainty by changing a longstanding custom. Foreign securities denominated in currencies depreciating against the yen, such as the New Zealand dollar, returned high nominal interest rates. Even though the institutions also experienced capital losses from exchange rate changes, they welcomed returns in a form which made them available for distribution. When this particular twist became less important and Japanese investment was more in the form of equity investment, New Zealand became relatively less attractive.

This kind of example is readily generalizable. In any policy debate, it pays to know, or to check with appropriate sources of information about, the decisions being made or likely to be made by significant players. It helps to know that experience disappointed those in the late 1960s who thought that management was itself a sufficient specialization and that conglomerates could operate in any market.

It is, however, longer term consequences of institutional change which are harder to decipher and to monitor. When central banks were being established in the interwar years, and, under the sponsorship of the IMF, as more countries became independent in the postwar years, there was little concern with the implications for inflation. But eventually a connection was made:

> Accordingly, I conclude that the only effective way to refrain from using inflation as a means of taxation is to avoid having a central bank. Once a central bank is established, the die is likely to have been cast for inflation.[12]

I was interested recently to listen to a senior official of the Reserve Bank of New Zealand reflect on the long-term experience of inflation in New Zealand, note that the average was much higher since the 1930s, and ask, in effect, whether Friedman was right. I do not think he was in the particular case of New Zealand. New Zealand's inflation rate remained more or less in line with international trends until the late 1960s or 1970s, and I do not think the existence of a central bank was the institutional change which then enabled New Zealand's rate to become unusually high. (Friedman may well be right to the extent that the existence of central banks contributed to the higher rate of international inflation in the 1950s and 1960s than in earlier years.) I suspect that what was important in the particular case of New Zealand was the abandonment of a fixed exchange rate. I have argued elsewhere that a fixed exchange rate was more a matter of faith and morality than of economic analysis for much of New Zealand's history, reinforced by the institutional fact that New Zealand's currency was long conceived as sterling which happened to be geographically removed from Britain, and that exchange rates were understood as bank charges for the geographic transmission of funds rather than the price of one currency in terms of another. Popular opinion contained strong elements of that until the devaluation of 1967 and even until the exchange rate regime became one of an adjustable peg in the 1970s.

The importance of being able to recognize longer run changes has itself increased because of changes in what we study, because people learn and adapt. Credibility has become a matter of great concern to policy-makers – and economic historians have found it a useful way of deepening understanding of past events, whether the greater flexibility of the British government than of the French during the Revolutionary Wars of the late eighteenth century, or reactions to policy initiatives during the 1930s. It can easily degenerate into circular argument, but there is a real sense in which the effect of policy often depends critically on the reactions it generates. There is a lot of useful economic thinking that can be drawn on, but it is the change in society which has made that thinking so useful. It is not, as sometimes thought, the result of a political choice about whose interests should be considered. Any part of society may be especially important for particular policies; when the concern is essentially about savings and investments, those most concerned with managing risk and making judgements about time preference – the financial markets – are likely to be prominent. The 'market reaction' which now plays a key role in budgetary policy-making is not deference to the relatively well-off; it is shorthand for a quick impression of social responses.

ECONOMIC HISTORY PROVIDES A GOOD TRAINING IN ANALYSING CONTEXTS

> As to what action the new National Government should take to try to improve the degree of co-ordination in the formulation of government policy, the obvious response is 'learn the lessons of our own history'.[13]

This is the conclusion, not of a self-interested historian, but of a former Secretary of the Treasury, reflecting on problems which have emerged from a re-organization of the public service. It provokes the question: what exactly does expertise in history provide? Nobody would take seriously the idea that there will be an exact repetition of past situations, and so it is not just a matter of enlarging memory. It is, I think, that an intelligent study of history increases sensitivity to institutional influences.

Policy advice, like economic history, draws on economic theory in an eclectic manner. In the summing up to a recent conference on 'Economic Reform and Internationalization: China and the Pacific Region', Alan Bollard noted the wide range of economic ideas and theories which had been drawn on in the discussion. They included terms and concepts from standard international trade theory, labour economics (especially on the implications of an imposed immobility of labour), production function analysis (especially on the significance of institutional change in agriculture), organizational theory and principal–agent analysis (especially on the future of state-owned enterprises), marketing, and others. (I cannot recall any specific reliance on Marxian economics.) But the discussion was far from confused. What gave it focus was a common concern with understanding the development which has occurred in China and its implications for the Asia–Pacific region, along with a shared background of most participants, especially their concern with resource allocation.

This particular exercise was directed towards greater understanding and was a long way from the formulation of specific policy advice. But its eclectic drawing on economic theory in the context of a specific context was precisely the process familiar to economic historians. It is also a process required for policy formulation. The latter also requires familiarity with other disciplines (although the discussion in China turned in large part on the related question of whether a change in economic direction would require change in the political system and whether it could be expected to induce the necessary change). In any case, economic historians are always well placed to extend their interests into any other aspect of history.

Not only can they use the natural 'imperialism' of economics, but they can relate to the emphasis on individuals which is common among historians who want to know about both social trends and individual experiences. In observing policy-making, I have often been tempted to reflect on another passage by Keynes, about 'practical men' being the 'slave of some defunct economist', or to think in terms of people being unable to accommodate new ideas after a certain age. As I have watched committees being assembled because individuals can be relied on to promote certain set ideas, I have realized that academics may be dogmatic, but they are more open to ideas than most people. Part of the context for any policy debate is considering the people playing key roles. It was not merely as a protective device that I began this paper with a description of my own background.

CONCLUSION

It might be said that this is a rather obvious argument – economic theory is not sufficient for policy analysis, economics is useful for policy purposes, so is an appreciation of the context in which any economics is to be applied, and economic history is a good means of understanding and practising the relevant kind of application. It could be put into an axiomatic form as economists – as a culture – generally prize,[14] but it hardly justifies such an effort. Nevertheless, it seems to me to have important implications, notably that in a teaching programme for future economists there should be adequate provision for developing an understanding of the kind of work in which graduates are going to be engaged. There can be many arguments for economic history: I personally put first not any argument based on policy considerations but that about allowing individuals to develop their intellectual capacities in the way they find most congenial, but there is also a very strong utilitarian argument. Longrun analysis is important, and economic history is the best way of developing it.

Let me conclude with a caveat. What is most needed in policy discussion is intellectual capacity. What gets very difficult is to preserve distinctions as policies are simplified for popular discussion. It is not merely a matter of preserving technical language such as 'public good'; it is a matter of discerning what really needs to be understood. 'Local autonomy within national guidelines' was a clever slogan which accurately caught an essential part of policy reform in educational management. It was not kept distinct in the political process from 'parents will be able to control the schools'. There is a sensible argument about corporatization and privatization within the public sector (and it draws on an appreciation of principal–agent relationships and the role of the capital market, including its limitations). It never got into the political process beside the apparent simplicity of selling assets to reduce debt. There are many skills required in the processes of policy formulation and implementation. Ability to handle long-range economic analysis, even with a due appreciation of context is not sufficient – but it is necessary.

APPENDIX: PUBLICATIONS OF THE INSTITUTE OF POLICY STUDIES, 1987–91

New Zealand in a Changing World: the Management of Economic Change, Wellington, Institute of Policy Studies, 1988, pp. 173.

The Producer Board Seminar Papers, Wellington, Institute of Policy Studies, 1988, pp. 124.

State Owned Enterprises: Privatisation and Regulation – Issues and Options, Wellington, Institute of Policy Studies, 1988, pp. i, 63.

Ashton, T. and St John, S., *Superannuation in New Zealand: Averting the Crisis*, Wellington, Institute of Policy Studies, 1988, pp. ii, 130.

Bale, G., *Wealth Transfer Taxation: an Important Component of a Good Tax System*, Wellington, Institute of Policy Studies, 1989, pp. i, 50.

Bird, R.M., *The Taxation of International Income Flows: Issues and Approaches*, Wellington, Institute of Policy Studies, 1987, pp. ii, 58.

Bollard, A., Holmes, F., Kersey, D. and Thompson, M.A., *Meeting the East Asia Challenge: Trends, Prospects and Policies*, Wellington, Institute of Policy Studies and NZ Institute of Economic Research, 1989, pp. ix, 186.

Bollard, A.E. and Thompson, M.A. (eds), *Trans-Tasman Trade and Investment*, Wellington, Institute of Policy Studies and NZ Institute of Economic Research, 1987, pp. ii, 86.

Boston, J., *The Future of New Zealand Universities: an Exploration of Some of the Issues*

Raised by the Reports of the Watts Committee and the Treasury, Wellington, Institute of Policy Studies, 1988, pp. iii, 103.

Campbell, C., Bollard, A. and Savage, J., *Productivity and Quality in New Zealand Firms: Effects of Deregulation*, Wellington, NZ Institute of Economic Research, IPS Studies in Productivity, no. 1, 1989, pp. 150.

Chen, M., *Women and Discrimination: New Zealand and the UN Convention*, Wellington, Institute of Policy Studies, 1989, pp. ii, 85.

Cleave, P., *The Sovereignty Game: Power, Knowledge and Reading the Treaty*, Wellington, Institute of Policy Studies, 1989, pp. iv, 92.

Dordick, H.S., *Information Technology and Economic Growth in New Zealand*, Wellington, Institute of Policy Studies, 1987, pp. 202.

Dugan, R. and Keef, S., *Company Purchase of Own Shares: The Case for New Zealand*, Wellington, Institute of Policy Studies, 1989, pp. i, 119.

Galvin, B., *Policy Co-ordination: Public Sector and Government*, Wellington, Institute of Policy Studies, 1991, pp. ii, 52.

Hastings, W.K., *The Right to an Education in Maori: the Case from International Law*, Wellington, Institute of Policy Studies, 1988, pp. ii, 39.

Hawke, G.R. (ed.), *Access to the Airwaves: Issues in Public Sector Broadcasting*, Wellington, Institute of Policy Studies, 1991, pp. 104.

Holmes, F., with Lattimore, R. and Haas, A., *Partners in the Pacific*, Wellington, New Zealand Trade Development Board, 1988, pp. 91.

Holmes, F. (ed.), *Stepping Stones to Freer Trade? Canadian, Australian and New Zealand Perspectives*, Wellington, Institute of Policy Studies, 1989, pp. ii, 72.

Holmes, F. and Pearson, C., *Meeting the European Challenge: Trends, Prospects and Policies*, Wellington, Institute of Policy Studies, 1991, pp. ii, 328.

Jones, G.W., *Privatisation: Reflections on the British Experience*, Wellington, Institute of Policy Studies, The First National Advanced Systems Lecture, 1987, pp. 48.

Kesselman, J.R., *Rate Structure and Personal Taxation: Flat Rate or Dual Rate?*, Wellington, Institute of Policy Studies, 1990, pp. ii, 87.

Krever, R. and Brooks, N., *A Capital Gains Tax for New Zealand*, Wellington, Institute of Policy Studies, 1990, pp. iii, 150.

Lloyd, P.J., with a commentary by Sir Frank Holmes, *The Future of CER: a Single Market for Australia and New Zealand*, Wellington, Institute of Policy Studies, and Melbourne, Committee for Economic Development of Australia, monograph no. 96, 1991, pp. ii, 47.

McKinlay, P., *Corporatisation: the Solution for State Owned Enterprise*, Wellington, Institute of Policy Studies, revised edition, 1987, pp. iii, 143.

McKinlay, P. (ed.), *Redistribution of Power? Devolution in New Zealand*, Wellington, Institute of Policy Studies, 1990, pp. i, 228.

McMahon, J.A., *New Zealand and the Common Agricultural Policy: Future Options for New Zealand*, Wellington, Institute of Policy Studies, 1990, pp. v, 131.

Martin, J., *A Profession of Statecraft? Three Essays on Some Current Issues in the New Zealand Public Service*, Wellington, Institute of Policy Studies, 1988, pp. ii, 55.

Morrison, P.S., *Labour Adjustment in Metropolitan Regions*, Wellington, Institute of Policy Studies, 1989, pp. ix, 254.

Orr, A., *Productivity Trends and Cycles in New Zealand: a Sectoral and Cyclical Analysis, 1961–1987*, Wellington, NZ Institute of Economic Research, IPS Studies in Productivity, no. 2, 1989, pp. 145.

Parston, G., *The Evolution of General Management in the National Health Service*, Wellington, Institute of Policy Studies, The Second National Advanced Systems Lecture, 1988, pp. 18.

Perrings, C., *The Cost of Tuition and the Options for Reform in the Public Funding of New*

Zealand Universities, Wellington, Institute of Policy Studies, 1988, pp. ii, 67.

Philpott, B.P., *Jobs and High Wages: The Implications of Productivity Trends*, Wellington, Institute of Policy Studies, (Studies in Productivity, no. 3), 1989, pp. ii, 50.

Poot, J., Nana, G. and Philpott, B., *International Migration and the New Zealand Economy: a Long-Run Perspective*, Wellington, Institute of Policy Studies, 1988, pp. iii, 217.

Prebble, J., *The Taxation of Controlled Foreign Corporations*, Wellington, Institute of Policy Studies, 1987, pp. iii, 67.

Prebble, M., *Information, Privacy and the Welfare State: An Integrated Approach to the Administration of Redistribution*, Wellington, Institute of Policy Studies, 1990, pp. iv, 135.

Prebble, M., *Integrated Circuit Cards: is it Smart to Use a Smart Card?*, Wellington, Institute of Policy Studies, 1990, pp. ii, 52.

Roberts, J., *Politicians, Public Servants and Public Enterprise*, Wellington, Institute of Policy Studies, 1987, pp. vi, 179.

Sandford, C., *Taxing Wealth in New Zealand*, Wellington, Institute of Policy Studies, 1987, pp. ii, 76.

Vann, R., *Trans-Tasman Taxation of Equity Investment*, Wellington, Institute of Policy Studies, 1989, pp. ii, 118.

Vasil, R., *Biculturalism: Reconciling Aotearoa with New Zealand*, Wellington, Institute of Policy Studies, 1988, pp. i, 45.

Wevers, M., *Japan: its Future and New Zealand*, Wellington, Institute of Policy Studies, 1988, pp. iii, 230.

Part II

URBANIZATION AND ECONOMIC DEVELOPMENT

5

LABOUR MARKET INTEGRATION AND THE RURAL–URBAN WAGE GAP IN HISTORY

Timothy J. Hatton and Jeffrey G. Williamson

Were labour markets highly segmented or well integrated in the past? Do they become better integrated over time as modern economic growth unfolds? These are important questions. Judgements about historical experience with industrialization, inequality, and accumulation often hinge on exploring the behaviour of wage gaps – 'big' gaps implying labour market failure. One key problem with this wage-gap approach, however, is that we are never offered a comparative standard. Well integrated compared to what? Not perfection, surely, since no country has ever achieved it, past *or* present. This chapter will argue that the assessment can only be made comparatively, across countries and over time. There is another key problem with this conventional approach: even these comparative assessments cannot be made in the absence of an economic model of labour market behaviour. Why? Because we must have a means by which asymmetric labour demand shocks can be isolated from the migration forces which serve to integrate markets. We will offer such a model in this chapter. Our argument will be illustrated by reference to one of the most persistent of wage gaps – that between urban and rural jobs.

Nominal wage gaps between farm and city are one of the most pervasive aspects of modern economic growth. So much so that they have become a key stylized fact of development economics. Indeed, a good portion of the literature on the Third World has focused on this problem at length, both in terms of labour market behaviour and in terms of policy formation in the face of factor market distortions. Yet wage gaps are not simply an institutional peculiarity of newly industrializing Third World countries since, as we shall see, they were even bigger in nineteenth- and twentieth-century Western nations. Furthermore, the evidence suggests that these wage gaps varied substantially over time.

The existence of these nominal wage gaps over the long haul of industrialization raises three questions. First, do they disappear when properly measured? Proper measurement would include the fact that cities are more costly places to live in, cities have greater disamenities, farmers also make in-kind payments to their workers, and farm labourers suffer seasonal unemployment. We will review the evidence which shows that, while much of these nominal wage gaps evaporate when adjusted for cost of living differences and for the perquisites paid to farm labourers, a residual gap remains to be explained.

Since the wage gaps survive improved measurement, a second question becomes relevant: are we observing equilibrium wage gaps? One of the most popular arguments for the equilibrium gap view can be found in the Todaro model, a pillar of development economics for more than twenty years. This model makes the plausible assertion that sticky industrial wages, urban unemployment, and flexible farm wages jointly account for the wage gap. Given the dominance of the model in the Third World literature, it may come as a surprise to learn that the idea has its intellectual roots in United States experience during the interwar years.[1] In any case, we will review some new evidence which will show that the Todaro model can explain only part of the historical time series on wage gaps.

Since equilibrium models, like Todaro's, cannot fully account for these wage gaps, we must move on to the third question: what disequilibrium forces account for these wage gaps and for their variation over time? By 1958 the early pioneers in development economics had a full appreciation of wage gaps, and they were central to debates over development strategy. Everett Hagen published an influential paper in that year on 'An economic justification of protectionism'. Based on evidence drawn both from advanced and underdeveloped countries, he concluded that 'The agricultural-urban wage differential exists in underdeveloped and economically advanced countries alike ... it is a persistent long-run phenomenon.'[2] Hagen's priors were very strong. He felt that these wage differentials were the result of unbalanced growth in the derived demand for labour. For him rapid industrialization creates an excess demand for labour in urban sectors while lagging labour demand in agriculture creates an excess supply in rural sectors. Since migration is never adequate to fully clear these two markets in any one year, and since the unbalanced growth persists year in and year out, a disequilibrium wage distortion will emerge. The more rapid the rate of unbalanced growth, the bigger the distortion.

These, then, are the issues, and the terms 'integrated' or 'segmented' labour markets are simply not up to the task. We need better evidence on the size of the true wage gap, and we need explicit economics which makes it possible to uncouple Hagen-like disequilibrating demand-side forces from Todaro-like equilibrating supply-side forces. Only then will we be in a position to assess how well labour markets have operated in the past and whether in fact they have improved over the past two centuries.

HOW BIG ARE THE WAGE GAPS?

Nominal wage gaps: historical evidence

These concerns with the nature of the development process, the costs of resource misallocation, and the framing of policy to promote development, all make the question of measurement paramount. If the gaps are large, then the presumption of labour market 'failure' is strong, the allocative and dynamic losses could be potentially large, and interventionist policies to remove the distortion (or to compensate for it) might be justified. Such concerns led in the 1950s and 1960s to a series of studies which sought to measure income and wage gaps between farm and non-farm sectors in both the industrialized countries past and the newly industrializing countries present. In the historical and contemporary Third World context, the central issue has been whether large wage gaps have been associated with labour market disequilibria generated by rapid rates of industrialization, urbanization, development, and growth.

In the pioneering studies of Clark and Kuznets, rural–urban income differences were seen as a common feature of economic development.[3] Indeed, this issue became the central focus of the important study by Bellerby, *Agriculture and Industry Relative Income*. Other studies examined levels and trends in the income gap for individual countries. For the most part these early studies were concerned with average income in farm and non-farm sectors rather than with wage rates. Income distribution was more the focus than was labour market integration (or lack of it). Some attention, however, was paid to relative earnings in agriculture and industry as an alternative measure of relative welfare.[4] Based on evidence from thirteen countries, Bellerby concluded that in 1938 the ratio of industrial earnings to farm earnings was, on average, 1.89.[5]

Are these the appropriate wage gaps to address the issue of labour market integration? Measures such as those presented by Bellerby are based on the comparison of wage rates for farm labourers with industrial wage rates which include both skilled and unskilled workers. Thus, in part, the wage gap reflects the premium for skill in the non-farm sector and would be affected both by the skill composition and by the size of the skill premium. In the late nineteenth and the early twentieth century the skill differentials of developed economies varied between industries and between countries, but typically ranged between 20 and 50 per cent.[6] Though the rural recruit to the urban sector might anticipate climbing the occupational ladder over time, comparable ladders existed in the rural sector (for example becoming a farmer or a rural craftsman). Given the difficulty of comparing different skills and given that typical rural–urban migrants were young and unskilled, the most appropriate comparison is between unskilled wage rates in both sectors.[7] This raises the question of which urban unskilled wage should be used. In practice the choice is usually between wage rates for building or manufacturing labourers: both were typical destinations for rural migrants.[8]

Our knowledge of nineteenth-century wage gaps has increased considerably in recent years, both in terms of their movements over time and across countries. For example, at the height of the British Industrial Revolution in the 1830s, weekly wages for building labourers were 36 per cent higher than those for farm labourers in the north, 106 per cent higher in the south, and 73 per cent higher for England as a whole.[9] Furthermore, the gap rose during the course of the

Industrial Revolution in Britain: urban common (not just building) labour wages were about 27 per cent higher than farm wages in 1805, 43 per cent higher in 1835, and 47 per cent higher in 1851.[10] Although they also rose in late nineteenth-century France, they were much smaller than in Britain throughout: the daily wage for urban ditch diggers was about on a par with farm labourers in 1852, but it was 18 per cent higher in 1882, and 27 per cent higher in 1911.[11] In the United States, the evidence from Vermont shows that the gap plunges during the Civil War decade, then recovers to 29 per cent in the early 1870s before surging to 66 per cent in the late 1890s.[12] For seven late nineteenth-century developing countries as a group, the wage gap was about 51 per cent,[13] a figure not too different from the 41 per cent for nineteen Third World countries in the 1960s and 1970s.[14] Even though there is plenty of variance in the size of these wage gaps, and even though there are problems of comparability in their measurement, nominal wage gaps have clearly been a fact of life since the first industrial revolution was launched more than two centuries ago.

Are the nominal wage gaps real?

Measuring wage gaps based on cash wages is a hazardous business. Ratios of cash wages may be a good guide to movements over time but, when it comes to the absolute levels, they may be seriously misleading. There are two important reasons why the nominal ratio of non-farm to farm wage rates overstates the true gap: in-kind payments in agriculture and cost of living differences between locations.

The most important form of in-kind payment was typically board. This usually covered food (at the farmer's table or otherwise), sleeping accommodation, and sometimes services such as laundry. These items clearly have significant value and were often a widespread feature of farm wage contracts. For example, as late as 1927, nearly half of all US farm labourers worked with board. Independent estimates of the value of board are few and far between and a common proxy has been simply to assume that the difference between the wage without board and the wage with board reflected the value of board. Using this approach, US statistics for monthly wage rates suggest that board was worth 32 per cent of the wage in 1890, 24 per cent in 1913, and 13 per cent in 1937.[15]

This proxy, however, ignores other prerequisites received by farm labourers. Often those not receiving board (and sometimes those who were) were given access to such resources as a house, fuel, garden space, pasture for animals, access to the farmer's, team, buggy or tools and equipment.[16] In a detailed survey of farm labourers in Michigan in 1893 we found that 28 per cent of labourers (with or without board) received at least one of these perquisites and in most cases several of them. Econometric evidence suggests that these were associated with lower cash wages, and should, therefore, be counted as part of the farm wage.[17] The most comprehensive evidence on the value of perquisites comes from a special survey conducted by the US Department of Agriculture in 1925.[18] Based on this evidence, it has been estimated that perquisites formed 40 per cent of total remuneration for non-casual farm labourers in 1925 and 30 per cent in 1941.[19] Relative to the estimate of total remuneration, the monthly cash wage without board for these years was 71 per cent and 80 per cent respectively.

Counting payments in kind can make a considerable difference, but was it significant only for the US? The extent of in-kind payments varied among countries according to the level of economic development, density of settlement, type of agriculture, and with different forms of labour contract.[20] In India in 1950–1 it is estimated that, of the total wage payment to casual farm workers (92 per cent of wage labour), 43 per cent was paid in the form of perquisites such as meals or other in-kind payments.[21] In late nineteenth-century Britain, it formed only a small addition to the cash wage (other items received from the farmer were typically deducted from the agreed cash wage), whereas in Sweden it accounted for perhaps 20 per cent of the total wage.[22] At the other extreme, in some European countries such as Finland, much of farm labour was supplied by cottagers and crofters, wholly in return for ground rent.[23]

What about differences in the cost of living between city and countryside? In the two most important expenditure categories, food and rent, rural prices were significantly lower. Furthermore, where food and lodging was received in kind from the farmer, these items were typically valued (if at all) at the farm-gate price. Since prices at the retail store have often been estimated at up to double those at the farm gate, this could make a substantial difference, even if only applied to a small part of the budget.[24] In addition, the urban cost of living varied across towns. It typically rose with the size of the town due to progressively higher rents, and hence the cost of living adjustment would vary accordingly.

One of the earliest attempts to measure these cost of living differentials between city and countryside was that made by Nathan Koffsky for the US in 1941.[25] His original estimates were for farm operator families and allowed for a large proportion of self-supplied foodstuffs, valued at farm-gate prices, but made no allowance for differences in rent. Making adjustments appropriate for labourers in both sectors gives the result (using low income city budget weights) that the urban cost of living was 20 per cent higher than the rural in 1941 and, extrapolating backwards, 25 per cent higher in 1925.[26] It is difficult to obtain estimates of the ratio before the First World War, but our recent investigation of relative prices for Michigan in the early 1890s suggests that urban prices were between 16 and 23 per cent higher than rural prices.[27]

In early industrializing Britain, the urban cost of living based on retail prices and rents was 23 per cent higher. Bellerby's estimates suggest that the cost of living ratio was 1.11 in 1904 and 1.04 in 1937/8. For Canada he reported a ratio of 1.13 in 1913 and a similar figure for 1938. This is consistent with Koffsky's findings for the US if the comparison is based on retail prices only.[28] The results of a study for Sweden by G.R. Allen are particularly interesting because an allowance was made for the farm-gate price effect and because his estimates go back before 1914.[29] Allen estimated that in 1870 the cost of living ratio was 1.24

when farm-gate prices were included, but 1.07 when retail prices were used. In 1913 the ratios were respectively 1.14 and 1.07 and, in 1934, 1.15 and 1.07.[30] Furthermore, these cost of living differentials for the nineteenth century are quite similar to currently developing Third World countries in Latin America and Africa.[31]

At the risk of overgeneralizing from a small set of observations, we are tempted to conclude that, based on retail prices, the cost of living in the towns was between 5 and 15 per cent higher than in the countryside in industrialized countries at the turn of the century, and that there was some tendency for the gap to diminish over time. When farm-gate prices are incorporated in the rural cost of living, this typically adds between 5 and 10 per cent to the differential. Where a significant part of the budget was bought or received at farm-gate prices, its size probably also decreased over time, reinforcing any decline in the retail price ratio.

How far do allowances for in-kind payments and relative living costs go towards closing the nominal wage gap? In the case of Michigan in 1893, the building labourers wage relative to farm labourers falls from 1.44 in nominal terms to 1.17 in real terms. At the aggregate level, the monthly wage ratio for manufacturing to farm decreases from 2.28 to 1.12 in 1925 and from 3.20 to 1.89 in 1941. For Sweden it appears also that a large part of the gap can be accounted for by these two adjustments.[32] For Britain in the 1830s, the retail price adjustment alone lowers the wage gap from 73 to 41 per cent. In Bombay in 1926, the real wage gap can be estimated at 8.5 per cent, and in Japan for the same year at 15.2 per cent.[33]

The evidence we do have supports the conclusion that a substantial part of the wage gap can be accounted for by these adjustments. However, when so adjusted the wage gaps do not dissappear completely. Even for the US, UK and Sweden, where the most comprehensive adjustments have been made, the real wage gaps still exceed 10 per cent and sometimes much more. Are there other omitted variables that might account for the remainder of the gap?

What about compensating differentials?

There are a variety of reasons why a rational farm labourer might decide not to migrate. Even though the wage gap might beckon the rural labourer towards the city, the appropriate basis of comparison is not between the consumption bundle available at the two locations, but between total utility available at each.[34] This raises the question of the quality of life in the city relative to that in the rural community. There is also the further question of whether the prospective migrant could expect to attain the same bundle as the average city dweller.

Nineteenth-century cities have a bad reputation, particularly in Britain. Sanitation was poor, the air was polluted, slums were crowded, disease was rife, and death rates were significantly higher than in the countryside. Here, above all, we might have expected a significant wage bribe to have been necessary to induce the rural labourer to migrate cityward. But what evidence is there on the size of these bribes?

This issue has been investigated in detail.[35] The method was to run hedonic regressions for the unskilled wage rate across towns with widely varying environmental characteristics. Urban disamenities were proxied by population density, town size, and infant mortality. The results indicated that disamenities raised the wage between the most pleasant and least pleasant towns in the midlands and north of England by 12 to 30 per cent in 1834 and by 3 to 7 per cent in 1905.[36] In the south, the premium was smaller, but still 8 to 20 per cent in 1834.[37] These disamenities were, therefore, significant. Interestingly, the most sensitive indicator of urban disamenities, infant mortality, was related more closely to urbanization (as measured by town size) than industrialization. In addition, for 1834, the availability of poor relief in rural areas needs to be taken into account. When all of these adjustments are applied, the wage gap for 1834 falls from 73 per cent to between 18 and 33 per cent for England as a whole, is larger in the south, but almost zero in the north.[38] By the early twentieth century the disamenities must have been considerably smaller as housing and sanitation improved.

It should be stressed that England in the 1830s was probably the most extreme case of urban disamenities. In other countries and in more recent times, it is doubtful that disamenities premia would be anywhere nearly as great, or even positive for that matter. We do not have comparable estimates for other countries, but the disappearance of urban–rural mortality differentials suggests that the premium probably evaporated in most countries after the turn of the century.[39]

What happened to the rural migrant when he or she got to the city? Did the migrant have equal access to the jobs and wage rates enjoyed by native city people? If not, then the move would seem less attractive to the marginal migrant despite the apparent gains based on average wages. Such questions have been at the heart of the development literature for some time. For example, the Todaro model argues that rural migrants, on entering the city, typically enter low wage casual occupations in the 'informal' sector or remain unemployed, at least for a while, before ascending the ladder to more permanent (and better paid) jobs. We will have more to say about one aspect of that debate below.

Evidence is available on this issue for nineteenth-century Britain.[40] It is based on information regarding individuals' characteristics, occupations, and places of birth from the enumerators' books for the 1851 census. Using a sub-sample of over 20,000 individuals in major urban centres, it is possible to distinguish the labour market experience of those born in rural areas and the city born (as well as the foreign born, mainly Irish). The results are striking. They suggest that rural migrants were not more prone to unemployment, nor were they more often in low wage occupations. True, the data do not make it possible to identify recent migrants, nor can we measure their individual wage, only the average for their occupation. Subject to these qualifications, however, the evidence suggests that immigrants from rural areas competed on equal terms with the natives.[41]

Does this evidence suggest that the probability of being unemployed or underemployed was not taken into account in migration decisions? Clearly not.

What it does suggest is that new entrants into an urban labour market faced similar prospects to everyone else. Given the inconstancy of employment, and often severe seasonal fluctuations in demand for labour (at least until the early twentieth century), we might expect jobs which were particularly prone to unemployment risk to command a wage premium, at least within a local labour market where the costs of migrating were small and information flows were good. In fact, recent research suggests that these premia are clearly identifiable.[42]

For Michigan in the 1890s, we have individual data for three groups of unskilled labourers, farm labourers, railway labourers, and building labourers – over 3300 observations in all. We first estimated equations for the probability of being unemployed and the length of time unemployed during the year of observation. We found that the incidence of unemployment was associated not so much with individual characteristics such as age, ethnicity, or family circumstances, but more strongly with the type of job, (for example, whether indoor or outdoor) and the length of the employment contract. In order to estimate the compensating differential for unemployment risk, we entered the predicted values from the first stage into an otherwise standard earnings function for each group. The results provide strong evidence in favour of compensating differentials for unemployment risk. For the farm labourers, an extra month of expected unemployment raised the monthly wage by 13.8 per cent, for building labourers, by 4.3 per cent, and for railway labourers, by 6.5 per cent.[43]

Evidence of this kind is unusual and we are not aware of similar studies for other times and places.[44] But the results indicate that expected unemployment was important in driving wage premia within a relatively homogenous local labour market. Would the same apply between rural and urban labour markets? More importantly, could differences in unemployment risk between the rural and urban sectors account for what remains of the wage gaps? Evidence is limited, but our suspicion is that it would not. The reason is that unemployment and underemployment seem to have been just as widespread in the rural as in the urban sector. For our Michigan labourers the average unemployment rates were 20.8 per cent on the farm, 25.8 per cent in building, and 10.8 per cent on the railways.[45] Evidence from the 1900 US census reported by Goldin and Engerman indicates unemployment rates over the year of 13 per cent for farm labourers and 15.5 per cent for non-farm labourers.[46] Much of this unemployment was seasonal. However, an important difference is that, though there were year to year fluctuations in demand for farm labour associated with weather conditions, urban employment was more prone to trade cycle variations extending over several years.

MIGRATION, MOBILITY AND LABOUR MARKET INTEGRATION

Measuring labour market integration

As we have seen, when we adjust for in-kind payments, the cost of living and various hedonics, rural–urban wage gaps look a lot smaller than they do at first sight. Can we conclude that labour markets were well integrated or not? One test would be to see if, when fully adjusted, the wage was identical in two locations. If not, then we would conclude that the two labour markets were not perfectly integrated. But this is surely too harsh a test. Clearly there will always remain some measurement error, especially when we try to account for inherently unobservable compensating differentials. One method would be to obtain significance tests for differences in the fully adjusted wage across labour markets or through time. Such tests have recently been applied to wage differences across cities in Britain and the US before the First World War. Examining 23 occupations in 12 US cities from 1870 to 1898, Rosenbloom found significant and persistent differentials both between and within regions.[47] He concluded that these reflected persistent disequilibria between local labour markets which were only loosely integrated. Evidence for British towns in 1905, however, indicates, at least at the regional level, that wage differentials were not statistically significant.[48]

Perfect labour mobility, either across regions or between rural and urban labour markets, has never existed. Even if the urban–rural wage gap was zero, we could not conclude that two labour markets were perfectly arbitraged. The reason is simply that wage gaps vary substantially over time. If we applied the zero gap criterion, we would conclude that the degree of labour market integration varied widely from year to year. This is graphically illustrated in Figures 5.1 to 5.3 which plot time series of the farm to 'industrial' wage ratio for eight countries in different epochs.[49]

Figure 5.1 plots wage ratios for three old world countries (the UK, Sweden, and Germany) in the late nineteenth century. All these exhibit sharp fluctuations, and there is some indication of a permanent rise in the ratio between 1875 and 1890. We shall comment on the UK case further below. Figure 5.2 plots the twentieth-century experience of Canada, Denmark, and New Zealand. Most notable in all of these is the surge in the wage ratio between the 1920s and the 1930s. The post–Second World War experience is varied: the wage ratio declines in Canada and Denmark but not in New Zealand. Finally, in Figure 5.3 we have the US and Australia. While they exhibit opposing trends, both document a surge in the wage ratio between the 1920s and the 1930s. We shall comment further on the impact of the Great Depression shortly.

These distinct variations over time suggest that major disequilibrating shocks to labour demand drove the wage gap over these periods. However, as we shall argue below, there were strong and persistent equilibrating supply side forces at work too.

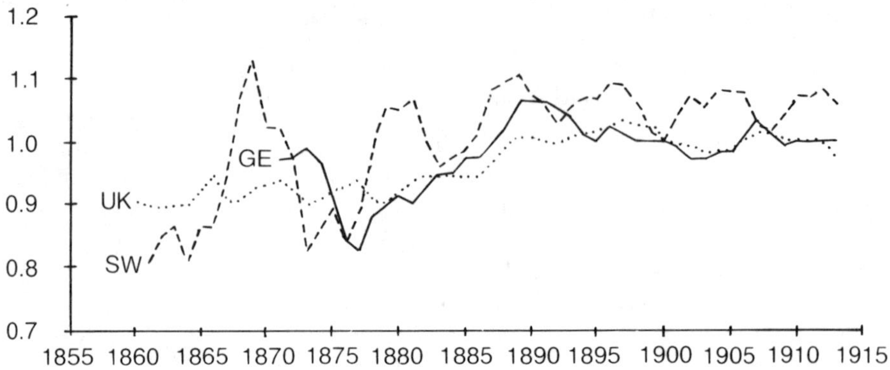

Figure 5.1 Late nineteenth-century urban–rural wage ratios in the United Kingdom (UK), Germany (GE), and Sweden (SW) (1900 = 1.0)

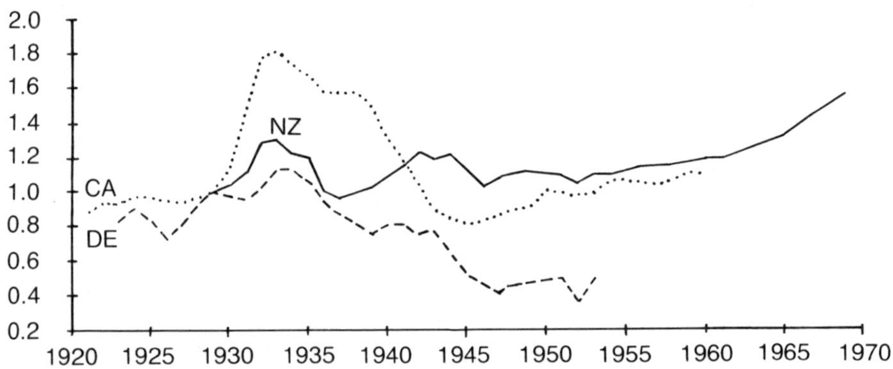

Figure 5.2 Twentieth-century urban–rural wage ratios in Canada (CA), Denmark (DE), and New Zealand (NZ) (1929 = 1.0)

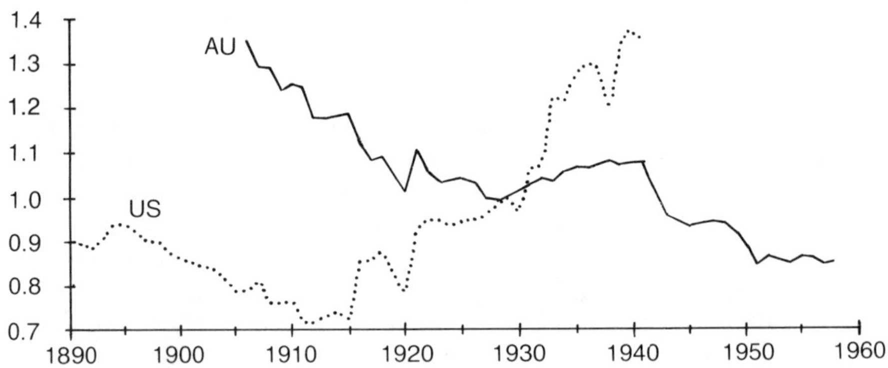

Figure 5.3 Twentieth-century urban–rural wage ratios in Australia (AU) and the United States (US) (1929 = 1.0)

Migration and labour mobility

The literature on domestic and international migration is enormous. Writers have often been moved by the evidence to comment on the degree of labour mobility. It is important to stress, however, that migration and mobility are not the same thing. Migration refers to an observed movement between locations, while mobility refers to the response to a given incentive to move. If the incentive to move were sufficiently large, there could be substantial migration even if labour was relatively immobile. Conversely, one might observe little migration if the incentive was small, even if labour was highly mobile.

In the context of rural–urban migration, it is useful to think in terms of the following simple migration function:

$$M = \mu[\log(WmEm/WaEa) - \log Y] \qquad (1)$$

where M is the rate of out-migration from the rural sector, W denotes the wage in each sector (Wm for urban or manufacturing and Wa for rural or agriculture), and E is the probability of being employed proxied by one minus the unemployment rate (following the Todaro model). In this model labour mobility is measured by the parameter which describes the elasticity of migration to a given (Todaro-adjusted) wage gap. Y is the equilibrium wage ratio which, in the absence of other compensating differentials, would be 1 ($\log Y = 0$). Zero migration would occur when WmEm/WaEa = Y. If the labour markets were perfectly arbitraged then this condition would hold continuously.[50]

We have tested this model on time-series data for off-farm migration in the US for the period 1920 to 1941. Since we have no time series on rural unemployment, we simply use the non-farm unemployment rate and unskilled wage ratio. Our equation is therefore:

$$M^1 = -\mu \log Y + \mu[\log(Wm/Wa)_{t-1} + \log(1-U)_{t-1}] \qquad (2)$$

where U is the urban unemployment rate. In estimation we also relax the restriction that the coefficients on the wage ratio and the employment rate are equal. This produced the following result (standard errors in parentheses):[51]

$$\underset{}{M_t} = \underset{(0.028)}{-0.048} + \underset{(0.033)}{0.095} \log(Wm/Wa)_t + \underset{(0.035)}{0.090} \log(1-U)_t$$

$R^2 = 0.58 \quad DW = 1.99 \quad rho = 0.50$

This estimate indicates that both the wage ratio and urban unemployment were significant determinants of migration and further that the coefficients are similar in magnitude, as the basic Todaro model would suggest. The elasticity of migration (our measure of mobility) is about 0.1. At first sight it may seem low, but it implies that a 10 per cent disequilibrium wage gap would induce 1 per cent out-migration per annum. In fact, during the 1920s about 2.2 per cent of the farm population left each year. This would, therefore, be consistent with a disequilibrium wage gap of 22 per cent (ignoring relative unemployment differences), which is somewhat larger than the fully adjusted wage ratio. We shall return to the 1930s again below.

Though we do not have comparable econometric findings for other countries, it seems likely that similar effects were at work elsewhere. A good example is offered by the British Industrial Revolution. Figure 5.4 graphs the ratio of farm labourer's wages to general non-agricultural labourer's wages from 1780 to 1870 against the out-migration rate from rural areas at five-year intervals. Clearly the two series do not move in an exact inverse relationship, no doubt because employment conditions were also important, particularly around the time of the Napoleonic wars. But there is a broad correspondence. In the late eighteenth century, when the wage ratio was low, out-migration was well below 1 per cent per annum. In the mid-nineteenth century, when the wage ratio was high, out-migration was well above one per cent.

Testing for labour market integration

Wage gaps between city and countryside have often been large in the past and they have certainly varied over time. Indeed, given the dramatic variations documented in Figures 5.1 to 5.3, one might wonder whether urban and rural labour markets were largely segmented in the past. This conclusion would be

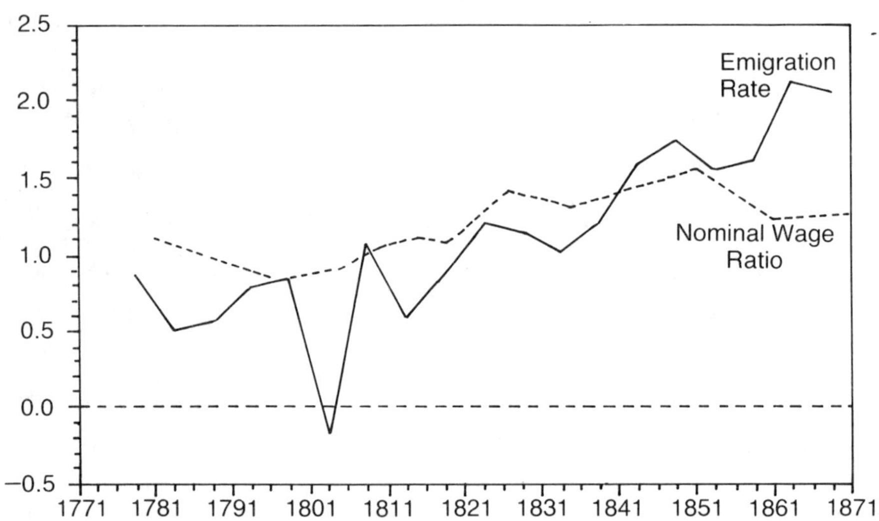

Figure 5.4 Rural emigration rates and the unskilled wage ratio, England and Wales, 1771–1871

Sources: Migration: J.G. Williamson, *Coping with City Growth during the British Industrial Revolution*, Cambridge, Cambridge University Press, 1990, p. 27. Wage ratio: J.G. Williamson, 'The structure of pay in Britain, 1710–1911', *Research in Economic History*, 1982, 7, p. 48.

hasty in the absence of any effort to isolate the disequilibrating economic and demographic shocks to these labour markets which may have produced large wage gaps in the first place. Debates over labour market integration or segmentation hinges, after all, on the presence or absence of equilibrating migration responses to such shocks.

How would we construct a test for labour market integration based on the type of evidence offered in Figures 5.1 to 5.3? One type of test commonly used, often in the context of goods or asset markets, and sometimes for labour markets, is to correlate changes in the relevant prices across two markets. For example, one could estimate the regression:

$$\Delta \log Wa_t = a_0 + a_1 \Delta \log Wm_t + e_t \tag{3}$$

Labour markets would be judged more closely integrated the higher the R^2 and the closer a_1 is to 1. However, this test of integration is flawed. For one thing, a high correlation between Wa and Wm could occur if there were common demand (or supply) shocks to both markets, even if they were completely segmented. Furthermore, if a_1 was exactly 1, then log(Wm/Wa) would be a random walk (with drift if $a_0 \neq 0$). Consequently, if e_t were random and serially uncorrelated, the wage ratio could wander over time without bound. Hence finding that a_1 was not significantly different from 1 would lead one to exactly the wrong conclusion.

A more appropriate test would be to see if there is a unit root in the (log of the) wage ratio (or equivalently, whether the wage ratio is integrated of order 0). This amounts to testing whether the wage ratio is a random walk. If so, then it would imply that a random shock to the wage ratio would be permanent, and there would be no tendency for labour market forces to drive the wage ratio back to some constant longrun equilibrium. More generally, since we know there are variables which influence the wage ratio, we can test whether the wage ratio and these other variables form a cointegrating set. To perform the test we first estimate the regression:

$$\log(Wm/Wa)_t = b_0 + b_1(X)_t + v_t \tag{4}$$

where X is a vector of variables determining the longrun wage ratio and v_t is the error term. At the second stage we run the regression:

$$\Delta v_t = c v_{t-1} + z_t \tag{5}$$

where v_t is the error term from equation (4). If c is significantly different from zero, we can conclude that the variables form a cointegrating set with the longrun solution given by equation (4). The test statistics are non-standard and several alternatives are offered by Engle and Granger.[52]

We have performed these tests on the experience of the eight countries for which the wage ratios were plotted in Figures 5.1 to 5.3.[53] We first tested the most naive model, namely for a unit root in the wage ratio. This is equivalent to equations (4) and (5) where b_1 is set to zero. We could not reject the hypothesis of a unit root in the wage ratio for any of the eight cases. We then tested whether the wage ratio was cointegrated with two variables: the log of the urban employment rate and a time trend. The results offered more support to the hypothesis of integration. On one test (the cointegrating regression Durbin–Watson statistic), the null hypothesis of no cointegration could be rejected in five cases, but on another (the augmented Dickey–Fuller test), in only two cases. Thus there is some weak evidence of integration despite the fact that these tests are known not to be powerful against the null hypothesis of no cointegration.

An alternative approach is to estimate an error correction model. Here, we specified the model as follows:

$$\Delta\log(Wm/Wa)_t = d_0 + d_1\,\Delta\log(Wm/Wa)_{t-1} + d_2\,\Delta\log(1-U)_t + d_3v_{t-1} + u_t \qquad (6)$$

where v_{t-1} is the lagged error from the cointegrating regression (4) which includes the employment rate and the time trend. If d_3 gives a significant (negative) coefficient, then it suggests that, within a dynamic model, deviations from the longrun equilibrium generate forces which drive the wage ratio back towards the longrun equilibrium. Our tests of this model produced five significant coefficients at the 5 per cent level and three at the 10 per cent level.

These tests confirm that labour supply responses did indeed generate equilibrating wage gaps in the longrun. But what were the potent disequilibrating forces on the demand side of these labour markets which produced the wage gaps in the first place?

WHAT DRIVES THE WAGE GAP?

The determinants of the farm wage

In order to uncover the forces driving the wage gap we first examine the determinants of the farm wage. We take the farm wage to be determined by the equilibrium in the supply of, and the demand for, farm labour. Farm labour supply is determined chiefly by out-migration and, as a simplification, urban labour market conditions are viewed as exogenous to the farm sector. Farm labour demand is determined by marginal value productivity in the farm sector.

Writing labour demand in logarithmic form:

$$\log La^d_t = A + \alpha(\log Wa_t - \log Pa_t) + rt \qquad (7)$$

where, as before, Wa is the farm wage, Pa is the output price, α the labour demand elasticity, and the term rt represents capital accumulation and technical progress. The rate of change of labour supply is determined by the balance of rates of natural increase, N, and out-migration, M:

$$\Delta\log la^s_t = N_t - M_t \qquad (8)$$

Converting (7) into changes, setting $La^d = La^s$ and substituting for M from (2) above (ignoring the constant) yields an expression for the rate of change of the farm wage:

$$\Delta \log Wa = \left(\frac{r - N}{\alpha}\right) + \Delta \log Pa_t + \frac{\mu}{\alpha}\,[\log(Wm/Wa)_{t-1} + \log(1-U)_{t-1}] \quad (9)$$

Thus, the farm wage is determined in the shortrun by labour demand in agriculture (farm prices and productivity) and by the 'pull' of the city as represented by the term in the square brackets (lagged employment and the wage gap). In the longrun (meaning when the Δs are all zero), the wage ratio is driven by rates of technical change, natural increase, compensating differentials, and urban unemployment.

We have estimated this model for the countries whose wage ratios are depicted in Figures 5.1 to 5.3. The first term in the model is proxied by a constant and a time trend, and we relax the restriction on the coefficients of the lagged wage ratio and the lagged employment rate. The results offer strong support for the model. The lagged wage ratio gives positive coefficients which are significant at the 5 per cent level in six cases, with only New Zealand failing the significance test at the 10 per cent level, and the coefficient averages 0.33 (average 't' value: 2.57). Lagged unemployment, also significant in six cases (with only Sweden failing at the 10 per cent level), gives an average coefficient of 0.63 (average 't' value: 2.72). Thus, urban conditions appear to have been very important in driving the farm wage, particularly unemployment. The rate of change of farm prices typically yields coefficients which are less than the expected value of 1, averaging 0.32, but is significant in seven cases (average 't' value: 3.95).

Let us illustrate further with a specific example, that for the UK, 1860–1913. Here we have augmented the model in two ways. We have entered a term for wheat yields as a proxy for farm productivity (which can be thought of as determining A in equation (7)). We have also entered a dummy for the spate of unionism among farm workers in 1872–6.[54] With these modifications the result is (standard errors in parentheses):

$$\begin{aligned}\Delta \log Wa_t = {} & \underset{(0.16)}{0.44} + \underset{(0.04)}{0.16}\,\Delta \log Pa_t + \underset{(0.03)}{0.09}\,\Delta Yld_t + \underset{(0.006)}{0.013}\,Dum \\ & - \underset{(0.0002)}{0.0004}\,t + \underset{(0.07)}{0.18}\,\log(Wm/Wa)_{t-1} + \underset{(0.07)}{0.26}\,\log(1-U)_{t-1}\end{aligned}$$

$R^2 = 0.63 \quad DW = 1.47$

All the coefficients are significant and the equation performs well in explaining changes in the farm wage. However, the impact of price, productivity, and union effects in the farm sector itself are relatively small (and are in any case transitory because output prices and yields enter as differences). For example, the fall in the farm wage after the early 1870s is often associated with the collapse of farm prices (due to the 'invasion of grains' from the New World) and in the short term with declining yields. A simulation of the model indicates that the effects arising from prices, yields, and unionism drove down the farm wage by a mere 4 per cent between 1873 and 1879 and a further 2 per cent between 1879 and 1887. More important was the fall in the non-farm wage, a slight rise in unemployment, and the trend term which was serving to raise the wage ratio.

Clearly, urban conditions were very important in determining the farm wage from the supply side. But those urban labour market conditions cannot really be treated as totally exogenous. Urban unemployment is determined by the interaction between the urban wage and labour demand, and also by the influx of migrants from the countryside. This suggests that the rise in the wage ratio in the UK between 1875 and 1890 may have been indirectly due to the fall in farm prices associated with the flood of agricultural imports from the New World. To see these effects we need to develop the model a little further to allow for interaction between these two labour markets in both directions.

Price shocks, sticky urban wages, and the Great Depression

In order to examine further the causes of shortrun variations in the wage ratio, we need to endogenize urban unemployment. Labour demand in the urban sector can be written as:

$$\log Lm^d_t = B - \beta \log(Wm/Pm)_t + vt \tag{10}$$

where Pm is the output price and vt the technical progress term. Labour supply to the urban sector is simply the total labour force minus employment in agriculture. In logarithmic form:

$$\log Lm^s_t = \frac{1}{1-s}\log L_t - \frac{s}{1-s}\log La_t \tag{11}$$

where s is the labour force share in agriculture and L is the total labour force. The log of the urban employment rate $[(\log Lm^d/\log Lm^s) = \log(1-U)]$ can be written as the difference between demand and supply:

$$\log(1-U)_t = B - \beta\log(Wm/Pm)_t + vt - \frac{1}{1-s}\log L_t$$
$$+ \frac{s}{1-s}A - \frac{s}{1-s}\alpha\log(Wa/Pa) + \frac{s}{1-s}rt \tag{12}$$

Having found an expression for the unemployment rate, we can substitute this into (8) to derive a dynamic model for the wage ratio. We have performed this task elsewhere but, for ease of exposition, we invoke the longrun equilibrium condition $\log(Wm/Wa) = -\log(1-U)$.[55] This gives, after some rearrangement, equation (13).

$$\log(Wm/Wa)_t = \frac{(1-s)(B+vt) + s(A+rt)}{1 - s + s\alpha} + \frac{1}{1 - s + s\alpha}\log L_t + \frac{\beta[(1-s)+s\alpha]}{1 - s + s\alpha}\log(Wm/Pm)_t - \frac{s}{1 - s + s\alpha}\alpha\log(Pa/Pm)_t \quad (13)$$

Equation (13) illustrates that, apart from trends in L and t, the wage ratio is driven by two variables, the product wage in urban industry and the intersectoral terms of trade. A rise in the urban wage will only increase the wage ratio if it is an increase in the real wage. This is essentially because it creates unemployment which deters rural migrants. The increase in the wage ratio will be less than proportionate if the elasticity of urban labour demand is less than one. A rise in the industry price would have a smaller effect because it operates indirectly on the wage ratio, by shifting the (nominal) urban labour demand curve. Similarly, a fall in the agricultural price level raises the wage ratio by shifting down the rural labour demand curve. Hence, in the absence of compensating changes in the industrial real wage, the terms of trade will have enduring effects on the wage ratio.

These effects worked with a vengeance in the US during the Great Depression. In the early 1930s the real manufacturing wage rose sharply and the terms of trade moved against agriculture. Both effects caused the wage ratio to rise. Our estimated model of the wage ratio (a dynamic version of equation (13)) allows us to measure their respective impacts. Between 1929 and 1934 the wage ratio rose by 19.7 per cent. The equilibrium rise is predicted to be 27.1 per cent, 10.8 per cent due to the real wage effect and 16.3 per cent due to the terms of trade. The dynamics imposed by migration cushioned the rise in the wage ratio initially but caused it to persist into the late 1930s.

Similar shocks occurred in other industrial economies with varying severity. For fourteen industrial economies it is estimated that the 27.2 per cent fall in the price of traded goods led to a rise in the industrial real wage of, on average, 13.8 per cent between 1928 and 1931. This in turn contributed over the same years to the fall of 14.2 per cent in industrial employment and a corresponding rise in unemployment.[56] In most countries, as in the US, rising urban unemployment stemmed the tide of rural out-migration. In Germany, in the face of a rise in unemployment to over 300 per cent, net rural–urban migration became negative in the early 1930s.[57] By contrast, in Japan the real wage did not rise and unemployment rose to only 3.8 per cent. The urban labour force swelled as rural out-migration increased and as farm wages fell because of the collapse in agricultural prices.[58]

In most countries the outcome of these forces was a rise in the wage gap. Among eleven European countries the wage gap increased between 1929 and 1934 in eight and decreased in three. In some cases the urban wage proved less rigid than in others, but more important in explaining inter-country differences was the magnitude of the economic shocks and the economic policy response. Those countries which left the gold standard early experienced a smaller rise in the real industrial wage and a less severe industrial depression.[59] Equally important was the move to agricultural protection which, in the countries concerned, served to attenuate the fall in farm prices, incomes, and wage rates.[60]

THE LONG HAUL: INDUSTRIALIZATION AND THE WAGE GAP

Disequilibrating labour demand-side shocks

One moral to emerge from this chapter is that, while wage gaps clearly signal disequilibrium, they do not necessarily signal market failure. Wage gaps between farm and city have attracted the attention of historians and development economists interested in industrialization because they are thought to imply market failure of significant proportions. Large wage gaps, after all, imply that urban industry is constrained by labour market distortions. In the vernacular of the development economist, the market cost of scarce city labour far exceeds the social cost of surplus rural labour, and these gaps have encouraged government intervention to offset the distortion. Without the intervention, not only is city labour demand choked off in the shortrun, but in the longrun the rate of urban accumulation may also be forestalled, given that scarce city labour implies a profit squeeze. Wage gaps, therefore, tend to put the brakes on industrialization. While all of this is true, it fails to explore the sources of the disequilibrium in the first place. The more dramatic the technological events favouring city growth, the greater the improvement in the industrial terms of trade favouring city growth, and the stronger the pro-urban policy bias favouring city growth, the larger the wage gap. Having said as much, wage gaps should be viewed as an indicator of *success*, not failure. Without those disequilibrating labour demand-side forces favouring the city, wage gaps would be modest and industrialization slow. Over the long haul of industrialization, large wage gaps are more likely to be an attribute of economic success, not failure. One of the best examples of this is offered by a comparison between nineteenth-century France and Britain. France had much smaller wage gaps between city and countryside and also underwent slower industrialization and city growth.[61] Another example is offered by Japan where the modest wage gap of the interwar period increased sharply with rapid industrialization in the 1950s and 1960s.[62]

Another moral emerging from this study is that the terms labour market 'integration' and 'segmentation' are simply not very useful. Wage gaps vary greatly over time, and thus judgements about labour integration or segmentation should as well. Such terms are convenient, but they mask the dynamics of disequilibrating shock and equilibrating adjustment, and these two forces must be uncoupled if we are to make any progress in understanding how labour markets have worked in the past and how they have evolved to the present. Fast labour supply-side adjustment between city and countryside can be shown to be consistent with large wage gaps in an environment of big and persistent demand-side shocks.

Equilibrating labour supply adjustments

To better understand the evolution of labour markets linking city to countryside, we need to learn much more about labour supply responses to market incentives and how they have changed over time. In the econometrics presented in this chapter, we have assumed that the parameters describing migrants' response to the (unemployment-adjusted) wage gap are constant. This assumption is unlikely to survive a more detailed scrutiny, but we are unaware of any historical research which offers the necessary evidence on cityward migration to do so. Our prior is that migration becomes more responsive to wage gaps as time wears on and for at least two reasons, both of which are a function of previous migrations. As the stock of past rural emigrants accumulates in the city, the flow of potential current emigrants is better informed about urban job prospects. Similarly, as the stock of past rural emigrants accumulates in the city, the flow of potential current emigrants should be augmented to the extent that past emigrants can serve to finance the move and job search. International migration studies typically find that the current flow of migration *is* positively related to the past stock of migrations, so it seems likely that the same would apply to migrations between countryside and city.[63]

There are other labour supply-side forces, in addition to the rural–urban migrations themselves, which are likely to influence the size of the wage gap given the disequilibrium demand-side shocks, but we have not explored them here.

First, what about the impact of foreign immigration? Whether the focus is on Britain in the 1840s or on America between the 1870s and the 1920s, the historical evidence shows that foreign immigrants to booming cities crowd out potential immigrants from the countryside. That is, the inflow of the Irish during the famine decade tended to crowd out potential English rural immigrants to the city, resulting in low rural emigration rates during the decade.[64] Another example is offered by the immigration of rural blacks from the American South to the urban North during the half century following the Civil War.[65] The presence of foreign immigration, pulled to booming cities, implies that wage gaps will be lower given some migration response of local rural labour to market incentives, while the wage gaps will be higher in the absence of foreign immigration. We need much more research to sort out these influences.

Secondly, in an economy closed to foreign immigration, demographic forces in city and countryside are likely to play an important role. Furthermore, those demographic forces are likely to be closely related to previous migrations. Migrations are dominated by young adults, since they have the most to gain over a lifetime from the move, and they have lower commitments to rural life. Thus, young adults are more responsive to market signals than are older adults. As migration from countryside to city takes place, young adults (for example, potential emigrants) become scarcer in the countryside, requiring a larger wage gap to induce the same aggregate migrations. If disequilibrating demand shocks of the same magnitude persist over time, then wage gaps are likely to rise over time as the size of the potential rural migrant pool contracts. On the other hand, the cities are better able to satisfy the same booming labour demands over time, since the young adult share rises (from past migrations), lowering the mortality rate (young adults being at lower mortality risk), and raising the birth rate (young adults being at higher fertility risk). Based on British experience during the Industrial Revolution, these demographic forces were important,[66] but we need more research to identify which of these forces has dominated wage-gap experience in the past.

Interacting labour, capital and commodity markets

The presence of wage gaps may tell us more about poor commodity market integration than about labour market failure. We have shown that a good share of the nominal wage gap disappears when deflators are applied. Furthermore, the higher cost of living in the city is, in good measure, attributable to higher rents. Dwelling services are, of course, non-tradables. Thus, one of the reasons why nominal wages facing city firms are higher than nominal wages facing rural farms is that the relative price of wage goods is higher in the city. It follows that, even if migration served to equalize real wages (deflated by the cost of living) between city and countryside, real wages (deflated by output price) facing the urban firm would be higher. Due to the presence of non-tradable wage goods, well integrated labour markets can still be consistent with large nominal wage gaps and scarce city labour. In short, we should be able to learn more about wage gaps by learning more about the evolution of urban rents over time.

Furthermore, trade theory tells us that integration in one market can be a substitute for integration in another. How much of the observed change in the wage gap over time can be explained by capital chasing after that cheap labour in the countryside? What role does the integration of capital markets between city and countryside play in accounting for wage gaps?

POSTSCRIPT: THE EVOLUTION OF GLOBAL LABOUR MARKETS

Everything we have said so far about wage gaps between city and countryside should be applicable to international wage gaps as well. Based on international migrations themselves, there appears to have been four epochs of migration experience since the early nineteenth century. Up to about 1870, international immigration was on the rise, and one wonders to what extent the experience served to erode global wage gaps, especially between the old world and the new. The period between 1870 and the First World War has been called the age of free migration of common labour. Do we also observe a convergence of wages and international labour market integration? The interwar period is one of industrial crisis and restrictions on migration. Did these events serve to augment international wage gaps and create greater segmentation? Finally, what about the post–Second World War period? Does it reflect a resumption of the pre–First World War period of global labour market integration?

We need some answers to these questions, and any research agenda on the evolution of a globally integrated labour market might well find it useful to begin by asking whether what we have learned about wage gaps between city and countryside can be applied at the international level. Early results suggest that it can,[67] but much more remains to be done.

6

CITIES AND ECONOMIC DEVELOPMENT: SOME LESSONS FROM THE ECONOMIC HISTORY OF THE PACIFIC RIM

Lionel Frost

I

To many observers, the city in its Third World incarnation is an awesome waste of human and environmental resources. It is easy to accumulate a list of modern city horrors: waterways in Bangkok, Manila, and Hong Kong fouled with sewage and industrial waste which sunshine turns into a toxin known as 'red tides'; vast towns of poorly served shanties, which in Guatemala City encroach to the very edge of railway lines and spread deep into ravines scarred by a 1976 earthquake; epidemics of cholera sweep through the shanty towns of Peruvian cities, and are spreading to neighbouring Ecuador, Colombia, and Brazil; the subsidence of cities such as Shanghai and Bangkok, due to excessive pumping of subterranean waters; chronic traffic jams as the number of vehicles increases far more rapidly than road capacity; air pollution so severe that in Mexico City outdoor exercise is ill-advised, while satellite photographs of north-east China fail to show the city of Benxi, buried beneath a layer of dirty air; and the sheer desolation of Manila's Smokey Mountain, where a thousand poor, sick, and dying scavengers live on a rubbish dump. From such anecdotes it is possible to build a picture of a developing world where the physical fabric of towns has been stretched almost to breaking point.

Small wonder, then, that the rapid growth of Third World cities this century, and the prospect of further dramatic increases to come, alarms many observers. The Third World is currently somewhere near the middle of a demographic 'modernization cycle', where population growth accelerates sharply as death rates fall but birth rates are maintained. This cycle comes to an end, with population growth flattening out, when birth rates are reduced through improved education, family planning, and higher consumer expectations.[1] From the mid-eighteenth century in Europe, and mid-nineteenth century in Japan, population grew massively. In the twentieth century, this phenomenal population growth came to an end, especially after the Second World War, and has approached zero in recent years. The Third World in general entered the cycle only in the last half-century: from 1950 to 1980, the population of the world's less developed regions grew by 3.3 per cent per annum, while in the more developed regions annual growth averaged only 1.2 per cent. Driven by this Third World growth, the world's population has swollen from around two billion in 1925 to four billion in 1975, and to five billion in 1987. The UN projects a world population of over eight billion by 2025.[2]

As in Europe and Japan during the nineteenth and early twentieth century, Third World demographic expansion has fuelled the growth of cities. From 1950 to 1980 the world's urban population increased by 4.7 per cent per annum, with the growth rate in less developed regions just under 8 per cent per annum. In 1950 the world's urban population numbered 0.7 billion, 39 per cent of it in less developed regions; by 1980 the total had increased to almost 1.8 billion, with the Third World's share 55 per cent. The UN forecasts a Third World urban population of an astonishing 3.9 billion in 2025, 77 per cent of the estimated world total. It predicts that by the end of the 1990s there will be a total of 22 megacities of over 10 million inhabitants (and only three of them outside Asia, Latin America, and Africa).[3]

II

There is a pessimistic strain of scholarly and popular writings which stresses the inability of the modern Third World city to cope with the pressure of rapid population growth. It has been argued that urbanization has distorted the structure of Third World economies by concentrating resources in towns with only weak industrial and thus employment-creating capacity, a situation which has been called 'overurbanization'[4] or 'pseudo-urbanization'.[5] Policies designed to build up urban industrial capacity, such as protective tariffs, tax incentives, and overvalued exchange rates, introduced an 'urban bias' to the economy which diverted productive resources from the countryside.[6] Furthermore, peasants migrated to the cities because they were either 'pushed' from the countryside by natural disasters or political and military strife, or were 'pulled' to towns by the prospect, however slim, of in time securing decently paying work.[7] Because high rates of natural increase have made a greater contribution to the growth of Third World cities than has rural-to-urban migration,[8] these cities have tended to grow under their own momentum, regardless of economic conditions. 'Overurbanization' manifests itself as a surplus and underemployed urban labour force, with the resultant ills of poor housing, sanitation, and other disamenities.

Despite the economic benefits they may offer, cities in the 'overurbanized' Third World are viewed as too large and too costly to run. City growth necessarily requires heavy investment in housing and infrastructure. Because such amenities can usually be provided cheaply in rural areas, it has been suggested that the redistribution of labour from country to city is characterized by diseconomies of scale.[9] Finally, the environmental costs associated with city-based manufacturing have led some writers to conclude that urbanization, and even economic development itself, is simply not worth the candle.[10]

Cities are places where characteristics of location and concentration provide a comparative advantage in the production of goods and services. The clustering of complementary producers and providers of subsidiary services, and the availability of labour supplies, can create substantial external economies. Because these benefits of concentration can encourage technical change and the creation of new secondary and tertiary jobs, healthy city growth is often held to be a *sine qua non* of economic development. Urban success encourages more labour to migrate from less productive primary occupations. The dilemma facing Third World countries is whether to encourage further growth of employment in cities which are already large, congested, and dirty, at the risk of accelerating rates of in-migration and intensifying urban disamenities. Or should city growth be discouraged, at the cost of foregone increases in living standards? The future, as seen through the pessimists' crystal ball, is of unmanageably large cities choking off any hope of economic development. Accordingly, many analysts favour policies which will check the runaway growth of cities and redirect resources to the countryside.

On the other side of the debate, economists have been chipping away, steadily and effectively, at the concept of 'overurbanization'. Allen Kelley and Jeffrey Williamson have developed general equilibrium models of Third World urbanization which stress the importance of endogenous limits to urban growth. They argue that rising costs associated with urbanization (such as site values and housing rents) can act as limits to city size by cutting disposable incomes and capital accumulation.[11] These price signals cause a market adjustment which slows city growth by discouraging in-migration, or by forcing industry in high-cost cities to pay higher wages to attract labour. Kelley and Williamson's model predicts that by the end of the century Third World urban growth rates will have slowed down markedly because of these limits to growth, as well as falling birth rates associated with the end of the demographic modernization cycle.[12]

Despite their polarity, there is at least one broad aspect of similarity between the views of the pessimists and those of Kelley and Williamson. Both sides assume that urban problems will automatically become more manageable when city growth rates slow down. Kelley and Williamson write that when rapid growth is checked 'fewer complaints will be heard from the urban planners, and reports of urban environmental decay will lose some of their popular interest'.[13] The crucial difference is that, while the pessimists see interventionist policies as essential correctives to the distortions in Third World economies which make for high urban growth rates, the more optimistic economists' view is of endogenous limits to city efficiency which in time operate to check the growth of cities and its associated problems.

III

In this important specialist debate, economic history is generally ignored. It is therefore implicitly assumed that the economic historian has little to offer. In this chapter the contrary case is argued that the economic history of cities is not irrelevant to current issues. Williamson's recent work on British towns during the Industrial Revolution[14] fruitfully draws parallels and contrasts with modern Third World city growth. The comparison, as Williamson notes, 'helps sharpen the historical issues', and one learns much about *both* types of city as a result. Williamson's comparative approach will be extended here, by examining *general* processes of city growth as revealed by cases scattered widely across time and space. Most of the cases are drawn from the Pacific Rim, a region for which diversity is the signal general characteristic.

An historical view of cities is usually discounted by modern analysts and policy-makers on the grounds that the Third World's city problems and rates of population growth are unprecedented. As one writer puts it: 'In short, the experiences of Europe and the rest of the industrialized world are not all that much help to Third World cities that today are up against a situation far more critical and demanding than any city anywhere, or at any time, has ever faced.'[15] These problems have occurred in cities where population growth rates generally average 4–5 per cent per annum. In fact, such rapid growth rates are by no means unprecedented.[16] Chicago grew by 17 per cent per annum during the 1860s, and by 10 per cent per annum in the 1880s. Detroit grew by 11 per cent per annum in the 1910s, as did Los Angeles during the 1920s. Calcutta's annual growth averaged 20 per cent from 1710 to 1750, and Bombay's 11.6 per cent from 1715 to 1744.

Though in the pre-modern period the overall trend was for towns to grow relatively slowly, there are many instances of quicksilver urban growth as a result of political factors, particularly the establishment of new capital cities. The transformation of Edo (Tokyo) from a fishing village to a city of over one million inhabitants during the seventeenth century is the best known example. When Hideyoshi unified Japan and established Osaka as his capital in 1583, the city's population, which stood at 60,000 in 1580, rose to 400,000 by 1600, a rate of increase of 28 per cent per annum. Isfahan, made capital of Persia in 1598, grew from 40,000 to 500,000 inhabitants over the next thirty years. Agra, a mere village when it was made capital of Mughal India in 1506, had become a city of half a million by the end of the century. After the Ottoman conquest of Constantinople in 1453, that city grew at an average of 6.4 per cent each year until 1500, and then at nearly 4 per cent per annum until 1552. These high growth rates were achieved with far more limited communications and building technology, weaker building materials, and poorer sanitation and fire-fighting techniques than are available to today's cities. There was no possibility of the pre-modern city developing the kind of coping mechanism which exists today.

From 1950 to 1980, the urban population of Pacific Rim countries grew at 4.9

per cent per annum, with the greatest rate of increase being in Central America (9.5 per cent), South America (8.3 per cent), and Southeast Asia (7.5 per cent). Table 6.1 shows the growth rates of a sample of the major Pacific Rim cities.

These growth rates have seen the average population of the above cities rise from 2.5 million in 1950 to 8.5 million in 1980. Many of them now account for a much larger proportion of their national population than they did in 1950: Mexico City accounted for 11.3 per cent of Mexico's population in 1950 and 21.6 per cent in 1980; Lima increased its share of Peru's population from 14.4 to 26.6 per cent; Seoul's share of South Korea's population rose from 5.4 to 22.3 per cent. Nevertheless, many cities further down the urban hierarchy have also grown at very high annual rates: for instance, Inchon, Chongju, and Pusan in South Korea, by an average of 7.1 per cent from 1960 to 1975; Pyongyang, North Korea, by 9.3 per cent (1960–74); Taipei, 9.2 per cent (1956–76); Wuhan, 11.2 per cent (1953–8); Quezon City, 9.4 per cent (1960–75); Kuala Lumpur, 9.6 per cent (1957–70); in Colombia, Bogota, 11.2 per cent (1951–64) and 8.2 per cent (1964–76), and Guayaquil, 9.1 per cent (1950–74); Tegucigalpa, Honduras, 12.6 per cent (1961–4); and Guatemala City, 12.3 per cent (1973–88).[17]

Like most Third World cities, these towns suffer from the effects of a dysfunctional physical fabric. In other words, they are ill-equipped to shoulder the load of growing numbers without suffering the effects of significant poverty and environmental damage. A number of planners and policy-makers consider that the problem lies with the fact that these cities are 'overurbanized' and have grown 'too fast', and accordingly see the solution as policies to slow city growth.

History argues strongly against such a diagnosis. Rates of population growth are a poor predictor of the quality of an urban environment. Constantinople, labyrinthine and poorly built, was extraordinarily disaster-prone. Agra was for the common people a mess of muddy lanes and thatched huts. Yet Chinese cities, many also large and fast-growing, were well-policed and administered, and

Table 6.1 Population growth rates of selected Pacific Rim cities, 1950–80 (% p.a.)

	1950–60	*1960–70*	*1970–80*
Bangkok	5.7	5.0	3.9
Hong Kong	5.9	3.0	3.1
Jakarta	5.6	6.1	4.9
Lima	5.5	7.1	5.9
Los Angeles	6.1	2.7	1.3
Manila	4.4	5.7	6.7
Mexico City	6.8	7.7	6.3
Seoul	11.8	12.5	5.7
Tokyo	6.0	3.9	1.4

Source: calculated from United Nations, *Estimates and Projections*, 1985 Table A-13.

adequately paved and drained. Edo was cleaner than its European counterparts.[18] Chicago in the 1880s grew from a half to just over one million inhabitants, and during those years developed severe housing and environmental problems. Los Angeles added as many inhabitants in the 1920s, yet coped with the growing numbers with ease by continuing its pre–First World War pattern of extensive development of suburbs, each of which, 'even the least pretentious, was touched by the materialized dream of a better life'.[19]

Furthermore, history shows that slowly growing cities may also be afflicted by a dysfunctional physical fabric. In the first half of the seventeenth century, London became dangerously congested and vulnerable to fire and disease, even though its rate of population growth – less than 2 per cent per annum – was by today's standards only moderate. As the demand for housing and workplaces close to the city centre increased, existing fire and sanitation regulations were overlooked and street cleaning arrangements were gradually discontinued. Nottingham, considered by many observers to be England's 'neatest' eighteenth-century town, was by the mid-nineteenth century blighted by a mass of crowded and dirty slums. From 1801 to 1851 Nottingham's population grew by 1.9 per cent per annum. The problem here was not so much with weight of numbers as with a serious shortage of building land because of the late enclosure of the fields surrounding the town.[20] Both London and Nottingham's institutions were ill-adapted to cope with even relatively gentle rates of population growth. The history of pre-modern towns is peppered with similar instances.

Where an urban environment is dysfunctional, the problem is not with the *rate* of urbanization but rather the *capacity* of the urban environment to absorb growing numbers. Where a city lacks an economic and institutional setting capable of responding effectively to population growth, rapid growth will exacerbate the problem of urban disamenity. But the more one looks at urban history, the clearer it is that there is no causal link between fast population growth and a dysfunctional urban fabric. The task is to identify the factors which make for dysfunctional urban environments, and those which prevent (or encourage) the development of a more accommodative physical fabric – a safe and efficient urban environment which can absorb growing numbers in a non-debilitating way.

It is perhaps the simplest principle of urban economics that in a growing city the advantages reaped by economies of location, scale, and agglomeration must exceed the costs associated with the building, equipping, and servicing of that city. These congestion costs include the capital, land, and labour required for housing and infrastructure, the need for adequate journey-to-work arrangements, the task of dealing with problems of pollution and waste disposal, and the risk and incidence of major losses of concentrations of labour and capital stock in times of natural disaster and warfare. If the level of congestion costs in a city rises, this necessarily leads to an increase in the price of one or more of the factors of production, which may put that city at a serious competitive disadvantage. If the city becomes in consequence a more costly and less efficient producer, its capacity to generate wealth will be impaired. Thus any city can be expected to build the type of physical fabric which minimizes congestion costs in relation to its economic advantages.

Congestion costs rise whenever a given use of resources, which may be of private benefit, create in an urban setting a rise in social costs. This occurs when individuals use scarce resources in a way which reduces the supply and quality of resources available to others, thereby creating externalities such as congestion and pollution. Because the market cannot put a price on fresh air, clean water, and road space which will ensure that users pay for all of the resulting costs, there is an incentive to overuse these resources. Such behaviour may be cheap for the individual, but will impose a heavy burden on the rest of society.

Such a use of resources may be the result of either under- or over-investment in city-building. Cutting investment by reducing housing standards will reduce congestion costs, as society will need to find fewer resources to meet its need for shelter. But cutting investment in, say, water supply facilities will raise congestion costs by reducing labour productivity through disease and the need to queue for water. High-density housing may reduce society's congestion costs by allowing large numbers of people to live near sources of employment, but such crowding may increase vulnerability to natural disasters or inflate rents. Lavish spending on things such as sprawling suburban housing, wide streets, and far-flung infrastructure can make for congenial cities, but only the most prosperous economies can afford the high associated social costs.

Endogenous increases in congestion costs are the key limit to urban growth in Kelley and Williamson's models. When congestion costs rise relative to economic advantages, one may assume that, given total rationality and perfect information, people will be less willing to live in or move to cities. In practice, city dwellers have responded to rising levels of congestion costs (and/or an undermining of their city's economic advantages) with strategies that work to minimize congestion costs. People who decide to migrate to cities have been prepared to suffer pain in exchange for the chance to improve their economic lot, as have cities' native low-income population. For low-income groups the cost of migration may exceed that of remaining in the city, even if work, housing, and amenities become more scarce. When rising costs or falling incomes threaten economic well-being, people tend to move into cheap slums rather than out of the city.

The way in which costs are reduced depends on a number of institutional and economic variables. These include site features and topography, ethnic stratification, population density, patterns of land use and ownership, spatial patterns of residence and workplace, building regulations and technology, the relative price of building materials, sanitation technology, proximity to water supplies, political structure, and the public sector's priorities, tax base, and administrative competence. The mix of variables differs from case to case, so in one city slums may be compacted near the centre, while in another they sprawl out at the edge; slums may be packed in at the rear of better quality residences, or segregated in intrinsically undesirable locations. One city may have adequate paving and sanitation arrangements but flimsy and small housing; another's housing stock might be fairly well-built but crowded and served poorly with infrastructure. Though the details of city form vary, the basic objective of cost-cutting is a city which is cheaper to build and run.

While cities offer a road to a better life, compared to the dead-end of the countryside, the road is punctuated with deep, hidden cracks to fall through. When cities need to adjust their congestion costs to maintain economic progress, the burden falls most heavily on those who get sick, those without skills, those without regular work, and those in low-income occupations. Thus the poorer the city (in terms of either economic weakness or the number of low-income inhabitants), the more dismal the environment.

The necessity for lower congestion costs is what accounts for dysfunctional urban environments. This is what unites, *mutatis mutandis*, the experience of rudimentary Third World cities and those of the industrial and pre-modern era. A city which can house and service large numbers at minimal expense can provide those who wish to improve their economic lot with affordable shelter, while at the same time releasing resources for investment in commerce and manufacturing. The result is faster, but messier, economic growth. What Williamson calls 'the ugly-city and industrialization-on-the-cheap development strategy'[21] was the hallmark of city growth in nineteenth-century Europe and North America, typified East Asian cities until quite recently, and is still common in the Latin American and Southeast Asian regions of the Pacific Rim.

In the 'ugly city', the efforts of housing and sanitary reformers to improve standards were unpopular with landlord and tenant alike, as they would have entailed higher congestion costs and driven up rents and taxation levels. Government decrees as to required housing form and standards were usually unenforceable for the same reason. When cities lack economic strength, the costs of collecting the taxes and enforcing the regulations required for urban improvement are very high in relation to social wealth. Thus in Hong Kong, though Building Ordinances in the 1840s and 1850s set minimum standards, housing shortages and the weight of population growth meant that houses were built back-to-back regardless. For the next hundred years property owners firmly resisted any government efforts at reform, while tenants themselves subdivided their lodgings to reduce their rent burden.[22] The extra costs required would have represented 'leakages' to the city economy, choking off investment and job-creation opportunities. City dwellers traded off commodities (obtained as a result of cities' ability to generate wealth) against environmental quality (which deteriorated through underinvestment in city-building), a preference revealed overwhelmingly by those who chose to migrate to the towns. In many cases, the 'limits to growth' simply made growing cities more crowded and dirty.

If a dysfunctional urban environment can be attributed to necessary adjustments to rising levels of congestion costs, can we expect an improvement in city wealth to lead to an improvement in the physical fabric? When incomes begin to rise on average as a result of faster economic growth, the brakes on congestion costs may be released somewhat. Rising incomes, preferably more evenly distributed, create new standards of expectations as to environmental quality, which governments are better able to meet because of an expanding tax base. Furthermore, a strategy which seeks to minimize congestion costs may create a physical fabric which over time becomes less and less efficient, leading to a *rise* in congestion costs. Leaving a town's streets unpaved will cut costs at first, but as population density increases commercial traffic will flow more slowly and expensive labour-intensive methods of waste collection will be required to avoid epidemics. Simply emptying chamber-pots into the street or back alleys will carry very low private costs, but the social costs of such a practice will rise faster than population density. A prosperous, but dirty city may face rising labour costs if workers are forever sick, or if wage bribes must be paid to attract reluctant workers from other towns or from rural areas.[23] A city with the resources to pave and sewer its streets can achieve substantial reductions in congestion costs. Thus there will be sound economic reasons for cleaning up investment-starved cities, if a slowing down of economic growth is to be avoided.

Such an explanation of urban improvement 'fits' the experience of many towns. But some towns failed to improve their physical fabric, despite rising average incomes. While rising incomes are clearly a precondition for a change from a dysfunctional to an accommodative urban environment, the improvement depends ultimately on the individual city's historically layered institutional structure.

Improving the physical fabric of cities is like opening a door which has two locks. One of the required keys is rising average incomes. The other depends on institutional structures appropriate to urban improvement. This is largely a matter of politics. Where government is stable and effective and has the will and tax base to tackle urban improvement, there is likely to be adequate provision of public goods. Where large areas of urban land are publicly owned (and then sold or used by government for housing or infrastructure) and where land ownership is subject to correct pricing policies, the sites needed for city-building are likely to be affordable and used effectively. Externalities can be contained by government intervention in the pricing of urban resources, so that people who use resources 'excessively' face taxes and penalties which increase the private cost of their behaviour to a level close to the social cost. When governments get this pricing right, they create disincentives to pollute and make inefficient use of scarce resources. In cities where average incomes are rising and government administration is competent, the transaction costs of such pricing (the costs of collecting payments and policing regulations) should become a less serious constraint on urban improvement.

As the recent experience of Singapore and Hong Kong shows, where the public sector gives urban improvement priority, its actions are most effective in high-density cities. Spatial compactness encourages efficient land use, creates economies of scale for efficient land use such as public transport and multi-storey housing, and reduces the need for costly commuting.[24] Governments in high-density cities can set correct prices for the use of resources more easily because the transaction costs involved are relatively low. The more compact the city, the easier it is to collect payments and enforce regulations.[25]

Not all cities have these characteristics, and so the ability to build and maintain functional urban environments is not evenly distributed. Crucial early decisions, relating especially to site choice and planning, exert an abiding influence on the subsequent development of the physical fabric, affecting matters such as population density, patterns of land ownership, and ease of infrastructure provision. Such institutions are powerfully inert and may continue to exert upward pressure on a city's congestion costs, even if income levels are rising.

Consider the case of Sydney.[26] That nineteenth-century Sydney was a city of high average incomes is beyond dispute: there was no large industrial proletariat, and no pool of illiterate former peasants; at the end of the nineteenth century wage rates for skilled and unskilled work were 50 to 100 per cent higher than those of London; working-class food bills were approximately half those of British workers. Yet the most powerful influence on Sydney's urban environment was the initial decision to site the city on a small peninsula on the doorstep of Sydney Cove. This constricted site, and the virtual absence of town planning, later made it expensive to provide the railway and tram facilities which would have dispersed the population to suburbs. The high value of land in Sydney encouraged the New South Wales parliament, which was dominated by rural interests, to underinvest in the city's public transport and sanitation. To live in Sydney, one had to adjust to high land prices and commuting costs, and these congestion costs were partially offset by high-density housing. Much of the city's housing stock was of a high standard, but the burden of cutting congestion costs fell heavily on the working population who lived in crowded, poorly drained slums close to central city workplaces. It was not until the twentieth century that major public transport improvements helped break down Sydney's compactness. But the implications of deeply rooted institutional factors, notably a sewerage system built 'on-the-cheap', are still yet to be played out.

In many Hispanic towns, notably Los Angeles and Lima, and in Anglo-Saxon towns such as Melbourne, Adelaide, Perth, and Christchurch, a key influence on the physical fabric has been the initial decision to site them at some distance from their major port. The separate port, and the typical layout of a large grid of wide streets, decentralized the towns from the start. Where Latin American cities were located near large areas of unwanted desert or swampland, low-income groups occupied the land illegally and built their own housing. In the Anglo-Saxon cities, even the most humble housing was relatively spacious, private, and set on large lots, and as the cities expanded this housing form was basically replicated. The dominant spatial characteristic of these cities – low-density sprawl – endures.

Inherent in urban sprawl is an inefficiency of land use which makes the cost-efficient provision of infrastructure difficult. It inflates social costs by creating major servicing difficulties. The economies of the Anglo-Saxon cities have been wealthy enough to carry these costs, but urban sprawl in Latin America makes for primitive sanitation and living conditions.

The past weighs heavily on cities' present problems and characteristics, and many cities have been unable to implement the policies needed to establish a set of institutions more conducive to urban improvement. Manila, for instance, has failed to levy or implement property taxes to encourage the use of urban land for productive purposes (rather than withheld for speculative gain), or to sort out which level of government (city or national) should pay to have the network of canals and open drains unblocked.[27] The cities best equipped to provide effective services and improve the quality of their environment are those which for historical reasons have managed to contain urban sprawl. Bogota, for example, was sited in the midst of rich farmland, and squatting on alienated land has been forcibly checked by the state. This has encouraged more consolidated land use: in 1985 the city's population density was nearly eight times that of Lima.[28]

IV

I have argued that the Third World's planners and policy-makers, few of whom have thought about the past at all, would do well to consider the lessons of the economic history of city growth. The past offers a number of cases where the problems of a dysfunctional urban environment – problems which in essence are being repeated in today's Third World cities – have been alleviated. In some cities, these problems have persisted. Rapid population growth will not always wreck urban environments: degradation occurs when cities adjust to economic weakness by skimping on the cost of repairing and expanding their physical fabric. History shows a complex of factors – economic and institutional – which either allow cities to break free of, or be trapped in, the awfulness of dysfunctional environments. Policies which simply slow city growth may ease the symptoms but will not solve the problem.

By endogenizing the development of institutions and the political and/or social factors which account for their persistence or change, economic history complements the useful econometric models of city growth. These models rely on the existence and operation of limits to city growth for their optimistic predictions of slower urbanization and of environmental improvement. In fact, history shows that such limits may, or may not, work in this way. Time and again cities have offset the limits to growth by adopting low-cost city-building strategies. As the social costs of such strategies rise, various institutional factors may either encourage or discourage the extra investment needed to improve the urban physical fabric. There are messy institutional and political structures which need to be taken into account if appropriate policies are to be devised and implemented successfully: such work is the economic historian's stock-in-trade.

Part III

LONGRUN ISSUES IN LABOUR, BUSINESS AND BANKING

7

OLDER WORKERS AND THE BRITISH LABOUR MARKET: ANALYSING LONGRUN TRENDS

Paul Johnson

The structure of the labour force in the developed countries has been transformed over the last hundred years by two fundamental behavioural changes – the increasing labour-force participation of married women, and the ever earlier withdrawal of older workers. While the first of these changes has been studied in some detail,[1] longrun trends in the employment and retirement of older workers have attracted little attention from historians in Britain.[2] This is surprising given both the magnitude and the pervasiveness of the decline in the labour-force participation of older people, particularly older men. Figures 7.1 and 7.2 present the basic data for France, Germany, the UK, and the USA, derived from unadjusted participation rates reported in national censuses and labour-force surveys. For men aged 65 years and over, the participation rates show a uniform decline from around 60 per cent in the 1880s to about 10 per cent by the 1980s. For women the picture is more complex; although France and Germany share with Britain a downward trend, the USA displays a more erratic pattern, with participation rates lower than those of the other countries in the late nineteenth century, but higher in the late twentieth century.

The economic impact of this withdrawal of older workers from the labour market is potentially large – for instance, if males over 65 years of age in England and Wales in 1981 had exhibited the same participation rates as this age group did in 1881, the economically active male population would have been greater by 1.9 million, or almost 14 per cent. Decreasing labour-force participation rates at higher ages have not only reduced the potential labour supply, but also greatly increased the cost of public welfare systems, because the non-active elderly receive a substantial degree of income support from the state. In 1910 state pension payments in the UK were equivalent to 0.44 per cent of GNP, a figure that rose to 2.6 per cent by 1950 and 5.4 per cent by 1981.[3] The rapid ageing of the population of the developed countries projected for the first three decades of the next century may further increase the cost of public pension schemes. The Organisation for Economic Co-operation and Development (OECD) has expressed concern that 'countries will face growing fiscal burdens as expenditures increase and the working-age population shrinks or remains constant in size',[4] and has suggested that efforts be made to reverse the decline in labour-force participation at higher ages.

But before trends can be reversed they first have to be understood, and explanations for the retirement trends of older people are not self-evident. International cross-section studies of participation rates show a clear relationship between levels of economic development and retirement, indicating that changes in labour-force participation at older ages are dominated by income effects.[5] On the other hand, in most developed countries high levels of poverty are found among the retired population, which suggests either unusual income/leisure preferences at older ages or the existence of non-income retirement effects. The array of potential non-income influences on retirement is very broad and the overall effect indeterminate. Increases in life expectancy over the twentieth century and possibly better health in old age may have increased labour supply at older ages, but parallel changes in the nature of work and the structure of the labour market may have reduced the demand for older workers. Many recent attempts have been made to explain retirement patterns, mainly by using cross-section evidence,[6] but, as Figure 7.1 shows, the trend towards lower participation rates for older men is long standing, and any adequate explanation must be of a longrun nature.

This chapter is a first step towards a longrun explanation of retirement in England and Wales since 1881. Because of data limitations the chapter deals rather more with men than with women, and with manual rather than white-collar workers; it makes use of data from the decennial censuses of England and Wales to trace longrun changes in participation rates, and evaluates alternative explanations of these trends. The chapter proceeds in four steps: Section I outlines the modern hypotheses about the causes of retirement, Section II analyses the census data, Section III uses the explanatory hypotheses to interpret the historical trends, and the findings are summarized in the conclusion.

I

Permanent withdrawal from the labour force in later life is a function of three types of factors – physical, financial and structural.[7] Poor health and physical disability are consistently found to have a negative impact on labour-force participation in modern studies of individual retirement.[8] How the influence of health status on individual retirement decisions relates to longrun changes in the aggregate participation rate of older workers is, however, unclear. Mortality rates for older people over this period have fallen almost continually, with life expectancy at age 65 in England and Wales rising between 1901 and 1981 from 10.6 to 13.1 years for men and from 11.75 to 17.1 years for women. On the other hand, the incidence and duration of sickness and disability may have increased, although the fragility of the data precludes any definitive conclusion.[9] Furthermore, fitness for work is a subjective measure which will change over time as social and medical attitudes towards health and sickness evolve and as the physical demands of work alter. It is possible that changes in the health status of older people since 1881 have interacted with changes in the health requirements of employment to reduce the functional ability of older workers to participate in the labour force, and this is one proposition that can be assessed with the data presented below.

Other labour-force changes are likely to result from economic motivations. Hannah has noted that 'voluntary retirement is, in a sense, a luxury good whose incidence would be expected to grow in a hundred year period in which general living standards have perhaps tripled'.[10] The normalization of retirement during the twentieth century may simply be the consequence of a rise in real income and an associated increase in rates of personal asset accumulation. Again this proposition can be tested. Falling retirement ages and rising life expectancy together greatly increase the stock of savings required to finance retirement. If retirement is consciously planned for and funded from accumulated savings, then we would expect to see the higher retirement rates preceded by significantly higher rates of asset accumulation by people during their working life as they consciously adopt a form of life-cycle savings. Just such a transition to life-cycle saving in later nineteenth-century America has been proposed by Ransom and Sutch as an explanation of the high savings rates and relatively high retirement rates between 1870 and 1900.[11] However, if retirement is financed primarily through public pension systems, we might expect retirement rates to increase as access to public pension schemes is widened and the value of public pensions rises relative to the earnings of older workers.

Structural factors – the state of the labour market and the nature of employment contracts – may also affect retirement behaviour. If labour productivity declines after some point in mid-career, older men may be viewed by employers as marginal workers, and so may be disproportionately affected by changes in the general level of labour-market demand. The introduction of rigid employment contracts which incorporate mandatory retirement rules are another example of the way in which labour market structures may affect participation rates at older ages.

II

These various propositions can be assessed through an analysis of census data relating to the age structure of the occupied population in England and Wales since 1881. Figure 7.3 presents the basic data. Working-age (15–64) male labour-force participation was more or less constant at something over 95 per cent between 1881 and 1961, whereafter it declined slightly as more younger adults delayed entry into the labour force by staying on in full-time education. For working-age women the participation trend has been strongly upwards since the Second World War, rising from around 40 to about 70 per cent. For older men there has been a long-term (though variable) decline in participation since 1881. For older women there has been a longrun decline, although participation rates rose from 1961 to 1971. This pattern is true whether older women are defined in the same way as older men – that is aged 65 years and over – or whether they are defined as those over the state pension entitlement age of 60 years.

Census data, it should be noted, cannot reveal anything directly about the *process* of retirement which for many people involves complex changes in labour-market status and labour inputs over a number of years.[12] Censuses and labour-force surveys typically classify older people either as being in the labour force or as being retired, and they make little allowance for the fact that the experience of retirement may have changed over time and varies greatly between individuals. However, the detailed age-specific information which the censuses contain about people in employment enables changes in the participation rates of particular age groups or birth cohorts to be traced over time.

Inferences drawn from successive censuses will only be valid if the enumeration policy at successive censuses is similar. Before 1881 retired people were enumerated under their former occupation, so earlier censuses are not usable for the analysis of the labour-force participation of older people. It is possible that employment trends observable in the censuses from 1881 are to some unknown extent an artefact of the data collection or classification process. A detailed examination of the consistency of census data by Clive Lee has concluded that 'the problem almost certainly diminishes with the passage of time and in relation to fuller and better data collection'.[13] Even so, problems of interpretation may arise because the concept of retirement has itself changed greatly over the past century. Recent analysis of older people's economic circumstances in late nineteenth-century London has shown that some elderly men described themselves as occupied in the census even though they were, in a modern sense, functionally retired.[14] There is no way of estimating the size of any bias this may introduce into a longrun analysis of census returns, but it seems likely that any overestimation of the 'true' participation rate would decrease over time. This suggests that census data for the late nineteenth or early twentieth century may overstate the functional labour-force participation rate of older people, a point to bear in mind when further adjustments to the data are introduced below.

In the case of married women, however, it has generally been argued that nineteenth- and early twentieth-century censuses under-report the true level of paid employment.[15] More recently Jordan has suggested that some reliable inferences can be drawn from the disaggregated female employment data.[16] Because of this uncertainty over the reliability of data on women's labour-force participation, and because women constitute a small proportion of the older workforce, this chapter reports census data on female employment but concentrates on explaining the more pronounced fall in labour-force participation rates for older men.

Tables 7.1 and 7.2 present the actual age-related labour-force participation rates for men and women for each census from 1881 to 1981, together with a best guess at age-specific and cohort-specific participation rates. In order to provide estimates of participation rates for quinquennial age groups and quinquennial birth cohorts from decennial censuses, some method has to be found to fill the many missing observations. The procedure adopted has been simply to interpolate age-specific participation rates for any empty cell from the age-specific data of the immediately preceding and succeeding cohorts. So, for example, to estimate the participation rate for the 1862–66 birth cohort of men when aged 40–44 years in Table 7.1, the actual rates of 97.8 per cent for the 1857–61 cohort (from the 1901 census) and 98.3 per cent for the 1867–71 cohort (from the 1911 census) have been averaged. In the table all numbers in bold type represent actual census data; all numbers in normal type represent interpolated data. This procedure is somewhat rough and ready, particularly between censuses which have reported data for differently delimited age groups; the greatest problems are likely to be with the 1881 census which adopted very wide age bands (details are given in the notes to these tables). Furthermore, it is a procedure that breaks down with the oldest, open-ended age categories, since these vary between censuses. The oldest category for the 1881 and 1891 censuses was 65 years of age and over, for 1921 and 1971 it was 70 years of age and over, and for all the other censuses it was 75 years of age and over. For this reason the right-hand side of the table has a jagged appearance as gaps have been left where no reasonable interpolations can be made. All final, open-ended age-group participation rates, whether interpolated or directly recorded in the censuses, are printed in italics.

These tables can be read in three distinct ways to distinguish between the age, period, and cohort effects on participation rates. Numbers in columns show the participation rate for each specific age group as recorded in censuses from 1881 to 1981 – this is the type of data used to construct Figures 7.1 and 7.2. Numbers in bold type running in diagonals from lower left to upper right show the age-specific participation rates recorded in successive census years – they represent cross-sections of the workforce at specific points in time. Numbers in rows show the age-specific participation rates for members of successive cohorts as they age through their life-course.

Looking first at the cross-section data from successive censuses in Table 7.1 (reading diagonals from lower left to upper right), it can be seen that the male participation rates for ages 25–64 years are very similar, but more recent censuses have progressively lower rates for both younger and older age groups. For women the pattern shown in Table 7.2 is very different. For censuses from 1881 to 1931 female participation rates are highest for the 15–19 age group, they decline sharply for women in their mid-twenties, and then continue a gradual decline with age. From 1951, however, female participation rates rise for women in their mid-thirties, and by 1981 women aged 40–49 years had the highest age-specific participation rate. Interesting though a census snapshot of the labour market is, it is difficult to interpret because it conflates what may be separate age and cohort effects.

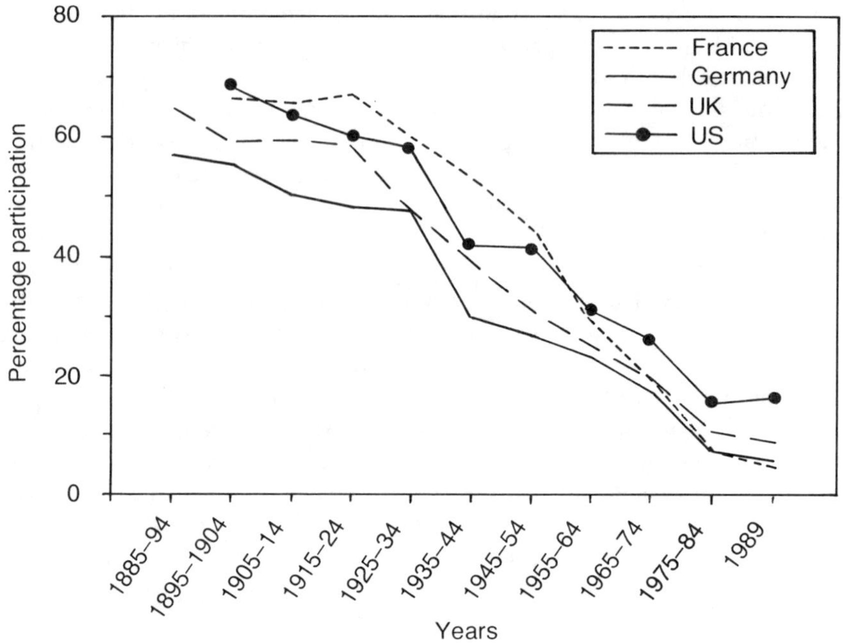

Figure 7.1 Labour-force participation rates for men 65+

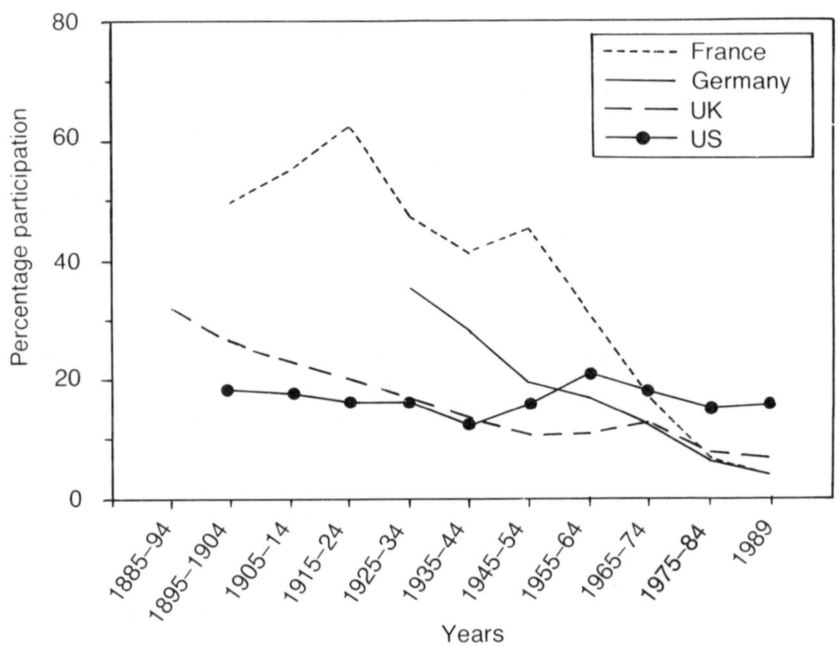

Figure 7.2 Labour-force participation rates for women 65+

To examine the role of age more closely it is necessary to focus on the participation rates for particular age groups over time by reading down the columns. From Tables 7.1 and 7.2 it is clear that both men and women under 20 years of age have experienced sharply declining participation rates since the Second World War, at a time when access to secondary and tertiary education has widened substantially. For men aged 25–44 years there has been little change in participation rates for over a century, but for men aged 45–54 years there is evidence of a slight but continuous rise in participation rates between 1891 and 1961, while for the group aged 60–64 years participation rates between 1891 and 1961 show no clear trend. Men over 65 years of age, however, seem consistently to have had significantly lower participation rates than those slightly younger; it appears, therefore, that 65 years of age was an important employment threshold well before the twentieth-century introduction of social security pensions or the widespread adoption of occupational pension schemes. The older age groups have also experienced a marked fall in participation rates over time, but the decline is not continuous; even when the varying age groups are collapsed into a single participation rate for men 65 years of age and over (as in Figure 7.3), the data show a slight rise in labour-force participation between 1911 and 1921. And the rate of decline should not be exaggerated; Table 7.1 shows that in 1951, with the postwar national insurance pension scheme firmly in place, almost half of men aged 65–69 years, and over a quarter of those in their early 70s, were still recorded by the census as being in the workforce.

Reading down the columns in Table 7.2 it is clear that participation rates for women aged 25 to 59 years have risen substantially between 1881 and 1981, though the increase has not been continuous, with the lowest age-specific rates generally occurring in the interwar period. For women aged 60–64 years the pattern is U-shaped, with the recorded participation rate in the late twentieth century matching that of one hundred years before, while for women over 65 years the longrun trend is more obviously downwards. The age threshold of 65 years noted for men in Table 7.1 appears to be less significant for women, as also does the threshold of 60 years, which since 1940 has been the age at which women with an independent contribution record have been entitled to draw a national insurance retirement pension. Despite this entitlement, participation rates for women aged 60–64 years actually increased between 1951 and 1981.

A third way to read the tables is to consider the lifetime employment experience of different birth cohorts (reading across the rows). Data for four illustrative cohorts of men born in 1832–6, 1872–6, 1907–11 and 1932–6 are plotted in Figure 7.4. This shows that these widely-spaced cohorts have experienced very similar labour-force participation trajectories over their working lives up to age 64, although the rates for the earlier cohorts are consistently, if only marginally, below the rates for the later cohorts. Beyond this age, the nineteenth-century workers experienced a reduction in employment rates, but it was drawn out over the following fifteen years, whereas the twentieth-century workers have experienced abrupt curtailment of employment

Table 7.1 Labour-force participation rates by age group for quinquennial birth cohorts of males, England and Wales

		Age group												
Birth cohort	*Census year*	*15–19*	*20–24*	*25–29*	*30–34*	*35–39*	*40–44*	*45–49*	*50–54*	*55–59*	*60–64*	*65–69*	*70–74*	*75+*
1812–16		–	–	–	–	–	–	–	–	–	–	***73.4***	–	–
1817–21		–	–	–	–	–	–	–	–	–	**95.0**	*69.1*	–	–
1822–26		–	–	–	–	–	–	–	–	**95.0**	92.4	***64.8***	–	**39.0**
1827–31		–	–	–	–	–	–	–	**95.0**	92.4	**89.7**	–	**68.9**	*35.1*
1832–36		–	–	–	–	–	–	**95.0**	95.4	**89.7**	89.3	**68.9**	66.7	***31.1***
1837–41		–	–	–	–	–	**98.1**	95.4	**95.8**	89.3	**89.0**	66.7	**64.5**	*29.0*
1842–46		–	–	–	–	**98.1**	97.8	**95.8**	95.9	**89.0**	89.3	**64.5**	–	*27.0*
1847–51		–	–	–	**98.1**	97.8	**97.5**	95.9	**96.1**	89.3	**89.6**	72.0	***40.5***	*24.9*
1852–56		–	–	**98.1**	98.0	**97.5**	97.6	**96.1**	96.4	**89.6**	89.2	**79.4**	**–**	***22.8***
1857–61		–	**97.1**	98.0	**97.9**	97.6	**97.8**	96.4	**96.7**	91.8	**88.7**	72.2	**41.7**	*20.3*
1862–66	(1881)	**90.2**	97.0	**97.9**	98.1	**97.8**	98.1	**96.7**	96.7	**94.0**	88.0	**64.9**	38.1	*17.7*
1867–71		90.7	**96.9**	98.1	**98.3**	98.1	**98.3**	96.7	**96.7**	94.0	**87.2**	60.5	34.6	*15.2*
1872–76	(1891)	**91.2**	97.1	**98.3**	98.4	**98.3**	98.1	**96.7**	96.7	**93.9**	87.3	56.1	31.0	***12.6***
1877–81		91.5	**97.4**	98.4	**98.6**	98.1	**97.8**	96.7	**96.7**	94.2	87.3	51.6	**27.4**	*11.1*
1882–86	(1901)	**91.8**	97.4	**98.6**	98.2	**97.8**	98.0	**96.7**	97.0	94.5	87.4	**47.2**	24.3	***9.7***
1877–91		91.7	**97.4**	98.2	**97.8**	98.0	**98.2**	97.0	97.3	94.7	**87.5**	43.5	**21.3**	*8.3*
1892–96	(1911)	**91.7**	97.2	**97.8**	98.1	**98.2**	98.3	97.3	97.5	**95.0**	89.3	**39.9**	–	*6.9*
1897–1901		92.8	**96.9**	98.1	**98.5**	98.3	98.4	97.5	**97.8**	96.0	**91.0**	35.2	***11.0***	*5.5*
1902–06	(1921)	**93.9**	97.1	**98.4**	98.4	98.4	98.5	**97.8**	98.2	**97.1**	88.8	**30.5**	–	***4.1***
1907–11		93.3	**97.3**	98.2	98.4	98.5	**98.6**	98.2	**98.6**	98.0	**86.6**	23.8	**9.8**	–
1912–16	(1931)	**92.7**	96.7	98.0	98.4	**98.6**	98.7	**98.6**	97.9	**95.3**	80.6	**17.0**	–	–
1917–21		90.5	96.1	97.8	**98.3**	98.7	**98.8**	98.3	**97.2**	93.5	**74.6**	–	–	–
1922–26		88.2	95.5	**97.6**	98.5	**98.8**	98.5	**98.0**	96.4	**91.6**	–	–	–	–
1927–31		86.0	**94.9**	97.7	**98.7**	98.6	**98.3**	97.6	**95.7**	–	–	–	–	–

1932–36	(1951)	**83.7**	94.0	**97.9**	98.3	**98.4**	98.0	**97.2**	–	–	–	–	–	–
1937–41		79.3	**93.2**	97.4	**98.0**	98.2	**97.8**	–	–	–	–	–	–	–
1942–46	(1961)	**74.8**	92.3	**97.0**	97.9	**98.0**	–	–	–	–	–	–	–	–
1947–51		69.7	**91.5**	96.7	**97.8**	–	–	–	–	–	–	–	–	–
1952–56	(1971)	**64.6**	91.0	**96.5**	–	–	–	–	–	–	–	–	–	–
1957–61		66.2	**90.6**	–	–	–	–	–	–	–	–	–	–	–
1962–66	(1981)	**67.7**	–	–	–	–	–	–	–	–	–	–	–	–

Notes: Figures in bold type are actual participation rates derived from the censuses.
Figures in normal type are participation rates interpolated from actual age-specific participation rates of the immediately preceding and succeeding birth cohorts.
Figures in italics represent participation rates for open-ended age groups, either 65+ or 70+ or 75+.

The age groups reported in the censuses and used to construct this table are as follows:
1881: quinquennial 15–24, vicennial 25–64, 65+
1891: quinquennial 15–24, decennial 25–64, 65+
1901 & 1911: quinquennial 15–24, decennial 25–74, 75+
1921: 16–19, quinquennial 20–24, decennial 25–54, quinquennial 55–69, 70+
1931: 16–19, quinquennial 20–34, decennial 35–54, quinquennial 55–74, 75+
1951 & 1961: quinquennial 15–34, decennial 35–54, quinquennial 55–74, 75+
1971: 15–20, 21–24, quinquennial 25–69, 70+
1981: 16–20, 21–24, quinquennial 25–74, 75+

Sources:
1881 Census, Ages (P.P. 1883, LXXX), Table 5.
1891 Census, Ages (P.P. 1893–4, CVI), Table 5.
1901 Census (P.P. 1903, LXXXIV), Table XXXXV.
1911 Census (P.P. 1913 LXXXVIII), Table 3.
1921 Census, Table 2.
1931 Census, Table 2.
1951 Census, Table 2.
1961 Census, Table 2.
1971 Census, Table 2.
1981 Census, Table 12.

Table 7.2 Labour-force participation rates by age group for quinquennial birth cohorts of females, England and Wales

Birth cohort	Census year	*Age group* 15–19	20–24	25–29	30–34	35–39	40–44	45–49	50–54	55–59	60–64	65–69	70–74	75+
1812–16		–	–	–	–	–	–	–	–	–	–	***18.3***	–	–
1817–21		–	–	–	–	–	–	–	–	–	**26.1**	*17.1*	–	–
1822–26		–	–	–	–	–	–	–	–	**26.1**	25.3	***16.0***	–	***7.5***
1827–31		–	–	–	–	–	–	–	**26.1**	25.3	**24.4**	–	**15.7**	*6.6*
1832–36		–	–	–	–	–	–	**26.1**	25.7	**24.4**	22.6	**15.7**	14.8	***5.7***
1837–41		–	–	–	–	–	**29.0**	25.7	**25.3**	22.6	**20.7**	14.8	**13.8**	*5.2*
1842–46		–	–	–	–	**29.0**	27.0	**25.3**	23.5	**20.7**	20.5	**13.8**	–	*4.8*
1847–51		–	–	–	**29.0**	27.0	**25.0**	23.5	**21.7**	20.5	**20.4**	14.6	*7.1*	*4.3*
1852–56		–	–	**29.0**	31.0	**25.0**	23.8	**21.7**	22.4	**20.4**	19.4	**15.3**	–	***3.8***
1857–61		–	**56.0**	31.0	**33.0**	23.8	**22.5**	22.4	**23.0**	20.2	**18.3**	13.8	**7.2**	*3.4*
1862–66	(1881)	**68.1**	56.9	**33.0**	31.8	**22.5**	23.3	**23.0**	22.0	**20.1**	17.3	**12.3**	6.6	*2.9*
1867–71		68.4	**57.8**	31.8	**30.5**	23.3	**24.1**	22.0	**21.0**	19.5	**16.4**	11.5	6.0	*2.5*
1872–76	(1891)	**68.6**	57.0	**30.5**	32.2	**24.1**	23.5	**21.0**	21.0	**18.9**	16.1	10.6	5.3	***2.0***
1877–81		68.3	**56.3**	32.2	**33.8**	23.5	**22.9**	21.0	**21.1**	21.2	15.7	9.8	**4.7**	*1.9*
1882–86	(1901)	**65.9**	59.2	**33.8**	33.7	**22.9**	23.7	**21.1**	24.6	23.4	15.4	**8.9**	4.8	***1.8***
1877–91		67.3	**62.0**	33.7	**33.5**	23.7	**24.5**	24.6	28.1	25.7	**15.0**	9.6	**4.9**	*1.6*
1892–96	(1911)	**68.8**	62.1	**33.5**	31.6	**24.5**	27.3	28.1	31.5	**27.9**	17.7	**10.3**	–	*1.4*
1897–1901		71.2	**62.2**	38.1	**29.6**	27.3	30.2	31.5	**35.0**	31.4	**20.4**	11.6	***3.1***	*1.3*
1902–06	(1921)	**73.5**	63.7	**42.7**	30.7	30.2	33.0	**35.0**	39.2	**36.9**	24.3	**12.9**	–	***1.1***
1907–11		75.6	**65.1**	42.2	31.8	33.0	**35.8**	39.2	**43.3**	44.1	**28.2**	10.3	**3.4**	–
1912–16	(1931)	**77.6**	65.2	41.7	32.8	**35.8**	39.1	**43.3**	51.2	**51.2**	25.3	**7.7**	–	–
1917–21		77.9	65.3	41.1	**33.9**	39.1	**42.4**	52.7	**59.1**	51.7	**22.4**	–	–	–
1922–26		78.2	65.4	**40.6**	35.3	**42.4**	51.5	**62.1**	61.3	**52.1**	–	–	–	–
1927–31		78.4	**65.5**	40.0	**36.6**	48.5	**60.5**	65.4	**63.4**	–	–	–	–	–

1932–36	(1951)	**78.7**	63.9	**39.5**	41.0	**54.6**	64.6	**68.6**	–	–	–	–	–	–	–	–
1937–41		74.7	**62.3**	41.4	**45.4**	58.7	**68.6**	–	–	–	–	–	–	–	–	–
1942–46	(1961)	**70.7**	60.7	**43.3**	49.4	**62.7**	–	–	–	–	–	–	–	–	–	–
1947–51		64.0	**59.1**	49.4	**53.4**	–	–	–	–	–	–	–	–	–	–	–
1952–56	(1971)	**57.3**	63.7	**55.5**	–	–	–	–	–	–	–	–	–	–	–	–
1957–61		58.2	**68.3**	–	–	–	–	–	–	–	–	–	–	–	–	–
1962–66	(1981)	**59.0**	–	–	–	–	–	–	–	–	–	–	–	–	–	–

Notes: as for Table 7.1.

Table 7.3 Actual and adjusted participation rates for males 65+, 1881–1971

	1881	*1891*	*1901*	*1911*	*1921*	*1931*	*1951*	*1971*
Actual	73.4	64.8	60.6	56.0	58.3	47.5	30.8	19.3
Adjusted for shift from agriculture	56.0	50.5	50.6	48.3	51.6	42.7	29.1	19.3

Source: as for Table 7.1. For details of adjustment procedure, see text.

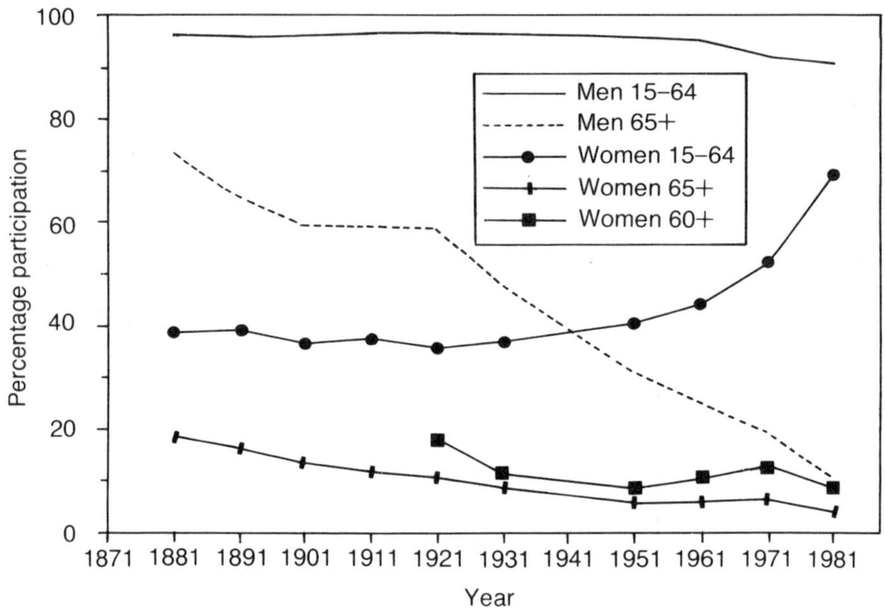

Figure 7.3 Participation rates for males and females in Britain

at age 65 and rapid decline thereafter. This reflects the increased age-structuring of the life-course over the last century; age has become an increasingly close correlate of labour-force participation as the probability of economic activity at low or high ages for men has declined significantly over time.[17]

Similar cohort data for women are plotted in Figure 7.5. This shows the striking changes to life-cycle employment patterns experienced by successive generations of British women. The two nineteenth-century cohorts show a general fall in participation over the life course, with a gradual tailing-off in old age. The twentieth-century cohort profiles, by contrast, show that these women left the labour market in their 20s and early 30s, and then returned to work between their late 30s and late 50s. The decline in participation from age 60 is much more abrupt than for earlier born cohorts, indicating a similar age-structuring of the life-course as for men.

Some of the recorded decline in participation rates at older ages may be a direct consequence of structural change in the economy if older workers are concentrated in particular sectors. In their study of labour-force participation rates for older US males, Ransom and Sutch found that the decline in the agricultural workforce from around 50 per cent to 25 per cent of the total US workforce between 1870 and 1930 had a major impact on measured labour-force participation rates because older workers were consistently over-represented in agriculture.[18] At first sight it might seem that similar sectoral shifts would have only a small effect on participation rates for older workers in Britain, because by the 1880s little more than 15 per cent of the workforce was employed in agriculture, forestry, and fishing, a figure which fell to 8.6 per cent by 1931. However, the concentration of older workers in the agricultural sector over the entire period since 1881 results in the sectoral decline in agriculture being a prime mover in the decline in labour-force participation rates. This can be seen when the actual labour-force participation rates for men 65 years of age and over since 1881 are compared with an adjusted rate which takes account of the shift away from agriculture.

The procedure adopted was to redistribute the male labour force recorded in each census between agricultural and non-agricultural employments according to the 1971 census rates (4.06 per cent agriculture, 95.94 per cent non-agricultural), and to apply to these artificial numbers the actual proportion of workers above and below 65 years of age in agriculture and non-agriculture as reported in each census. This produces the agriculture-adjusted male labour-force participation estimates shown in Table 7.3. A similar adjustment for females has a negligible effect – a consequence of the smaller proportion of both the total female workforce and the aged female workforce employed in agriculture. For men, however, the results are striking – adjusted labour-force participation rates fall from 1881 to 1891, but are marginally *higher* in 1921 than in the three preceding censuses. Overall the adjusted data in Table 7.3 suggest that the incidence of retirement in Britain would have been virtually constant between 1881 and 1921 had it not been for substantial structural change in the economy. This finding corresponds with that of Ransom and Sutch for the USA, and of Conrad for France and Germany – virtually all the observed decline in the labour-force participation of older men between the 1880s and the 1920s can be accounted for by the decline in size of the agricultural sector.[19] From this two important conclusions can be drawn: first, that retirement rates for male manual workers aged over 65 years in towns were as high as 40 per cent as early as the 1880s and remained at about this level until after the First World War; secondly, that the origins of a new retirement regime for the majority of older men should be sought not in the late Victorian period but in the 1920s or 1930s.

III

What can these multiple readings of census data tell us about the determinants of the labour-force participation of older people in Britain? When combined with a limited amount of information from other sources, the evidence from the censuses can be used to distinguish between the competing explanations of retirement behaviour discussed in the first section of this chapter. The first hypothesis, that rising retirement rates result from a worsening in the average health status of older workers relative to the health requirements of employment, receives no support from the census data. As Figure 7.4 shows, the labour-force participation rates between ages 45 and 64 years for men born 1832–36, 1872–76 and 1907–11 rise across birth cohorts, a finding which is consistent with other evidence about improving nutritional status and physical stature for British males over this period.[20] Yet despite the higher prime-age participation rates for the later-born cohorts, old-age participation rates are much lower and decline after the age of 65 much more rapidly for the later-born. For women (Figure 7.5) the case is even clearer – participation rates for later-born cohorts when in their 50s are much higher for earlier generations, but the rate of decline after 65 years of age is much faster. For this pattern to be explained by changes in health requires that the incidence of some specific diseases of old age should have increased greatly over time, and should have become much more acute at or around age 65 for successive birth cohorts. No evidence exists of any such dramatic and peculiarly structured developments in morbidity.

The second possibility is that the evolving pattern of labour-force participation rates reflects the improving financial status of the elderly. If retirement is a luxury good purchased with the fruits of past saving, then it should be possible to detect substantial changes over time in savings rates. The evidence again gives little support to this hypothesis. No direct estimates of the longrun private savings rate of British workers are available, but some plausible guesses can be made. If the annual change in the stock of household encashable assets is treated as net household saving and income from employment taken as household income, a proxy household saving rate can be constructed, which has a mean value of 4.4 per cent for the period 1880–1914, 5.1 per cent for the period 1920–1939, and 5.9 per cent for the period 1946–1962.[21] This proxy savings rate takes no account of two important assets – owner-occupied dwellings and occupational pensions. Neither element, however, was of much significance for manual workers before the Second World War. In 1914 perhaps 10 per cent of the UK housing stock was owner-occupied, and a negligible share of this was owned by manual workers.[22] Although owner-occupation spread in the 1930s with the introduction of 90 per cent mortgages, these loans were available only to young or prime-age workers, and therefore the value of real estate was unlikely to have been a significant influence on working-class retirement decisions until the prime-age workers of the interwar period approached retirement in the late 1950s or 1960s. Similarly, although total membership of occupational pension

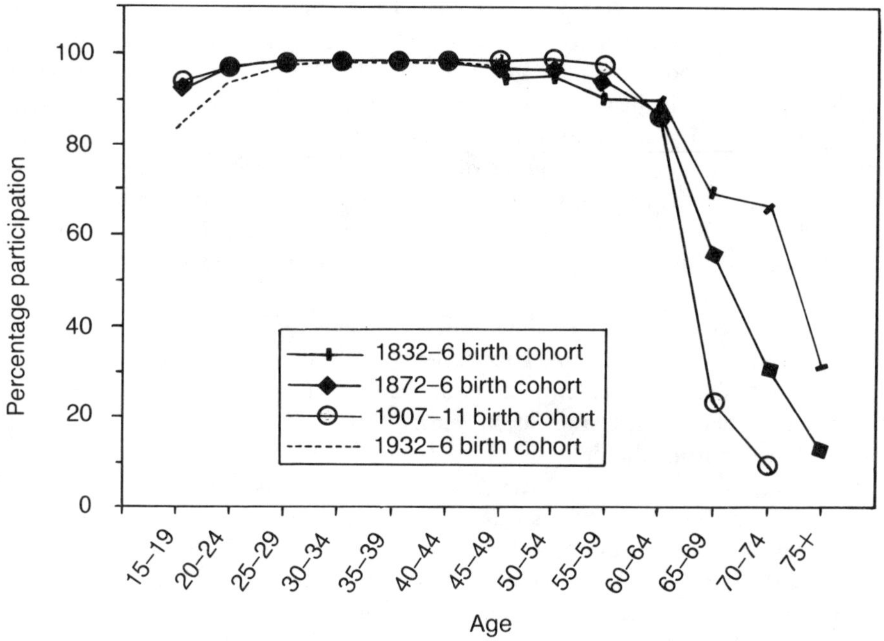

Figure 7.4 Age-specific participation rates for successive cohorts of men

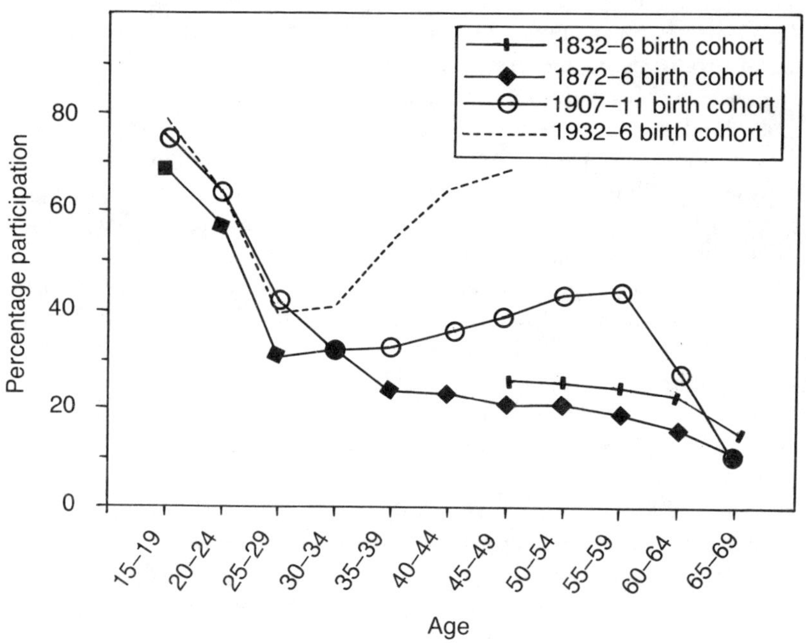

Figure 7.5 Age-specific participation rates for successive cohorts of women

schemes rose from perhaps 5 per cent to 13 per cent of the workforce between 1900 and 1936, the number of older persons receiving occupational pensions in the interwar period was small. In 1936 around 200,000 occupational pensions were being paid, inclusive of widows and orphans pensions and pensions to persons under 65 years of age. With 3.9 million people aged 65 years and over, this indicates a maximum coverage of 5 per cent of the elderly population.[23] A detailed study of the living conditions of the elderly has led Thomson to conclude that 'in the 1930s not more than 2 to 3 per cent of the aged population could have been maintained by regular superannuation payments under such schemes'.[24]

The adjusted retirement rate in Figure 7.4 begins to decline after 1921; if this was a consequence of planned retirement resulting from conscious life-cycle saving, there should be evidence of savings rates rising at least thirty years earlier. In practice there is little indication, either from the calculation of the proxy saving rate or from the analysis of other asset holdings, of household savings rates rising substantially before the Second World War. Furthermore, the actual savings rate for manual workers was almost certainly much lower than the proxy rate suggested here, since working-class assets in 'small saver' institutions amounted to only 10–15 per cent of total household encashable assets over the period 1901–1936.[25] This suggests that the net savings rate for working-class households before the Second World War was very low, and certainly not sufficient to sustain a lengthening period of retirement. The savings hypothesis does not seem to fit well even for the more recent and more abrupt decline in participation rates for men over 55 years of age since the mid-1970s. According to Treasury statistics, rising retirement rates over the past two decades do not coincide with any observable increase in the ratio of personal wealth to GDP.[26]

If household savings were low and increasing only slowly before the Second World War, how did people no longer active in the labour force support themselves? The adjusted labour-force participation rate in Table 7.3 suggests that between 1881 and 1921 in industrial parts of the country perhaps no more than half the male population over 65 years of age was occupied. It seems unlikely that retired people received substantial financial assistance from their children, although aged parents who co-resided with their adult children may have received assistance in kind. Peter Laslett has recently concluded: '[It is] improbable that much actual money would have passed from elderly son to very aged parent, or from children of any age to their mothers or fathers in later life. Where there was property the direction of assistance was from the old to the young rather than the other way round.'[27] In fact, the most important source of financial support for the non-active elderly from 1881 until the payment of the first old age pensions in 1909 appears to have been the Poor Law. Using official Poor Law data Charles Booth estimated that in 1891 the proportion of men over 65 years of age in receipt of Poor Law relief was 39.5 per cent in London, 28.5 per cent in other urban and suburban areas, and 25 per cent in rural or semi-rural areas.[28] If we assume that there was little overlap between the occupied population over 65 years of age and the pauper population over 65 years of age,[29] then it is apparent that the majority of the non-occupied elderly were in receipt of Poor Law assistance.

Although in theory the Poor Law allowed support only to individuals who were destitute, in practice local administrators adopted flexible criteria, frequently allowing assistance equivalent to a very small pension to people over 65 or 70 years of age.[30] This, together with occasional help from family, friends, charity, or savings, was the normal lot of the non-employed elderly in late Victorian Britain. The payment of a means-tested old age pension of 5s per week from January 1909 to people over 70 years of age widened access to public financial support, but the scale of this should not be exaggerated. In March 1912, 642,524 pensions were being paid in England and Wales, of which 37.5 per cent were paid to men.[31] These male pensioners represented 29.8 per cent of the total male population of England and Wales aged 65 years or over, a figure very close to Booth's estimate that 27 per cent of men 65 years of age or over in England and Wales in 1891 were in receipt of Poor Law relief. Some upward adjustment to the 1912 figure would be required to take account of those men aged 65 years or more who were still in receipt of Poor Law relief, but this was a relatively small group. The implication is clear – the introduction of old age pensions in 1909 served largely to replace existing Poor Law relief. It is not surprising, therefore, to see only a small dip in the adjusted labour-force participation rate in 1911.

The payment from 1928 of insurance-based pensions to manual workers aged 65 years who had an adequate national insurance contribution record may have induced some decline in participation rates, but the effect appears to be small. The proportionate decline between 1921 and 1931 in participation rates for the 65–69 age group covered by the new pensions was the same as that for men aged 70 years and over who already had access to means-tested pension.[32] These insurance pensions, however, involved neither a means test nor a retirement test, and even in the late 1930s over 55 per cent of pensioners remained at work at age 65.[33] Paid at a rate of 10s per week, the pension was a useful top-up to other income, but was scarcely enough to sustain an independent life at a reasonable standard. The 1908 pension of 5s per week was around one-sixth of the average earnings of an adult male manual worker, and the 10s per week pension payable in the 1930s represented an almost identical share of the average male manual worker's wage.[34] After 1946 the pension was paid to men over 65 years of age on condition that they withdrew from the labour force, but it remained at a below-subsistence level and each year between 1950 and the early 1970s one-quarter of all state pensioners received a means-tested supplement to raise their income above the poverty line.[35] In the early 1970s a study of low-income households noted that 'old age remains the main systematic cause of poverty'.[36]

The relative value of the state pension increased somewhat from the mid-1970s, but its consistently low level over the period 1909–1971 means that it is not a sufficient explanation of the labour-force participation trends shown in

Figure 7.3. Changes in state pension entitlements could explain changes in participation rates at particular times, though the expanded entitlements in 1909 were more apparent than real, and the insurance pensions of 1928 had a limited impact on labour supply because they were paid as an entitlement unrelated to either income or continued employment. The retirement condition attached to pensions after the Second World War must have depressed participation rates for men over 65 years of age and would be one reason for the much lower participation rates in 1951 (a boom year) than in 1931 (a depression year), but this cannot explain the further decline in participation rates thereafter. Furthermore, if pension entitlement was the crucial factor, then the reduction in 1940 of the public pension age for women from 65 to 60 years should have precipitated a substantial fall in the female participation rate for the age group 60–64 years between 1931 and 1951, but this did not happen. The post-war expansion of occupational pension schemes undoubtedly also increased the financial attractiveness of retirement for some workers; by 1956, eight million workers, almost one in three of the workforce, were enrolled in occupational pension schemes, a figure which had further increased to 11.1 million by 1971.[37] Yet this expansion in coverage had only a limited effect on pensioner income until the late 1970s; in 1971 occupational pensions accounted for just 13.6 per cent of pensioner incomes compared with 54.1 per cent from social security benefits, and only just over half of newly retired men were in receipt of any income from a pension fund.[38]

Financial factors – particularly state and occupational pension entitlements – have undoubtedly contributed to the decline in participation rates at older ages, particularly since the Second World War, but they do not *explain* these trends. It seems most unlikely that between 1921 and 1971 an increasing proportion of 65-year-old men have voluntarily withdrawn from the labour force in order to receive a pension income that consigns them to a bare subsistence existence. The third possibility, therefore, is that their rising rate of withdrawal from the labour force is a consequence of the way in which the labour market and labour contracts have been structured.

In a depression the incidence of unemployment among older workers might be particularly high, and so might induce high rates of labour-force withdrawal. Just such a process may have been working in 1931, resulting in a fall relative to 1921 in the participation rate for both men and women over 65 years of age, but this is clearly not a valid explanation of the fall in participation rates during the long boom from the end of the Second World War to the early 1970s.

Another structural possibility is that the nature of labour contracts has changed over time, with employers increasingly adopting mandatory retirement rules in combination with seniority wage systems and occupational pension schemes. There can be little doubt that this has been an important influence on retirement rates since the Second World War, but the low labour-force participation rates of the 1970s and 1980s make it clear that retirement at or before 65 years of age has become the norm, not just for workers enrolled in the occupational pension schemes of public-sector and larger private-sector employers. Hannah argues that this age structuring of labour markets through the interaction of retirement rules and pension schemes offers an explanation of the longrun decline in labour-force participation rates for older men since the 1880s. However, this is almost certainly an overstatement – the limited scope of occupational pensions and mandatory retirement rules before 1939, and the fact that even in the early 1970s almost half of newly retired men over 65 years of age had no occupational pension income whatsoever, must caution against an exaggeration of the specific role of formal pension and employment contracts.

A third structural factor may be a change over time in the type of work available, which has put a premium on newly acquired skills and made older workers increasingly functionally redundant. In the 1890s it was widely believed that the pressure of modern employment practices was forcing workers out of employment from their early 50s.[39] In evidence to the Royal Commission on the Aged Poor in 1895, Charles Booth joined forces with spokesmen for the friendly societies and trade unions to argue that it was becoming increasingly difficult for workers to obtain a position after the age of 50.[40] Yet the participation rates for men aged 50–54 and 55–59 years appear to have increased over the thirty years from 1891, although these rates probably fell slightly between the 1881 and 1891 censuses. There also seems to be a fairly stable participation rate for 60- to 64-year-olds between 1891 and 1911, although rates for men 65 years of age or over do clearly fall between 1881 and 1911. It is possible, of course, that the case made to the Royal Commission reflected labour-market changes of the preceding twenty or thirty years, for which no census data are available, but the language used by witnesses in their submissions implied that the problem was a current and continuing one. Alfred Jephcott, a prominent engineering union and friendly society member, stated that 'because of the great stress of work as we arrive towards old age, the difficulty of men as they emerge towards old age is increasing year by year in their effort to get employment'.[41] In fact, the participation rates up to age 64 for men born in the late 1820s, who would have suffered from any constriction of employment prospects in the 1880s when they were in their fifties or early sixties, were almost identical to the participation rates of their male children born twenty-five years later in the 1850s.

IV

No single hypothesis proffered in the modern literature on retirement rates and retirement behaviour can stand on its own as a convincing explanation of the course of labour-force participation rates in England and Wales over the one hundred years since 1881. The almost continuous longrun decline in the participation rate of older men, on which a number of commentators have attempted to place an interpretation, has been shown to a large extent to be a result of structural change in the economy. The implication of the adjustments presented in Table 7.3 is that non-agricultural labour-force participation rates for men over 65 years of age were considerably lower in the late nineteenth century than has hitherto been believed, but did not begin their secular decline until after 1921.

The health status of older workers is probably the most important explanation for the observed labour-force participation patterns of men over 65 years of age in the late nineteenth century, with gradual loss of strength and mobility whittling away the proportion of active workers as each cohort grew older. On the other hand, it has been shown that illness or decrepitude cannot provide a plausible account of the much more abrupt decline in participation witnessed in the twentieth century. Hypotheses about the economic causes of retirement are also inadequate as a complete explanation. The low level of financial-asset accumulation by manual workers, at least until the Second World War, and the extensive poverty of the retired population indicate that retirement for most people was not a simple function of rising wealth or more generous or more easily available public pensions. Although the inducement from the state to retire at age 65 may help to explain downward movements in participation rates in the late 1920s and late 1940s, it cannot adequately account for the further decline from 1951. Moreover, as late as the early 1970s, the majority of working men who left employment at or around age 65 did so without any occupational pension entitlement and with little prospect of being able to enjoy above subsistence living standards in retirement. Not until the 1980s have substantial numbers of the newly retired been able to withdraw from the workforce with substantial assets and reasonably secure and generous retirement incomes. Nor can unemployment or an increase in the intensity of work or an expansion in the coverage of occupational pension schemes provide an adequate account of longrun trends.

It seems more likely that, rather than movements in retirement rates having a single cause, it has instead been the interaction of state pension rules, rising individual wealth, and more strictly age-structured labour contracts that have created ever-rising expectations among successive birth cohorts that paid employment will cease at some age around 65 years. This normalization of retirement expectations and the retirement experience has been a major social as well as economic innovation in twentieth-century Britain, and to be properly understood it requires both a more detailed and a more wide-ranging investigation than the census data allow for. But even on the basis of the summary evidence presented in this chapter, it is clear that a longrun view of the labour-force participation of older workers reveals the historical specificity (and sometimes the analytical implausibility) of many recent 'explanations' of retirement behaviour. Before national governments, or the OECD, implement policies designed to reverse the retirement trends of the last hundred years, they should first try to understand the complex history of retirement. Only when the longrun development is properly understood can confidence be placed in policies designed to alter retirement practices in the future.

8

THE NEW BUSINESS HISTORY: THEORY, QUANTIFICATION AND INSTITUTIONAL CHANGE

Stephen Nicholas

INTRODUCTION

During the last decade, transaction cost theory has transformed the writing of business history. Standard neoclassical theory found little favour among business historians, in part because the black box production function approach to the firm assumed away the question of organizational design. Yet Chandler's *Strategy and Structure* (1964) showed that internal U-form and M-form structures were important and Hannah's *The Rise of the Corporate Economy* (1976) and Chandler's *The Visible Hand* (1977) argued cogently for the efficacy of hierarchical firms over markets.[1] Transaction cost theory provided the analytical framework. Innovation in U-form and M-form organizations was explained in transaction cost terms by Oliver Williamson,[2] while Chandler and Hannah relied on Coase's insight that 'firms replaced markets until the costs of organizing another transaction within the firm became equal to the costs of carrying out the same transaction through exchange in the market' to describe vertical integration in the hierarchical firm.[3] The transaction cost model focused attention on the internal organization of firms and on the distribution of economic activity between firms and markets. The study of institutional arrangements was back in fashion, and business history was integrated into the wider literature on institutional change and economic growth.[4]

Economic institutions structure economic activity, constraining economic, political, and social interaction. They evolve through time, changing their organizational structure – that is, changing their rules, regulations, customs, and taboos. Such institutional changes are generally assumed to capture efficiency gains, since institutions reduced uncertainty and the costs of transacting. History matters because institutional evolution is mediated through existing economic, social, and political structures. Institutional evolution, then, can lead to economic growth or to stagnation and economic decline. Together, history and transaction cost theory promise an organizing framework for understanding institutional change in the longrun.

As a model of institutional change through time, transaction cost theory is not without its limitations. The choice between market or hierarchy, the vertical integration issue, is justified on the simple expedient of hypothesizing high enough transaction costs in the market place and low enough costs of internal firm administration.[5] Making the same point, Williamson admitted that the Coasean model tended to be tautological and that the transaction costs of markets and firms had not been operationalized, nor was it obvious how they could be.[6] Besides being static, the firm–market dichotomy was too narrow, depicting firms as islands of planned coordination in a sea of market relations.

In response to this last criticism, the firm–market paradigm was extended and modified to include intermediate institutional arrangements, such as agencies, franchises, dealerships, joint-ventures, and long-term contracts, between spot market transactions and the hierarchical firm.[7] This allowed business historians to describe the growth of American, British, and European firms through well-defined stages, from using the market to selling through independent distributors or agents, then to establishing sales branches, and finally to investing in regional production plants. As firms integrated vertically and diversified, U-form and M-form internal structures evolved within hierarchical firms.

These changes in organizational design remain largely descriptive, poorly informed by theory, and not operationalized in an analytical way. Recent developments in the theory of contracts offer new insights into the costs of organizing transactions within and between markets, intermediate modes, and firms. The second section of the chapter develops a theory of contracts model for firm growth. The third section operationalizes the model using the agency problem in the Hudson's Bay Company, contractual relations between independent firms, and quantitative tests of the transition between alternative contractual arrangements as examples. It also addresses the role of 'culture' in shaping organizational design.

THEORY OF CONTRACTS MODEL

The theory of contracts model depicts economic institutions as nexuses of explicit or implicit contracts for transacting in services or goods.[8] Contracts specify incentive structures, and they bond, monitor, and enforce contract provisions between the parties to the exchange. Markets, firms (hierarchy), or intermediate modes, including subcontracting, franchises, licences, and long-term contracts, form the spectrum of economic institutions for structuring exchange contracts. If information was perfect, exchange contracts could be costlessly and completely written, monitored, and enforced. But uncertainty and asymmetries in information between the contracting parties give rise to hidden action (moral hazard) and hidden information (adverse selection). Hidden action is most typically related to the effort of the agent. The amount of energy an agent puts into task completion cannot be unambiguously determined by the principal from the agent's output, and even when inputs can be observed directly they may be difficult to measure.[9] Hidden information relates to observations available to the agent but not to the principal. The principal cannot easily determine whether the agent uses information in the way best calculated to serve the principal's interests. Knowledge is power, and behaviour by agents that is not in the best interests of the principal is labelled opportunism.[10]

The existence of hidden action and hidden information makes the contractual relationship between the agent and principal a problem of decision-making under uncertainty. Most contracts do not specify sets of actions by the agent and principal for every possible contingency, since it is prohibitively costly to specify performance for every eventuality. Such contracts are incomplete. Contracting may be incomplete in a second sense: future states of the world within which the contract exists may be unknown, making explicit contracting impossible. The design of contracts, including decision-making structures, incentive schemes, and information flows, depend on the 'completeness' of contracting.

Contract incompleteness presents special problems when agents can 'hold up' the principal by opportunistically appropriating quasi-rents from durable transaction-specific capital investments (such as machines or advertising signs), idiosyncratic investments in reputation and brand name, and unique human capital investments (including skilled manpower) made by the principal.[11] Idiosyncratic investments may be necessary to support the exchange of services or goods, but such investments have been dubbed 'hostages' to exchange when idiosyncratic capital acts simply as a bond to contract performance. Unequal bargaining power can shape the contractual arrangement, where the weaker party is forced to invest in idiosyncratic capital – unnecessary for exchange, but forfeited for 'non-performance' – determined by the stronger bargainer.

Besides power in the bargaining arrangements, the level of idiosyncratic investment depends on the nature of the product and the frequency of transacting. Perishable products, or complicated machinery, require physical and human capital specific to transportation, display, demonstration, and repair; one-off transactions do not warrant investment in transaction-specific capital while frequent transacting may. Assets with appropriable quasi-rents impact directly on organizational design, influencing the structure of the contract, especially the need for costly contract performance monitoring.

A contract is too frequently viewed simply as an act. While certain contracts may be invariant over the term of their lifetime, in many cases the contractual arrangements are not independent of the institutional setting of the contract.[12] When adjustments are made to contract arrangements, because of shocks external to the contract or because one (or both) of the parties wishes to modify the contract, such contracts have been labelled relational.[13] Relational contracts are sustained, dynamic economic and social relationships, modified for unforeseen events according to the relative bargaining power of the parties. Typically, such contracts involve frequent interaction between the parties, and are usually of long standing.

In a survey of inter-firm contracts, Macaulay discovered that the exchange relationship ranged from formal contracts (with well-defined legal and economic sanctions) to informal, unwritten, customary understandings.[14] For example, contracts between manufacturers and their parts suppliers in the US auto industry were 'carefully planned agreements ... designed that the supplier will have only minimal, if any, legal rights against the manufacturers'.[15] In contrast, firms in other industries entered into mutual understandings which relied on 'a man's word', a handshake, or 'common honesty and decency'.[16] Such informal agreements are typical of contractor–supplier relationships in the Japanese auto industry, and have recently been adapted by American auto firms.[17] These informal arrangements depended on repetitive transactions and the creation of social relationships across the boundaries of the two firms.

Within the firm, social relationships define a culture, a stock of common knowledge acquired over time and shared by the firm's employees. Culture prescribes rules and habits of behaviour which employees accept, follow, and use as the basis of action. Recurrent transactions between agents and principals builds trust, cooperation, and reputation, allowing successive modifications to the firm's culture through on-going learning. History matters because the creation of a corporate culture is a cumulative investment in shared values – or a collective memory – passed on from the present generation of employees to the next. To act opportunistically towards the group, whose norms of trustworthiness and cooperation have been accepted, invites retaliation and a loss of reputation.

Reputation, cooperation, and trust create a culture that reduces the costs of transacting by attenuating opportunism. To trust someone or to cooperate with someone is to refrain from promoting your self-interest at the expense of the other party. Cooperation and trust are particularly important when it is costly to write a formal and complex performance contract, or when the performance conditions of the contract are expensive to monitor. Trust and cooperation allow implicit contracts or non-specific contracts to substitute for costly-to-write formal contracts with detailed performance and monitoring provisions. The parties to such informal or implicit contracts are confident that modifications required to offset shocks will be cooperatively and cheaply bargained away. Contracting with a cooperative and trustworthy party reduces the likelihood of contract default, since a party will avoid default to protect his or her reputation. When contract default is difficult to identify, for example when the quality of supply is hard to verify by inspection, reputation attenuates opportunism. Default and opportunism are especially costly when one party has made transaction-specific investments that yield a large appropriable quasi-rent. Trusting another party reduces the costs of contract monitoring and lessens the threat of 'hold-up' when the parties have made transaction-specific investments. Culture directly affects the structuring of incentive contracts.

TESTING THE MODEL

Internal organizational design: the firm

Formed in 1672 the Hudson's Bay Company was an early multinational company that faced the problem of structuring an internal organizational design to attenuate opportunism within the firm.[18] Managers or 'officers' in Canada were employed by the London Committee to trade in furs with the Indians and, secondly, to supervise the workforce of canoemen, carpenters, cooks, and labourers on the Bay post. Asymmetric information between the agents on the Bay and the London Committee posed problems of agency. By trading for furs with the Indians and supervising the Company's servants, the managers on the Bay gained better and different information than did the London Committee. The London Committee could not always determine whether this information was used in the best interests of the Company. Moral hazard was a potential problem since, from the furs the post took, the Company could not determine unambiguously the amount of energy managers put into supervision or trading. The severity of the winter, the reliance on the Indians to trap furs, and the activity of competing companies might reduce the intake of furs for an energetic manager relative to an unenergetic one.

The London Committee addressed the agency problem in the formal employment contract. Each manager's contract specified the number of years to be spent on the Bay, the salary, and other stipulations, such as the care of wife and children in case of death. Implicit in the contract was the provision of housing, food and transportation. Salaries were high, ranging from £50 to £200 per annum. In the early years of the Company's existence in Canada, the managers' formal incentive contracts gave them considerable discretion in their trading relations with the Indians, and originally gave managers the right to trade for furs on their own account. The London Committee quickly recognized that discretionary private trade provided a powerful vehicle for opportunism, and within two years it was declared illegal. But private trade was not easy to eradicate. The principals in London first looked for solutions to the private trade problem within the formal contract structure. High salaries, by increasing the opportunity cost of opportunistic behaviour, helped to reduce such activity, as did salary increases, commendations, gratuities and, during the early years of the Company's history, end-of-year monetary rewards, which were not necessarily tied to increased output levels. The Company's records show that the London Committee believed that monetary rewards, gratuities, and salary bonuses increased work effort. Agents were also required to take oaths that they would not engage in private trade, and to post bonds as a guarantee against private trading.

Further experimentation by the London Committee led to the introduction of a new incentive scheme within the formal contract structure – the right of managers on the Bay to trap fur. However, private trapping gave opportunistic managers a mechanism for masking private trade and also opened the opportunity for unscrupulous managers to substitute Company furs for their own poorer quality furs. To attenuate this problem, the conditions for private trapping, and the penalties for cheating, were carefully specified. Furs had to be warehoused before the beginning of the trading season and an upper limit on the value of privately trapped furs was set at £100. Concealing furs led to the forfeiture of the furs, the bond and also the manager's salary. In 1770 private trapping was declared illegal, and to compensate for the loss of private trapping salary scales were revised upwards and a bonus of 3s per score of beaver traded was paid.

Besides an incentive structure, the Company's ability to control the conduct of managers, and to ensure that they performed satisfactorily, required a system of monitoring and internal controls. To wipe out private trade, ships and ships' captains – the main conduit for contraband trade – were monitored: all the men's baggage and mail was searched, each ship was searched before it left London and when it returned, and all legal consignments of liquor and trade goods were sealed. However, the most important control mechanism was the Company's accounts, which were also an information system. Information from these accounts provided the Company with absolute and relative performance measures of its Bay managers.

The Company's accounting system employed a commodity unit of account, known as a 'Made Beaver' (the price of a single prime male beaver skin): the *Official Standard* denominated all trade goods in this unit, while the *Comparative Standard* assigned Made Beaver values to all furs received from the Indians. The *Official* and *Comparative Standards*, neither of which varied much over time nor between posts, provided a device for detecting cheating by denying the managers any price discretion in their trade with the Indians, and by reducing costly inter-post competition. But, without the scope for price bargaining, the *Official Standard* disadvantaged the Company, and hampered trade with the Indians who required ceremonial gift giving and discretionary presents as part of the trading process. As a solution to this problem, managers were allowed to reduce the amount of trade goods paid to the Indians for furs. This price reduction occurred in those commodities amenable to small reductions in quality such as cloth, brandy, and tobacco. This not only freed up trade goods for use in ceremonial practices, but also provided the means by which opportunistic managers could cheat the Company.

To ensure that these goods were used to the Company's advantage and not to that of the manager, the London Committee required the managers to incorporate the *Overplus* (the bundle of goods freed up by paying the Indians below the *Official Standard*) into the system of accounts sent back to England each year. These accounts included the *Account Books*, *Post Journals*, and the *London Correspondence Inward-Official* that were kept according to precise instructions and regulations. Using the information on the inventory of trade goods, furs obtained, commodities traded, and the *Overplus* from the various account books, the Company created indices for comparing one agent's performance with another's. Comparisons of the net return (the difference between the *Overplus* and the expenses of the post) and the terms of trade (total return of furs divided by the value of trade goods) between posts were used to discipline (demote, relieve, and recall to London) and reward (through salary increases, gratuities, and commendations) its managers. Thus, the Company's accounting system created a flow of information that formed the basis of the London Committee's decision rules for rewarding and disciplining managerial performance. Over the longrun, the Hudson's Bay Company's contractual arrangement with its managers evolved new incentive, monitoring, and information structures to attenuate the agency problem. In so far as survivorship is a measure of organizational success, the Hudson's Bay Company overcame the costs of agency.

Intermediate organizational design: agency contracts

Contracts between British multinational enterprises and their independent agents abroad raised similar problems of agency to those in the Hudson's Bay Company, and called forth similar solutions. A sample of contracts from twenty-one British multinationals in the period 1870 to 1939 was analysed to evaluate the evolution of the incentive structure, information flows, and monitoring and enforcement mechanisms.[19] Input requirements, such as the amount of travelling, advertising, and showing – specified to ensure a high quality service – formed the centre-piece of agency contracts. Every agency contract contained vague (and unenforceable) clauses requiring the agent to 'push the sale' of the principal's product – a direct recognition of the moral hazard problem. But agents could sit back and wait for orders. Sales flowing from the principal's investment in brand name, goodwill, product differentiation, and advertising could be captured by the unenergetic agent at the cost of rudimentary paperwork. The agents' better information concerning the local market meant that adverse selection was also a potential hazard. To attenuate such opportunism, service monitoring and enforcement provisions were designed as part of the incentive contract.

Commissions that tied income to the level of sales encouraged a high level of sales effort. Agency contracts also required the agent to carry stock and to employ engineers or other technical staff. Stocks held by the agent ensured prompt delivery and acted as advertising when displayed in the agents' offices and showrooms. Consignment stock carried by the agent allowed the principal to advance credit to customers. Engineers hired by the agent, or jointly by the agent and principal, ensured demonstration, installation, and after-sale service. Stock and engineers were forms of transaction-specific investments that bonded the agent to the principal.

Even with such requirements, principals could not be sure that agent performance was adequate. Direct monitoring was necessary, and contracts provided for the flow of information. Stocks were monitored by weekly, monthly, and half-yearly stock lists. Agents might be required to send to the principal the terms of each sale (including the customer's name) or simply the name of the customer. The principal would then execute the order directly with the customer. These controls were strengthened by the right of the principal to inspect the stock and books, and to appoint the agent's book or storekeeper. The principal's technical representative, who worked from the agent's office, was an effective, if costly, form of direct monitoring. All principals employed travelling representatives who monitored their agents. The final sanction was non-renewal of the agency agreement, and non-renewal was the typical form of contractual termination between agents and principals.

The payments system was also open to agent opportunism. Of course, stock monitoring and the right to inspect the books also allowed the principal to supervise payments. Such methods were superfluous when the principal insisted on direct execution of orders to customers. But the agent, by misinforming the principal, could collect a commission by passing orders of non-creditworthy customers. As a result, contracts specified that the agent should take every precaution to pass orders only of creditworthy customers, in order to advise the principal as to whether credit should be given. Some contracts explicitly allowed principals to refuse orders or to make the final approval of orders. Despite such safeguards, bad debts were common under the agency system. There were also risks in receiving payment for stocks on consignment when customers paid agents for goods that were the property of the principal. A common arrangement was the requirement that agents pay by bill of exchange or letters of credit drawn on a London or European merchant house. Principals also encouraged payment by charging interest on outstanding payments, and by offering a discount for cash within one to three months of sale – usually 2.5 or 3 per cent. Agency contracts shared much in common with the incentive contracts within firms, specifying a complex incentive structure, creating a flow of information, and instituting direct monitoring of the agent to overcome the problem of agency.

Transition from agents to sales branches

Incentive contracts with independent agents provide one solution to the agent–principal problem; vertical integration provides an alternative solution. The shift from agents to sales branches in my sample of twenty-one British multinational firms depended on interaction between the structuring of incentive contracts and the frequency of transacting, the nature of the product, and the need for idiosyncratic (transaction-specific) investments by the agent and principal. The larger the volume of sales, the greater were the monitoring costs of the agency system, and the greater the actual or potential losses through agent opportunism. There was a minimum sales volume, or transaction frequency, before an investment in a sales branch was undertaken. For example, Ransomes, a firm of agricultural machinery makers, calculated that a £10,000-a-year trade would be required before a Paris depot could economically compete with an agency trading on less than £2,000 per year. The costs of running branch sales offices were not insignificant, as the 1929 costs of Fowler's Budapest branch of £11,593 and George Wostenholm's New York City branch of £15,700 per year showed. The wholly-owned sales subsidiary incurred higher fixed costs, but lower marginal costs, of extending sales relative to employing an agent.

The nature of the product determined whether idiosyncratic investments in distribution and marketing facilities, including advertising, credit facilities, demonstration, assembly, and repair, were necessary for exchange. Such investments created a quasi-rent vulnerable to exploitation by an opportunistic agent. Organizational design is sensitive to the nature of transaction-specific assets, leading machinery and engineering firms to replace agencies with sales branches. Vertical integration frequently protected quasi-rents from idiosyncratic investments more effectively than did contractual arrangements with agents. Williamson found that hierarchical firms have superior monitoring and dispute procedures, providing an efficiency advantage over inter-firm contractual arrangements.[20] The shift from agents to sales branches reflects the longrun evolution of contractual arrangements; it is a study in institutional change.

Transition from sales branches to production plants

The shift from sales branches to production plants – the last stage in the historical growth of large firms – involves re-contracting within the firm. To operationalize the transaction cost model, I use a logit model to estimate the production, location, and transaction cost factors in the sales branch/production plant decision. Locational choice and production cost factors received most attention in the plant investment decision, that is until economists asked why firms invested overseas, or regionally, in production plant rather than simply licensing know-how to independent firms. This question directed attention to the firm as a device for protecting firm-specific knowledge and information, with strong public-good characteristics. There is no formal model of the sales branch/production plant choice and, in the quantitative model estimated below, production, location, and transaction cost factors enter the model *ad hoc*.

The data comprise information on 448 British multinational firms that invested in a sales branch or production plant between 1870 and 1939. Information was collected from business histories, firm archives, the *Stock Exchange Yearbook*, and data in public record offices.[21] Empirical work on pre-1939 forms of overseas investment is hampered by poor data on production, location, and transaction costs variables. Proxy variables were defined so as to capture the production and location costs factors. Six broad two-digit Standard Industrial Classification (SIC) groups (food/drink, chemical, engineering, metal manufacturing, textile, and the excluded group) were used as proxies for production costs. In so far as each industry can be characterized by a unique technology, product group dummies may reflect the underlying scale and production cost factors. In recent work on American firms before 1914, economies of scale were significant in the food and drink, chemical, metal, and engineering industries, but not in textiles.[22] Of course these product dummies are also likely to reflect other factors, such as transportability of the product. In addition, many British multinationals began production on a small scale in host economies, using outdated plant and equipment. Therefore, the product dummies, as measures of production costs, are not particularly robust and must be treated with a good deal of caution.

MARKET – the percentage of the labour force in each host economy in manufacturing in 1923 – and DEVELOP – a qualitative dummy variable – provide proxies for market size, relative per capita income levels, and the level of economic development. DISTANCE is a dummy variable that measures whether an overseas investment location is 'near' or 'far' from Britain, and is a proxy for transportation costs. PSYCHIC proximity, a binary variable taking the value 1 if English was the 'native' language and 0 otherwise, measures the factors that encourage the flow of goods between markets and depends upon similarities in the level of economic and social development, education, language and culture, and political, institutional and legal systems between home and host economies. It is expected that costs of investing fell with psychic proximity and rose with psychic distance; the sign of DISTANCE is expected to be negative while that for MARKET and DEVELOP should be positive.

Transaction costs can not be measured directly. Archival studies of the timing of plant investments by Wellcome, Babcock, Bryant and May, Callender Cable, Albright and Wilson, and British Insulated Cable showed that each firm concentrated its overseas expansion into a very few years. The bunching of foreign direct investment (FDI) decisions, shown in Table 8.1, was uniform across countries, product groups, and firm sizes. The bunching contradicts the popular model in which multinational enterprises (MNEs) go abroad through a 'process of incremental problem solving' in each host country with a 'sequence of moves from more to less familiar countries'.[23] The bunching can be explained by transaction cost factors. Two types of transaction costs were internalized within the production branch: the rents from production-based knowledge which are not easily codified and patented; and secondly, scope economies related to managing at a distance. Knowledge of operating multilocational firms has strong learning-by-doing characteristics and is embodied in human capital organized as

Table 8.1 Bunching of foreign direct investment in production branches (%)

Gap in years	*All firms*	*Firms with 3+ FDIs*
0	26	26
1–3	19	22
4–10	21	19
11–25	18	17
26–39	7	9
40+	7	8

teams, such as boards of management.[24] Such knowledge gives rise to scope economies when the costs of organizing production in several locations within one firm are less than the costs of organizing production in separately owned plants.[25] In addition, such knowledge, which is not easily codified, is difficult to transfer through arm's-length markets in which there are high costs of recognition and disclosure. The production subsidiary is a contractual arrangement that attenuates these transaction costs.

Three proxies are constructed to measure transaction costs: NUMBER, which is the number of branches each parent firm operates abroad; DIVER, the number of different two digit SIC product groups for each firm; and RAW, a binary dummy variable measuring whether the parent had backward vertical contracts of integration. NUMBER, whose sign is expected to be positive, captures directly the idea that managerial knowledge yields scope economies related to managing numerous branches at a distance. DIVER and RAW proxy managerial expertise related to diversified product lines which encourage simultaneous investment in two or more markets. The expected sign of both these variables is positive. The dependent variable is a qualitative variable taking on the value 1 for a production plant and 0 for firms with only a sales branch.

Since each firm faced the binary choice of investing in a production plant or operating a sales subsidiary, limited-dependent or qualitative-choice models provide an appropriate characterization of the investment decision. For firm i, given the vector of explanatory variables denoted X_i, we assume the probability of investing in a production plant, P_i, can be described by the logistic function

$$P_i = \frac{1}{1 + \exp(-\beta X_i)} \quad -\infty < \beta X < \infty \tag{1}$$

where β is the coefficient to be estimated. Since many observations are not available for each firm, P_i must be estimated by maximum likelihood techniques. For T observations, the likelihood function is

$$l = \prod_{i=1}^{T} P_i^{y_i} (l - P_i)^{l-y_i} \tag{2}$$

where

$$y_i = \begin{cases} 1 \text{ with a probability } P_i \\ 0 \text{ with a probability } 1 - P_i \end{cases}$$

which is estimated by the Newton–Raphson interative procedure for maximizing non-linear objective functions.[26]

The results of the logit equations are reported in Table 8.2, where the reference firm (in equations 1–4) produced all product groups other than food, drink, and chemicals. In models 1–4 the product dummies are significant, suggesting that, in so far as the dummies captured production costs, these costs increased the probability of forming production facilities. In model 5, a larger number of product group dummies were introduced, but they were not significant. On the basis of a log likelihood chi square test, the additional dummies in model 5 can be excluded and models 1–4 are adequate representation of the production cost aspects of the sales branch/production plant decision. More generally, the hypothesis that all the coefficients are equal to zero, implying that all alternatives are equally likely, can be rejected on the basis of the reported likelihood ratio tests for all equations.

The location variables returned mixed results. PSYCHIC proximity is positive and significant. The greater the psychic proximity, the greater the likelihood that British MNEs invested in production plants. DISTANCE is negative and insignificant, but the variable is not particularly robust and the result may be due to measurement error. The binary measuring the level of development, DEVELOP, is positive, implying that British firms were more likely to invest in production plants in developed markets, but is insignificant. MARKET is an imperfect proxy for market size and maturity, but it is employed because of data limitations on variables such as income per head. However, the insignificant results are not inconsistent with the model; if the bunching of FDI is driven by internal scope economies, then market size would not be expected to be as important an explanatory variable as is usually assumed.

The economies of scope hypothesis receives statistical support from the transaction cost proxies. There is evidence in model 2 of multicollinearity between DIVER and RAW, with a significant change in the coefficient of DIVER when both variables are introduced into the same equation. According to a likelihood ratio test for variable inclusion, RAW should remain in the model; so model 2 in Table 8.2 is the preferred model. The results on the transaction cost proxies support the hypothesis that firms invest in production facilities to attenuate transaction costs related to appropriating production based knowledge and scope economies. In terms of institutional change, the production plant decision is the final stage in the longrun evolution of the multilocational firm.[27]

CULTURE AND CONTRACTUAL FORM

The agency models above have treated the relationship between the principal and agent as an act, rather than as a continuing economic and social relationship. Yet hierarchical organizations involve well-defined social relationships which foster trust, cooperation, and reputation. The Hudson's Bay Company created a corporate culture, or a corporate social system, as an implement for attenuating the costs of agency.[28]

The London Committee invested in corporate culture by indoctrinating its managers and workers with a unique set of corporate values. This was made easier by selecting its managers and workers from two separate homogeneous groups. Beginning in 1689, the Company recruited apprentices from Christ's Hospital in London, and they were sent to Canada as the first of a new managerial class. These 'Blue Coat Boys' were educated in writing and

Table 8.2 Logit models for the sales branch/production plant decision[1]

	1	*2*	*3*	*4*	*5*
Food/drink	1.77 (3.27)	1.44 (2.53)	1.79 (3.27)	1.75 (3.21)	1.70 (2.98)
Chemical	1.01 (2.86)	0.90 (2.48)	1.01 (2.83)	1.00 (2.83)	0.91 (2.33)
Engineer					0.04 (0.14)
Metal					−0.39 (−0.85)
Textile					−0.37 (−1.00)
Psychic proximity	0.86 (3.29)	0.85 (3.28)	0.86 (3.30)		0.83 (3.16)
Distance	−0.25 (−0.93)				
Develop				0.45 (0.69)	
Market			−0.008 (−0.46)		
Diver	0.69 (3.60)	0.30 (1.19)	0.66 (2.88)	0.71 (3.08)	0.66 (2.94)
Number	0.18 (2.65)	0.17 (2.39)	0.17 (2.62)	0.12 (1.77)	0.18 (2.70)
Raw		2.63 (2.51)			
Constant	−0.46 (−1.86)	−0.45 (−1.80)	−0.26 (−0.50)	0.16 (0.84)	−0.37 (−1.29)
χ^2 likelihood ratio	53.08	64.34	53.28	54.49	54.95
DF	6	6	6	5	8
Cases	380	380	380	380	380

Note: [1] t-statistics in brackets

arithmetic, which was required for the careful keeping of the *Account Books* and *Post Journals*, and they were trained to supervise the labourers on the Bay. By the beginning of the nineteenth century, it was from this group that many of the Company's managers regularly came. Similarly, beginning in the mid-1680s, the Company started to hire its labourers from the Orkney Islands, and by 1700 this area was the sole source of labour. The apprenticeship of 'Blue Coat Boys' and the hiring of Orcadians established the preconditions for the creation of a Company 'culture'.

The 'Blue Coat Boys' and the Orcadians were imbued with the 'culture' of the Company. The Company had very strict expectations about the behaviour of its employees – they were supposed to be sober, industrious and, by and large, celibate. The formal swearing of oaths bound the men to be loyal and true to the Company. In turn, the Company bound itself to the men by providing care for the wives and children of managers (who had behaved with courage and fidelity) who died in Canada. These were the formal elements that created interlinking obligations and commitments between the London Committee and their managers.

The Company's correspondence is replete with positive encouragement and praise, commending managers for their work and rewarding them with large gratuities. The ethics of the Company's culture encouraged cooperation, reputation-building, and trust, while investments in reputation and cooperation by managers engendered honest behaviour, reducing the costs of monitoring. The ethical system encouraged agents to share the same goals as the principal. This had practical advantages for the Company's monitoring system. By creating a moral code, both for managers' private and work lives, the Company was able to encourage and sustain a system that reduced goal-divergence and opportunism. For example, informing the London Committee of suspected malfeasance was an accepted part of a manager's duty, frequently leading to the recall to London of managers to explain allegations of private trade. Yet the Company's culture also provided guarantees for recalled managers; managers knew that all hearings would be fair and impartial. This Company's culture reduced the agency problem in two ways: by aligning the workers' goals to those of the Company, and by having a very high probability of detecting managerial opportunism.

CONCLUSION

To demonstrate the longrun evolution of contractual arrangements within and between firms requires microeconomic data. Most studies of vertical integration have not relied on the structure of contracts between firms. In part, such data are hard to get or are no longer extant; in part the transaction cost model has been a convenient hook upon which to hang the process of vertical integration, thereby avoiding the need to analyse the structure of inter-firm contracts. To 'explain' vertical integration by the expedient of assuming high enough transaction cost in the market relative to the firm is really no explanation at all. Similarly, organizational design within firms, especially charting the U-form and M-form structures, has been described by business historians, but how these structures overcame the problems of agency has largely been neglected.

The theory of contracts approach to the firm offers one avenue for operationalizing transaction cost economics. Each of the studies in this chapter addressed the question of agency – how principals implement explicit and implicit contracts in order to structure incentives and to bond, monitor, and enforce non-opportunistic agent behaviour. These studies have been concerned with longrun changes both in the contractual arrangements for managers in the Hudson's Bay Company and for overseas agents of British firms, and also in the shift in contractual form from agency to sales branches and then to production plants. By employing micro data on contracts, it can be seen that the use of incentives (pay rises, bonuses, praise, discounts for early payment), bonding (investment in stock, engineers, and showrooms), monitoring (accounting-information systems, searching of ships, and visits by travelling company representatives), and enforcement (recall to London and non-renewal of agency agreements) provide the framework for explaining the evolution of contracts.

The shift from sales branches to production plants is an important stage in the growth of large firms. While transaction cost explanations are implicit in many historical descriptions of the decision to invest in overseas or regional plant, the transaction cost factors have rarely been explicitly discussed or modelled. For British multinational firms, an economy of scope explanation for the choice of production plants over alternative contractual arrangements (such as licensing) was presented and operationalized. The modelling and quantitative testing are relatively crude, but suggest directions for the operationalization of transaction cost approaches to the evolution of firms.

In all the cases studied, contractual arrangements were analysed within their historical context. History matters, especially the creation of a 'corporate culture' or collective memory within firms, which attenuates opportunism. Linking social relations within firms to the theory of contracts provides a framework for understanding trust, cooperation, and reputation, which forms an important element of everyday life in hierarchical institutions. The integration of history and the theory of contracts promises to provide new insights into institutional change in the longrun.

9

CULTURAL DETERMINANTS OF ECONOMIC PERFORMANCE: AN EXPERIMENT IN MEASURING HUMAN CAPITAL FLOWS

Leslie Hannah

I

Economic historians are constitutionally averse to the view that national culture can have a pervasive and longrun effect on economic performance, though much empirical work in the subject points in that direction. They are, of course, right to look for other factors before resorting to cultural factors as a catch-all residual. Much of the modern debate on, for example, whether the Japanese are (or are not) economically efficient because they are culturally different has underlined the importance of resisting too facile an emphasis on cultural explanations. In this chapter it will be argued that a more systematic approach to measuring the role of cultural factors is both desirable and possible.

II

Many commentators (and particularly those from overseas) have remarked on the unusually strong anti-industrial, anti-enterprise, or anti-business strands in British culture. The high point of this literature, copiously bolstered by damning quotations from novelists, poets, and opinion makers over more than a century, was Martin J. Wiener's 1981 book, *English Culture and the Decline of the Industrial Spirit 1850–1980*.[1] A Texan professor of history, Wiener chronicled the development of gentlemanly anti-business ideals, their transmission through the public school and university systems, the myths of rural innocence lost in industrialized Britain, and the middle classes' persistent ambivalence towards science, innovation, and entrepreneurship. He warmed to his theme in picturesque and often grotesque detail, with the shocked reaction of a Texan sophisticate clearly visible through the scientific detachment of his analysis, somewhat like the pioneer anthropologist viewing with wry distaste the strange sexual mores of a newly discovered tribe. Nor did he shrink from drawing the clear policy message:

> At the end of the day it may be that Margaret Thatcher will find her most fundamental challenge not in holding down the money supply or inhibiting government spending, or even in fighting the shop stewards, but in changing this frame of mind. English history in the eighties may turn less on traditional political struggles than on a cultural contest between the two faces of the middle class.[2]

The natives were extremely agitated by this timely (and best selling) contribution to the debate on the British disease, but deeply divided in their reaction. Businessmen added substantial weight to Wiener's case by an enthusiastic endorsement of his central thesis.[3] To many of them, it seemed that Wiener had bravely exposed anti-business prejudice, which they saw lurking not only among left-wing politicians, but also in the corridors of power, in the media, and in the schools and universities.[4] None the less, government ministers welcomed the cultural diagnosis of failure as enthusiastically as businessmen, and claimed their own pro-enterprise policies as the proper response to the need for changed cultural attitudes.

Opinion poll evidence, meanwhile, stubbornly refused to confirm either Wiener's interpretation of grass-roots alienation from industry, or Mrs Thatcher's hopes for a substantial change in attitudes. For most people, the reality of lifetime experiences and the common sense of the need to make a living produced simpler (and less easily ridiculed) views: according to the pollsters, industry and business were generally well thought of in the abstract, but were distrusted because of their perceived inability to deliver and sustain job security. The pollsters found that Mrs Thatcher's emphasis on enterprise and self-reliance may even have created greater, rather than less, awareness of these shortcomings.[5]

Such evidence may have dented Wiener's thesis slightly, but the most devastating attacks on his interpretation of anti-business culture came from his fellow academics.[6] Academic refutations of Wiener were wide-ranging and magisterial. Evidence was produced of the flimsiness of the alleged correlation between literary culture and businessmen's behaviour. After all, anti-business prejudices were just as powerful in Britain's heyday as the workshop of the world as in her twentieth-century decline. Equally, the bitter socialist rhetoric of Brecht, or the anti-Westernism of some Japanese novelists, has not prevented their countries enjoying modern economic miracles. Wiener's critics even speculated on a reversal of his hypothesis, arguing that successful entrepreneurs everywhere have typically come from 'outgroups' like the Jews, Quakers, or immigrants. On this view the creative destruction of the established order by the socially disapproved businessmen is the mainspring of economic progress, and Establishment 'support' for business its death knell. Certainly British aristocrats, far from shunning business (as alleged by Wiener), appeared to have more enthusiastically adopted 'bourgeois' business pursuits than their more conservative, agrarian continental counterparts, without that obviously boosting British growth.

The debate became 'academic' in the worst sense: scholars inconclusively attacked great but impenetrable issues in over a century of British historical decline, while those in the world of affairs (already convinced that the phenomenon of anti-business culture was real) were intent on rectifying it. The blanket academic rejection of Wiener left policy-makers with no proper guidance from well-conceived analyses of the dynamics of cultural change and its potential effects. But that did not necessarily prevent their policies being effective. How far *has* Britain been culturally transformed by the changes that men of affairs have promoted?

III

There are many dimensions in which cultural attitudes can be measured: indeed, the difficulty of tying down generalizations about national cultural attitudes was what gave the academic nitpickers their boisterous field-day of inconclusive debate. Yet some of the points they were debating *can* be reduced to measurable and testable propositions. There is a wealth of historical material on the social and cultural background of British businessmen and on how they differ from their overseas counterparts. It is also possible to use more recent biographical data on businessmen to assess how far things have changed in the 1980s. We can only scratch the surface of such an extensive topic here, but the subject is too important to be left where the academics left it.

One area of plentiful information is businessmen's educational backgrounds: in Britain's 'old school tie' society, establishment figures are rarely reticent about their school, and social commentators have made the most of this. There are, for example, two common cultural stereotypes of the impact of the public schools on British business. The oldest stereotype is part of the general left-wing critique of the British Establishment. According to this, businessmen (and more particularly top businessmen and financiers) are born into the wealthier classes and educated at public schools *for* leadership positions, which they inherit (or wangle on the old boy network) rather than qualify for. Wiener and others, by contrast, see the public schools as a major force directing young men *away* from business careers, instilling a sense of the inherent superiority of other, more 'gentlemanly' callings.

It is not difficult to imagine that there is a great deal of variety in the impact of different schools, or of the same school at different times, and thus some truth in both views. It is correspondingly easy to 'disprove' any generalizations: for example, evidence can be produced that many public schools in the post-war years have increasingly inclined to recruit the sons of businessmen, to encourage boys to go into business, and to educate them to as high a level in the sciences as they were accustomed to in the classics.

If one has to choose between the rival stereotypes of British culture, I have little doubt that what I have called the left-wing view is nearer to the truth. Countless surveys of the social and educational origins of businessmen have shown the disproportionate representation of public school boys in senior management positions in industry. Indeed, in the 1920s, 1930s, and 1940s – when the post-war generation of business leaders who figure in the early surveys were being educated – it was not unusual for firms recruiting trainee managers to specify that they would primarily consider public school men of 'character', or those with personal introductions, and from a good family.[7] Open recruitment by merit was confined to a relatively small part of the business sector.

Complementing this, there was sometimes a disdain for the academically inclined, and particularly for the university graduate. Thus international comparisons of the higher education of businessmen typically show that directors of British companies were paragons of under-education. In the 1950s, only a third of top British businessmen had been to university – a level already exceeded in the business elites of major industrial competitors like America, Germany, France, or Japan *before the First World War*.[8] More up-to-date surveys suggest that, while the proportion of graduates in top management has slowly increased in Britain, this lag relative to other countries has persisted in recent decades.[9] This was, moreover, not obviously a general failing of British society or education, for other elites became significantly more meritocratic and open than the business elite in the course of the twentieth century.[10]

Now it is entirely possible that the British business leaders' relative lack of (and unusually socially exclusive form of) education is quite irrelevant to their firms' poor economic performance. Business – like most callings – requires a good deal more than the effort and intelligence measured by university degree courses. British universities have a different social and even educational role from those elsewhere: only in recent decades, for example, has it become *de rigueur* for bright upper-class children to attend university in Britain, while vocational training (particularly business training) has certainly been a weak spot in British universities. There is no precise social and educational equivalent of the public school abroad, but other countries similarly restrict access to business leadership positions by parallel means, some of which are no more conducive than British public schools to the training needs of business. In Britain, allowing bright and effective non-graduate employees to progress to top positions could even be seen as a strength, while insisting on degrees as a prerequisite for entry to senior management positions (like the British professions or most leading overseas businesses) could be a damaging artificial barrier to the success of the ambitious.

Such views, usually honestly based on direct experience with single cases and on reasoning from first principles, have been repeatedly advanced over the last one hundred years by those claiming that British avenues of promotion, social mobility, and leadership recruitment have many virtues. The arguments in themselves are not implausible. There are few things worse for economic efficiency in modern technologically progressive societies than an under-valuation of education, but in the extreme, perhaps, credentialism – excessive reliance on paper qualifications – can compromise meritocracy. Yet postwar Britain can hardly be accused of meritocratic extremism! Of course, ardent British devotees of the present system have never had their confidence in it dented in the slightest bit by the inconvenient fact that its flowering has coincided with economic decline relative to other nations which curiously appear to have different systems of recruitment and promotion of business leaders.

We can no longer be so sanguine. At the very least, it has increasingly been recognized that the onus rests on those wishing to maintain the established system to prove the case for its benign influence. More incautiously, we might consider signs of movement towards the more economically successful norms established by our overseas business competitors as a sign of potential improvement in the quality of British business leadership.

IV

At first thought, it did not seem very likely that there had been any great changes in the 1980s in the kind of people who had reached leadership positions in business. The networks of influence, the prestige of schools and universities, the nature of training and education, the ladders of promotion within large organizations: all of these factors change not by the month or the year, but by the generation. They have in Britain been extraordinarily stable over many generations. The American economist, Mancur Olson, in his *The Rise and Decline of Nations* (1982), identified British-style stability of established economic elites as a profound source of weakness in all countries that had not experienced the upheaval of revolution or defeat in war, an experience which in much of continental Europe and Japan dislodged old entrenched elites and stimulated economic growth.[11] Two Cambridge sociologists – Philip Stanworth and Anthony Giddens – illustrated British elite stability between 1905 and 1971 in their study of the chairmen of 199 of the largest industrial and commercial companies.[12] They found that public school men – particularly those from top schools such as Eton or Harrow – were dominant throughout the period, and there was only a gradual (and small) increase in the minority of chairmen who had attended universities.

The events of the 1980s could surely not have significantly dented the systems of recruitment and promotion that had bolstered this extraordinary stability over the whole twentieth century? There was, it is true, a remarkable 1980s anti-Establishment upheaval in the political world, as Mrs Thatcher's confidence and power were reinforced by political success. Many Etonians (who had long dominated Conservative cabinets) were unceremoniously passed over or dismissed by a lady who distrusted their style and was determined to brook no opposition from the traditional grandees of the Conservative Party. This provoked shocked Establishment growls, such as that attributed to her one-time Secretary of State for Defence, Francis Pym: 'The trouble is we've got a corporal at the top, not a cavalry officer.' As *The Guardian*'s political correspondent remarked of the (Old Etonian, ex-Lancers) Pym, he 'epitomised, in manner and class and cunning habit and squireish paternalism and innumerate dedication to the feel of politics rather than the facts of economics, everything that she wanted to defenestrate from the Conservative citadel'.[13] She did not hesitate to do so when she felt strong enough: Pym was promoted to Foreign Secretary, then sacked. Political power in Britain is firmly concentrated on the prime minister in cabinet, and Mrs Thatcher used it. Beyond the cabinet room, however, her writ ran in company boardrooms only in the public sector, and even there its run was being rapidly reduced by privatization.

V

None the less, it seemed worthwhile to examine how far the small changes which were painfully working their way through up to the 1970s – trends such as the slowly increasing representation of graduates in the business elite – were sustained in the 1980s. There were, moreover, many journalistic claims that the whole cultural fabric of British business had been turned upside down in the 1980s. As *Business* magazine asserted in 1989: 'A new class of managers has emerged from the ranks ... The Young Turks had fewer hang-ups about status. Many had degrees or a professional qualification such as accountancy ... the cult of the amateur was over.'[14] The problem with accepting such claims at face value was that they had been made at regular intervals over the post-war decades, without having much measurable impact on the composition of the business elite.

Researchers at the London School of Economics have, therefore, taken a preliminary look at how the career and educational backgrounds of chairmen of the leading industrial and commercial companies in Britain changed between 1979 and 1989. The results for the top fifty companies (shown in Table 9.1) are striking. Far from confirming the relative stability of earlier studies, they show a marked acceleration of the pace of change in the background of the business elite. The most striking shift is in the secondary education of business leaders. Once dominated by public school boys, this group now has a majority of chairmen who went to grammar schools or to schools maintained by the state. The top public schools showed a substantial loss in membership of the business elite. Eton, which in 1979 had educated the chairmen of five of the top fifty companies (paralleling its dominance in other areas of the Establishment), had none of the top chairmen by 1989. The representation of public schools as a whole has more than halved in the decade.

The rising stars in the top boardrooms were the grammar school boys: comprehensives were, of course, rare when this cohort of chairmen were school boys.[15] The gainers included famous direct grant schools, like Manchester Grammar School, which, when these chairmen attended (prior to most of these schools going independent after 1974), offered many free places and had low fees; and there were also more chairmen from local grammar schools in the state sector. Typical of these new men is Sir Peter Walters, chairman of Britain's largest company, BP. With just a light touch of the new elite's inverted snobbery, he describes his background as 'intelligent working class':[16] one of his grandfathers

Table 9.1 Secondary education of the chairmen of the top fifty companies

	1979	*1989*
'Top' public schools[1]	9	1
Other public or fee-paying schools[2]	20	11
'Top' grammar schools[3]	4	8
Other grammar schools	5	12
Other maintained schools	9	15
Educated abroad	3	3
Total	50	50

Notes: 1 These are defined as the original 'Clarendon' schools (Charterhouse*, Eton*, Harrow, Rugby*, Shrewsbury*, Winchester*, Westminster, Merchant Taylors' and St Paul's); only the asterisked schools were actually represented in our samples for 1979 and 1989.

2 These are mainly members of the Headmasters' Conference (HMC) and boarding schools. Two chairmen in 1979 and one chairman in 1989 came from lesser fee-paying schools which were not members of the HMC.

3 These are schools listed as direct grant grammar schools by the Department of Education and Science or Scottish Education Department in 1964. Most of those represented in our sample were members of the HMC. These were mainly day schools which at the relevant time took a socially wider range of pupils, including many not paying fees, though they became fully independent and fee paying after 1974.

was a school teacher, another a police constable, and his father joined Birmingham City Police Force at 18 and became its youngest Chief Inspector at 32. Walters himself was educated at King Edward High School in Birmingham, a direct grant school. Entering Birmingham University to read law, he switched within two weeks to the commerce degree, before national service and his rise to the pinnacle of success at BP. Like many who benefited from the direct grant and grammar school system, he is unashamedly meritocratic and regrets the school's demise. Yet such upward mobility was not only possible from the grammar schools. Even the less prestigious 'other maintained' sector contributed fifteen chairmen in 1989 – six more than in 1979 – to make up for the falling representation of the independent fee-paying sector.

These changes should not be exaggerated: they are based only on the top fifty companies[17] and, given the problems of state education in the 1970s and 1980s, may not be sustained. Yet, the apparent changes in this one decade of the 1980s are more substantial than those recorded in previous studies of the business elite over *all* previous decades of the twentieth century *taken together*.

VI

This astonishing change can be interpreted in a variety of ways. One possibility is that the social elite and the wealthy (who traditionally sent their children to public schools) have recently become more alienated from business than in earlier decades. Just as, at the end of the nineteenth century, they reduced their exposure to the risk of farm landholdings in the agricultural depression, so they are now reducing their risks in business when it is exposed to the winds of world competition. This, however, seems implausible: for where is there now in the British economy to go that is *not* suffering the winds of competition?[18]

A more plausible interpretation is that ex-public school boy chairmen had often been protected by family influence and other networks, or merely projected towards the top by the privileged educational opportunities offered by those schools for a person of any given IQ level. This enabled them to gain top business positions in the past, but now such influences have declined: whether as a result of changing social ethics, widening educational opportunities for others, or increased competition and professionalism in business. The public school men who are in top jobs now are, on this interpretation, much more likely than their predecessors to have obtained their position by merit: like their grammar school contemporaries, they are likely to be more hard-working, more intelligent, and more competitively successful than their predecessors. It might be objected that, even now, the independent fee-paying sector is far more highly represented than one would expect from the small proportion of children it has educated. In fact, it is now represented at almost exactly the level one might expect from the relative size of sixth forms in the state and fee-paying sectors when these chairmen were young.[19]

There have been more genuinely open opportunities for the more successful pupils from the state schools, often from modest, though still rarely from unskilled working-class backgrounds, to climb to the top of the business ladder. The improvements in the state education system after the Second World War, and the effective recruitment of able school leavers and, more especially, of university graduates, have together created a more open career ladder in business, which at last is showing through at the top.

That formal education (rather than merely traditional staples of 'character', 'enterprise', or 'business genius') is an important aspect of their route to the top is clear from the chairmen of 1989 who attended the (disadvantaged-sounding) 'other maintained schools'. On the whole, these were *not* 'City barrow boys': undereducated geniuses who thrived on being rejected by grammar schools at age 11+, and who were insufficiently affluent to pay public school fees. Many of these 'other maintained' schools were highly selective and academic, some grammar schools in all but name, and their chairmen were clearly academically gifted: in fact, twelve out of fifteen of them went to university.

Overall changes in the university education of the 1989 chairmen (Table 9.2) are less striking, but support the meritocratic interpretation. The increase in the proportion of business leaders attending university (already apparent in the earlier post-war decades) continued in the 1980s. Only fourteen of the top fifty chairmen of 1989 (mainly public school boys and a few self-made men with no educational qualifications) did not attend university. There has, moreover, been no decline, as precipitate as that of the elite public schools, in the aggregate representation of the elite universities of Oxbridge,[20] nor of London (which, for

Table 9.2 University education of the chairmen of the top fifty companies

	1979	*1989*
Oxford	5	11
Cambridge	14	5
London	4	4
Birmingham	2	5
Other British universities	3	8
Overseas universities	3	3
No university education	19	14
Total	50	50

Sources: as Table 9.1. Sir Owen Green (BTR) is not counted as attending Oxford, for his university studies were brief, being interrupted by the Second World War. Others for whom no information on university was available were assumed to have had no university education.

top businessmen, means mainly the LSE). This is as one might expect from their increasingly meritocratic status: with rising state financial support these elite universities have recruited more on the basis of academic merit than wealth since the Second World War (certainly significantly more so than the fee-paying public schools).

However, Oxbridge and London no longer dominate the graduate playing field. The chances of graduates of 'other British' universities reaching the top more than doubled in the 1980s – these are the established 'redbrick universities', not the new 'plateglass' foundations of the 1960s, which came too late for most of this generation of chairmen. Birmingham University led the way; with its long tradition of industrially inclined vocational courses, it produced as many of the 1989 chairmen as Cambridge.

VII

These changes in the business elite in the 1980s no doubt have a range of causes as various as the distinguished careers that lie behind the statistics of the two tables. We suggested earlier that Mrs Thatcher seemed unlikely to be the cause. In fact, she can take the credit for some of the appointments: the top fifty companies of 1989 include half a dozen nationalized, and recently privatized, companies whose chairmen she and her ministers appointed or promoted at an earlier stage, and public school men were rare among these. Yet this cannot explain the bulk of the changes in the private sector. Any relation to Mrs Thatcher – who was more attached to the virtues of small business than the large corporate bureaucracies headed by most of these men – is, of course, tenuous. As Sir Owen Green, chairman of BTR, puts it: 'I think you could say that I am an outsider. I am not in the Thatcher "mafia" and I am not a political animal. But I am a supporter of Thatcherism, in the sense and to the extent that it has helped to bring about some necessary changes in the environment.'[21] That almost certainly describes the only link of most of his colleagues at the top to Thatcherism. Some in Mrs Thatcher's immediate political circle were, moreover, inclined to celebrate the virtues of self-taught business genius pulling itself up by the bootstraps, and to despise 'paper' qualifications as irrelevant credentialism: hardly attitudes calculated to promote the changes we observe.

That did not prevent Thatcherism having an indirect effect. Some of the changes in the tables are the result of upheavals among the leading companies, resulting from the strong competitive pressures and restructuring of the 1980s Thatcher whirlwind. Companies like BTR and Saatchi & Saatchi – relatively small in 1979 – joined the top fifty companies, along with the privatized or about-to-be privatized companies. Other companies, like Amalgamated Metal and C.T. Bowring, fell well below the fiftieth mark as their markets collapsed in the 1980s, and they have not recovered their position since. Yet half the companies appeared in both the 1979 and 1989 lists and within this group there were also substantial personnel changes, suggesting that the move to meritocracy was due to changes within companies, not just to the reordering of the top businesses under the pressure of increased competition and privatization.

It seems certain, moreover, that the foundations for such widespread changes were laid not in the 1980s but much earlier: when the business leaders in question were being recruited, trained, and promoted. The average age of the chairmen of 1989 was 59 years. They had typically finished their education in the 1950s, and progressed through middle management positions in the 1960s and board promotions in the 1970s. These were decades of widening educational opportunity, but also, we are now prone to forget, of profound changes in attitudes both within and towards business. As the major continental European countries began perceptibly to overtake British living standards during the 1960s, social and cultural changes accelerated, stimulated by the increased contemporary perception of the national, industrial, and personal importance of business success. Concretely this was reflected in the inauguration of business sections in the quality newspapers, and by the foundation (eighty years after the pioneering American business schools) of major new centres of business education like the London and Manchester Business Schools. There was possibly also an acceleration of changes in the wider cultural fabric of Britain described by Wiener that are less easy to convey, given the problems of generalization about national culture. So much of our culture is unspoken and intangible that it is not easy to make a convincing case for the reality of change by example or by quotation, as Wiener's academic critics made painfully clear.

Anecdotally, I have the impression that such changes did have a tremendous effect on promotion procedures and professionalism within the leading British firms, but it is difficult to substantiate such impressions statistically. We can, however, observe the effects of these changes on the people that businesses were able to recruit, notably in the career choices of university graduates. The small numbers of graduates among the postwar business elite suggest that in the first half of the twentieth century, when that generation was recruited, business careers were a minority taste at British universities. This is confirmed by the scattered contemporary statistics: possibly only a third of graduates then opted for careers in business.[22] By the 1960s, however, the proportion of the (then much increased numbers of) university graduates opting for a career in industry and commerce reached two-thirds and it has remained around that high level since.[23] While the data are not strictly comparable, it seems, moreover, that the postwar enthusiasm of Japanese and German graduates for business careers may have been waning in the 1980s. Thus Britain's *relative* position could be picking up even more rapidly than her own apparent shift in cultural attitudes – if that *is* what lies behind the changes – alone suggests.

There has been an equally remarkable transformation in the *quality* of British students who opt for careers in business. Those who make the choice early – for example, by opting for undergraduate courses in engineering, accountancy, or business management – are not only increasing in numbers but also improving in quality, as measured by 'A' level examination scores relative to the scores of those in more traditional academic subjects.[24] In the increasingly popular business-orientated courses, 'more' has certainly not meant 'worse'.

There are also clear indications that the best students in *all* undergraduate disciplines, not just in those orientated to business, are showing more interest in business careers than used to be the case. It was once not uncommon for questionnaire surveys to show as reasons for entry into a business career that the candidate had failed his civil service exams or obtained a poor degree: business was the choice only by default. Wiener quoted Margaret Drabble's novel *The Ice Age*, set in early 1960s Cambridge, to illustrate the survival of this view:

> It must be said that it never once crossed Anthony Keating's mind that he might get a job in industry. Rebel he was, but not to such a degree: so deeply conditioned are some sections of the British nation that some thoughts are deeply inaccessible to them. Despite the fact that major companies were at that time appealing urgently for graduates in any fields, despite the fact that the national press was full of seductive offers, the college notice boards plastered with them, Anthony Keating, child of the professional middle classes, reared in an anachronism as an anachronism, did not even see the offers: he walked past them daily, turned over pages daily, with as much indifference as if they had been written in Turkish or Hungarian. He thought himself superior to that kind of thing: that kind of advertisement was aimed at bores and sloggers, not at men of vision like Anthony Keating.[25]

This view was in fact already becoming obsolete in 1960s Cambridge, and it is now emphatically not the view of the brightest graduates, at least judging by their career choices. As Figure 9.1 shows, the increased output of British university graduates with first class honours in the postwar period, and particularly in the 1970s and 1980s, has gone almost entirely to the business

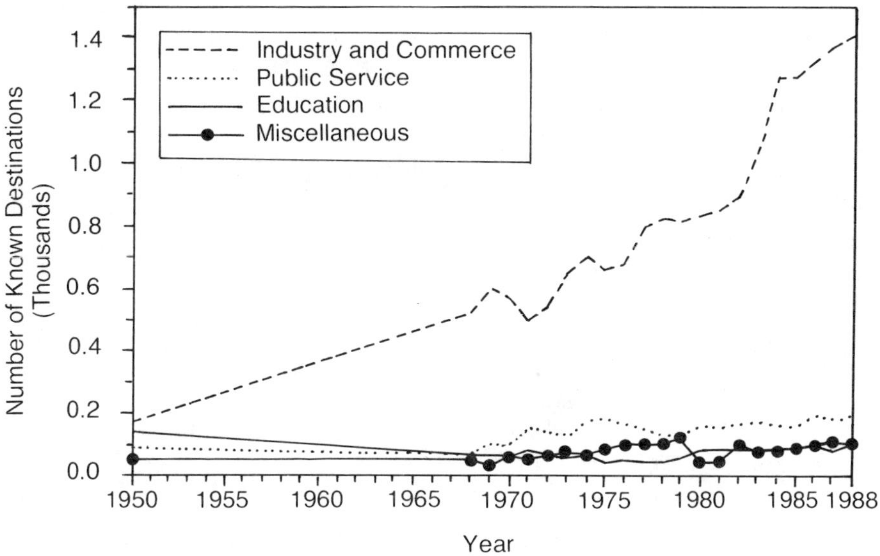

Figure 9.1 Male graduate first class degree: known home employment destinations (1950 and 1968–88)

sector. This contrasts strikingly with the experience of the academically weaker graduate recruits: business has not recruited an increased proportion of the graduates with third class honours or pass degrees, who have also been produced in increasing numbers. That distinction, if that is the word, belongs to the public sector and particularly to the local authorities.

The trend favourable to business is, moreover, now firmly established, with continuing success in business recruitment of first class honours graduates apparent in all recent decades. It seems that not only has there been a revolution at the top in the boardroom, but that this revolution is firmly rooted in evolutionary cultural and educational change. This laid firm foundations for a society where graduates increasingly recognized the worth, challenge, and rewards of a career in business, and where business had many of the brightest brains in their generation to work with.

VIII

To be optimistic about the effects of these longrun changes on business efficiency in the 1990s, we need to have some confidence that academic degree results reflect in some way the combinations of effort, intelligence, and other factors which are also conducive (though no doubt by somewhat contrasting processes) to business success. Certainly those with first class honours were well represented among the top company chairmen of 1989: James Prior of GEC (a 'first' in estate management from Cambridge), Maurice Saatchi of Saatchi & Saatchi (a 'first' in sociology from LSE), Sir Robert Haslam at British Coal (a 'first' in civil engineering from Birmingham), Sir William Barlow of BICC (a 'first' in electrical engineering from Manchester), and Sir Christopher Hogg of Courtaulds (a 'first' in English from Oxford). Some of the new men of 1989 have also topped off their education with a postgraduate business degree: two (Hogg and the American R.P. Bauman of Beecham) with a Harvard MBA, and one (Ian Vallance of British Telecom) with the equivalent from the London Business School.

Of course, most graduate chairmen (like most successful graduates elsewhere) obtained second class honours degrees. Further, indeed, the best 'seconds' among them were fully a match for the 'firsts': this is as true in business as in most other callings. What is clear is that the relatively few 'firsts' – whose increased recruitment by business happens to be measurable – include a significant portion of the cream of their generation. Certainly recruiters for the large corporations, though careful to stress their search for the rounded individual, tend to favour the academically successful when making offers. They have for some decades looked, among other things, not explicitly for 'firsts' but rather, consciously or not, for the same qualities as are reflected in the award of a 'first'. Salary surveys show that firms – though often not knowing degree results when making an offer – in fact pay more to 'firsts' than to other recruits; moreover, this differential still persists in business salaries years later.

All the signs are, then, that the British business world is now substantially more meritocratic than it was a generation ago. The men already at the helm of the top British businesses in the early 1990s are largely drawn from the intellectual cream. It is, moreover, quite clear that their successors in the late 1990s will also be drawn from an impressive pool of first-class talent. It would take a curiously myopic and self-satisfied academic to feel that these trends alone – deep-seated and longrun though they are – will guarantee Britain's business success in the 1990s. But, equally, it would take a peculiarly British form of cultural deformation to argue that the shift towards meritocracy and positive graduate attitudes towards business will not greatly strengthen the capability of British businesses to further improve their strategic performance in the increasingly competitive markets they now face.

IX

This chapter has shown that it is as important to measure the direction of the flows as the changing stocks of human capital, which have hitherto been the major concern of historical growth accountants. There is, however, much more work to be done in this area. It is critical, for example, that explicit international comparisons are made. While differences in national educational systems make such an exercise hazardous, preliminary results suggest, for example, that Japan, the USA, and continental European countries all had higher proportionate flows of university graduates towards business careers than did Britain between the

1920s and the 1960s. However, there is evidence of more recent convergence: there is a slight trend away from business careers in Japan and Germany, while other countries like Australia show a pro-business trend as in Britain. The significance of such differences for economic growth will, of course, depend on the marginal productivity of human capital in alternative uses in the different economies. While salary data produce some evidence for resolving the issues, it has been difficult so far to make significant progress along those lines because of problems of comparability.

It is possible, none the less, to conclude on an optimistic note, both for economic historians and for policy-makers. Economic historians will, it is hoped, welcome the possibility of human capital flow accounting as a way of testing the Wiener hypothesis, particularly as it appears that relevant data are available, albeit largely neglected. For policy-makers, the conclusion that 'culture' is important is sometimes seen to have pessimistic implications. Culture is seen as unchanging and unchangeable. Our initial measurement suggests, however, that this need not be so. Even a conservative society like Britain's can undertake substantial reappraisal of itself and change dysfunctional cultural traits after observing that they are damaging to its longrun economic health. We have a choice; but we do not need to change our culture if we value it for 'non-economic' reasons.

10

BANK DEREGULATION IN AUSTRALIA, YESTERDAY AND TODAY: LESSONS OF HISTORY

David Pope

INTRODUCTION

Perhaps the most celebrated event in the Australian economy in recent years has been financial market liberalization. Deregulation of the financial system – including 'freeing' the exchange rate, the establishment of fifteen foreign trading banks, the removal of interest rate ceilings on all trading and savings bank deposits, and other bank deregulations – has initiated structural change not only in banking but also in other sectors of the economy. Moreover, it has been the experience of financial deregulation that has largely motivated policy-makers to call for microeconomic reform of other key sectors of the Australian economy, including transport, the labour market and, more recently, telecommunications.

The road to free banking was broadly paved by the Campbell Committee (1979–81) and by the proposals of the Martin Review Group (1983–84). Much was expected from increased competition, namely through increased efficiency and diversity of bank products. Certainly product innovation and technological change quickened. Yet there is another side to the story. In the last years of the 1980s, the lending policies of the deregulated banks were coming back to haunt them in the form of bad and doubtful debts in association, at least in part, with spectacular corporate collapses. Late in 1990, the Australian Treasurer berated the banks, arguing that their customers had been 'poorly served' and that the banks had become 'mesmerised' by spiralling asset prices and afflicted with speculative fever. A parliamentary inquiry followed.

Questions of the beneficial effects or otherwise of deregulation involve the influence of deregulation on banking efficiency and costs, bank profitability, and the pricing of bank services. Interwoven is the issue of risk management in financial institutions. Economic historians are fortunate to have a laboratory of sorts, provided by the past sweep of experience, in which to examine questions relating to past and present. In this regard, in the second half of the nineteenth century, Australia had attained the state of 'free banking'. This period (1860–1914) in Australia's banking experience provides a powerful perspective on today's problems.

The chapter is divided into three sections. The first section looks at the growth of regulation and the forces for deregulation in the late 1970s and 1980s and contrasts these developments with deregulation in the second half of the nineteenth century. The second section looks at the consequences in terms of the banks' performance post-deregulation and also demonstrates the strong parallels between the two eras. The final section offers conclusions, which draw out the strengths of long-term studies of our economic past.

FORCES FOR DEREGULATION: 1980s AND THE VICTORIAN AGE

The Royal Commission of 1936 and the Campbell Committee, 1979–81

The banking controls which the deregulators of the 1970s and 1980s sought to remove were pre-eminently a legacy of the Second World War. The depression of the 1930s tipped the scales in favour of central banking. However, the process of centralization through expanding the functions of the government-created Commonwealth Bank (established in 1912) was slow. The report of a Royal Commission, published in 1937, concluded that greater economic stability and improved efficiency could be achieved by strengthening the Commonwealth Bank as a central bank.[1] The Commission recommended the introduction of a variable minimum deposit requirement, endorsed the fixed exchange rate regime, and argued that a central bank was needed to supervise, indeed take control of, any bank unable to meet its obligations. In this it was clearly influenced by the history of the bank crisis of the early 1890s. Minimum capital requirements were proposed and, in order to assure compliance, the commissioners argued that the banks should be licensed.

The Commission was also concerned with the industrial structure and performance of the trading banks. It adopted the view that high industry concentration and low competition had spawned supernormal profits. Banks were deemed to enjoy a privileged position (supplying industry with credit) similar to a public utility supplying goods and services to the public. This led to the question of whether or not bank profits should be regulated.

Not surprisingly, the private banks vigorously opposed the draft legislation based on the Commission's recommendations, and this delayed their implementation. With the outbreak of war in 1939, however, the Commonwealth government lost little time in introducing regulations under its defence powers. Between 1939 and 1942, these involved exchange controls, the granting of powers to call the trading banks' surplus investible funds to special account at the central bank and to issue directives to the banks with respect to the asset composition of their balance sheets, and the imposition in February 1942 of interest rate controls. These wartime regulations were incorporated into permanent legislation in 1945.

The adoption of central banking and 'policy activism' at this time was not, of course, unique to Australia. Regulatory systems based on the public utility model were being built in other Western economies. Similarly, the deregulation of the Australian financial system which followed the release in 1981 of the *Final Report* of the Inquiry into the Financial System (the Campbell Committee) occurred at a time of an almost global march away from regulatory regimes in financial markets. This is not to deny that the Campbell Committee – and the banking commissioners of 1936 – played a role in focusing debate and in shaping particular solutions.

By the close of the 1970s certainly many in the community were dissatisfied with the controls that existed in banking and finance. It was this dissatisfaction that prompted the government to appoint the Campbell Committee.[2] Deregulation was recommended on the grounds that efficiency would be improved in three senses: allocative efficiency – the extent to which funds are directed into the most productive (highest yielding) areas of investment; technical efficiency – the extent to which resources are used up in the intermediation process (for example, the size of banking margins); dynamic efficiency – its capacity to generate financial innovations. Efficiency gains in banking won through deregulation would flow into efficiency gains to the economy as a whole.

The Committee concluded that most of the prevailing regulations were ineffective or even counter-productive. Interest rate ceilings had some perverse distributional effects in that some depositors had low incomes while some of the beneficiaries of concessional interest rates were high income earners.[3] Moreover, restrictions on entry to banking and the prevention of price-competitive behaviour through interest rate ceilings made the banking sector inefficient, with wide margins between borrowing and lending rates. The inability to compete on the basis of price (interest rates – which were an instrument of the government's monetary policy) prompted banks to engage one another in non-price competition. This led to the proliferation of banks' branch networks. As the Australian Bankers' Association submission to the Campbell Committee noted:

> For much of the period since World War II the use of official monetary policy largely precluded the banks from competing through price with one another and with financial institutions not subject to the Banking Act. The banks attempted to attract business through quality of service and convenience of location.[4]

More price competition and less branching would, it believed, benefit customers through lower charges.[5]

Some commentators also argued that the banks had become inefficient, using excessively conservative lending practices. Because the demand for funds typically exceeded the supply at the regulated interest rates, the banks were more involved in credit rationing than in the development of innovative financial instruments which would assist business. As a matter of evidence, most financial innovations developed in this period arose in the non-bank sector and many of them had the objective of avoiding regulation.[6]

The major area of economic policy in which financial controls were used was monetary policy. Post-1945 restrictions on bank lending affected M3 growth and a similar outcome was also achieved by varying the Statutory Reserve Deposit (SRD) ratio. In practice the effectiveness of monetary policy was diluted by the regulations, in that they promoted the growth of 'near money', deposits with non-bank financial intermediaries (NBFIs), over which the central bank had no direct control. As the trading banks' share of all financial assets declined, so too did the power of the authorities to conduct monetary policy.[7]

While the 1936 Royal Commission had endorsed the then existing fixed (sterling) exchange rate, members of the Campbell Committee argued in favour of a flexible regime. For one thing, it was thought that the authorities could regain control of domestic monetary conditions – surrendered to world monetary conditions under a pegged exchange regime. Public and private (bank) interests in deregulation were mutual. The authorities stood to regain some measure of control over financial activity through monetary policy, which had eroded under regulations that had stunted the banks' market share (relative to NBFIs). For the banks, deregulation offered the chance of regaining lost ground and the possibility of expansion into fresh fields. Ackland and Harper suggest that it was this conjunction of public and private interest in deregulation in Australia that explains why financial deregulation was adopted so quickly and thoroughly.[8]

The removal of interest rate ceilings on all trading and savings bank deposits occurred in December 1980. Major deregulations ensued, including reductions in minimum term on trading bank deposits in 1981 and 1982; the end of quantitative lending guidances, 1982; the floating of the Australian dollar, 1983; the invitation of banking licences to sixteen foreign banks, 1984; the removal of remaining ceilings on bank interest;[9] the replacement of the 'liquid assets and government securities' (LGS) convention with the Prime Assets Ratio (PAR), 1985; and the reduction in 1988 in the SRD ratio to 1 per cent – down from 7 per cent. In the same year PAR was reduced from 12 to 10 per cent, and the distinction between trading and savings banks with respect to PAR and SRDs was removed.

Deregulation in Victorian Australia

While Australian banks entered the Second World War largely unregulated, this had not always been the case. The British Treasury first set down its ideas on conditions under which colonial banks must operate in 1840, these regulations being revised in 1846. The main points in the Colonial Banks Regulations, as revised in 1846, were:

1 Advances on land were not to be permitted – banks must confine transactions to discounting commercial paper and negotiable securities and other legitimate banking business.
2 A company was not to hold its own shares or make advances on them.

3 Advances to a director or officer were not to exceed one-third of the total.
4 Liabilities, other than deposits, were not to exceed three times paid-up capital.
5 Note issue was to be limited to the amount of paid-up capital.
6 A bank was to be constituted as a body corporate, initially for a period of not more than twenty-one years; each extension of its life was similarly limited.
7 Liability of a banking company was to be twice the amount of subscribed capital.
8 Statistical returns of assets and liabilities were to be furnished, half-yearly or yearly.[10]

Governors of all British colonies were instructed to observe these 'general principles'. Of particular interest to the subsequent history of Australian banking is the first principle, which asserted the 'real bills doctrine' of British banking, namely the restriction of lending to discounting short-term, self-liquidating commercial bills of exchange arising out of transactions in real goods and services as opposed to the speculative use of credit, as in land; and also the fifth, which sought to constrain the note issue of the commercial banks. Both can be seen as restraining *inside money*, the latter by directly limiting the private note issue, the former by tying down the domain of advances, and hence the creation of additional deposits.

On the matter of the note issue, the British Treasury was to moderate its views. In acts of incorporation, Australian colonial banks sought more elastic issues and the limits were raised to paid-up capital plus coin and bullion. Progressively more weight was placed on the liquid assets held by banks than on shareholders' funds, and by 1856 the Bank of Australasia had secured Treasury licence to print private notes up to the value of three times its specie and bullion holdings. Following the arrival of responsible government in the 1850s (in Western Australia, 1890), several Australian colonies (the status of 'state' came with federation of the colonies in 1901) permitted new banks to be formed under individual or general companies acts, and in these cases Treasury neither had, nor sought, a regulatory role. In Queensland the local legislation for the incorporation of the Bank of Queensland in 1863 included the exceptional clause which stated that the bank's note issue was not to exceed the amount of uncalled capital and other securities that the directors may for the time being have on hand.[11] However, in this and in state-initiated general companies acts the overriding rule was that a bank had unlimited liability for its note issue. In the course of the 1860s and 1870s Victoria, New South Wales, and Tasmania applied this simple principle to all banks in their territories, whether formed under new or already established acts. Nor, by this time, were the banks constrained by the old Treasury rules. The quarterly returns, which the banks were obliged to furnish under the 1846 Regulations, show that the note issue for the banks was well below the maximum set by the rules.

There were rules limiting banks' total indebtedness (to two or three times liquid assets, or paid-up capital, coin, and bullion). However, these were never restrictive, as deposits were excluded from the calculations. Moreover, a bank's liquid reserves were permitted to do more than one job. Reserves held against the note issue were simultaneously reserves against deposit withdrawal.

Both Treasury and the bankers of Lombard Street continued to espouse the real bills doctrine. Land was not a legitimate mortgageable asset and, by the doctrine, advances should be directed to trade paper which was the *non plus ultra* of the English bankers' profession.[12] Yet Treasury regulations and English bankers' sentiments soon came to nought. The power and interest of the British Treasury in colonial banking waned with responsible government, as discussed above. Nor were the formal Treasury codes taken very seriously. In the vernacular of the times, bankers drove a coach and horses through the hampering limitations of the legislation. The National Bank lent on land almost from its inception. In the final months of 1859 it granted half of the requests of farmers for overdrafts on the security of land and two-thirds of the applications of businessmen for overdrafts on the security of suburban land.[13] What the National was doing, so too were the others, with land-based advances possibly accounting for as much as two-thirds of the banks' total advances business by the 1880s. According to H.G. Turner, banker, historian, and litterateur, 'the limitations [of the acts and charters] are practically ignored, in some cases by a special adaptation of the form of the book entry, but frequently by an entire disregard of them'.[14] Why this retreat from English principles? Turner supplied the broad logic:

> Had the banks absolutely restricted their operations to what would have passed the ordeal of Lombard Street, two, or at the most three of them would have been ample for the operations. As the discountable paper of the colony does not amount to nearly one-half of the deposits held by the banks, they would have had no inducement to offer interest to attract savings, nor to open branches throughout the country.[15]

Australian bankers' advance business reflected local conditions. Wrote the *Australasian Insurance and Banking Record*: 'the policy of Australian banking has gradually adapted itself to the requirements of a country differing widely in all essentials from the motherland'.[16] These requirements were largely related to the alienation and development of land.

To conclude the picture of Australian banking before 1914, it should be noted that there were no controls on interest rates, which as we have seen were to become a pervading feature of Australian financial markets after 1939. These, as well as currency exchange rates, were matters for the private banks themselves. And there was no central bank. The Commonwealth Bank, established in 1912, did thereafter manage the government account, but its main purpose was to compete with, not to regulate, the private commercial banks. It came at a time when state Labour governments were busy establishing state-owned brickworks, fishing fleets and, in one state, even butcher shops, all with much the same intent.

While the federal government did establish the Australian note issue under Treasury at the end of the period, in 1910, for much of the second half of the nineteenth century – certainly the third quarter – banking regulations were not stringent. Free banking was a reality.

Expectations

The deregulations of the 1980s were direct and explicit. In contrast, those of the second half of the nineteenth century were more subtle. Treasury formulae of control became more elastic with time and, in any event, formal codes of banking and the tenets of Lombard Street were progressively ignored by Australian bankers. Regulation, in a sense, withered.

The expectation among the Australian banking fraternity in the latter half of the nineteenth century was for considerable bank growth. This was to be delivered through increasing the scale and number of branches. Land was seen as a legitimate mortgageable asset and advances could be so secured. Parenthetically, in another part of the Empire, Canada, a land-abundant country like Australia, bankers stuck more firmly to the real bills doctrine. Related or not, Canada escaped systemic bank failure in the 1890s.

In Australia, deposit growth was expected from population and economic expansion, together with the tapping of the savings of British investors. In general, expectations were buoyed by the promise of a rapidly expanding economy, a physically dwindling frontier, and the 'unearned increment' on land (inflation). Henry Giles Turner, sometime president of the Bankers' Institute, Australasia, was later to call the 1880s the 'age of extravagance'. 'Non-performing loans', 'investor fall-out', bank closures, or terms with the same meanings, were not in the vocabulary of Australia's bankers. The mood was euphoric. Few saw virtue in prudence.

The next era of financial deregulations a century later occurred in, and fuelled, a similar psychological state of mind. Bankers and the authorities were supremely optimistic about the benefits of deregulation. The banks were optimistic about their own growth, the authorities about their control of monetary growth. Consumers would gain too through the reforms which would improve efficiency and, along with the entry of new banks, reduce the margin between banks' borrowing and lending rates. The industry would be more competitive and bank interest margins lower. There would be less non-price competition, specifically some rationalization of banks' branch networks, and more innovation in the provision of services and the 'unbundling' of service charges on accounts.

WHAT HAPPENED? BANKS' PERFORMANCE POST-DEREGULATION

1980s and early 1990s

Competition through bank entry

Sixteen new bank licences were offered in response to forty applications. Fifteen were taken up, many by subsidiaries of major international banks. However, entry alone does not guarantee effective competition. The new banks have found it difficult to compete with the big local banks – ANZ, Westpac, National, and Commonwealth – especially at the retail level. This reflects advantages held by the 'big four' in terms of customer loyalty which, until this time, has also supplied these banks with cheap deposits (from pensioners). To the extent that there are scale economies, overseas banking firms face higher unit costs in establishing and running their operations. The two foreign-owned banks which have enjoyed high returns have done so by steering clear of retail trade and by exploiting wholesale niches. Seven new domestic banks were established in the course of the 1980s, all involving a conversion of NBFIs into banks. Like the foreign-owned banks, the new 'domestics' have been slow in gaining ground. New domestic and new foreign banks combined account for little more than 10 per cent of all bank assets.[17]

Market Share

Deregulation of interest rates led to an increase in the banks' ability to compete for deposits with unregulated intermediaries such as finance companies, building societies, and credit unions. Figure 10.1 shows the split of market share of assets between banks and non-banks. Among the non-banks, building societies' share in total assets of all financial intermediaries fell substantially. This could reflect the effect of bank competition, but it also followed from the fact that some building societies became banks. The share of finance companies fell even more sharply. This reflected a decline in bank-affiliated finance companies, both of existing and new banks. Their business was merged with the general banking business of the parent companies.

Bank margins and profitability

Bank interest margins had been higher in Australia than in comparable countries.[18] Deregulation was expected to change this situation. Increased competition would, it was thought, increase the banks' cost efficiency, while interest ceilings, especially on deposits, would be removed. Competition for deposits would place upward pressure on borrowing rates and bank entry downward pressure on loan rates. The aggregate picture is of a downward trend

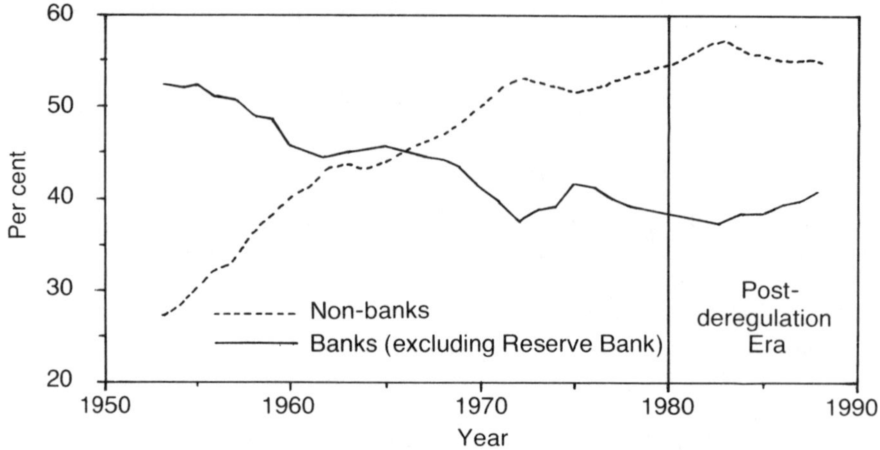

Figure 10.1 Market shares – banks and non-banks in Australia
Source: R. Ackland and I.R. Harper, 'Financial deregulation in Australia: boon or bane?', paper presented to the *Economists Conference*, University of New South Wales, Sydney, 1990

in interest rate margins (Figure 10.2). However, when disaggregated into *wholesale* (large transactions through money/capital markets) and *retail* (small household/business transactions through bank branches), the former has fallen while the latter has risen, causing the aggregate to rise from mid-1980s, that is, since new bank entry.[19] What explains this result? Milbourne provides two answers. First, the new foreign banks mostly avoided retail trade because of the high cost of establishing branch networks. Secondly, 'non-performing' loans and provision for doubtful debt rose sharply from the mid-1980s and the banks sought to recover outlays and losses through higher interest margins in the less competitive retail market.

Profitability appears to have declined. Table 10.1 is based on a Reserve Bank of Australia (RBA) survey, regrettably discontinued in 1986/87. This suggests that the banks' profitability has fallen to nearer to the level of industrials. At a more disaggregated level (Table 10.2), the major banks have recovered their former profitability (1988/89); new foreign and state banks have generally performed poorly, while the new domestic entrants have generally performed most strongly.

Efficiency, branching, and scale economies

Some evidence of the banks operating closer to the minimum points of their longrun average cost curves (providing gains in cost efficiency) is provided in Table 10.3. The ratio of operating costs to assets of the banks fell by around 14 per cent.[20] Moreover, real deposits per employee increased by around one-third

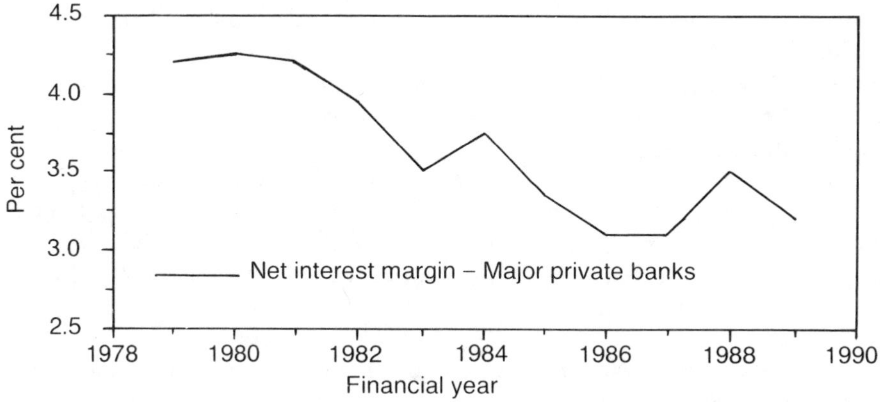

Figure 10.2 Bank interest rate margins (net interest income ÷ average assets)
Source: R. Ackland and I.R. Harper, 'Financial deregulation in Australia: boon or bane?', paper presented to the *Economists Conference*, University of New South Wales, Sydney, 1990

Table 10.1 Net returns to assets (%), 1983/4–88/9. Major financial groups in Australia

	1983/4	*1984/5*	*1985/6*	*1986/7*	*1987/8*	*1988/9*
Banks	0.9	0.85	0.68	0.6	0.75	0.63
Merchant banks	0.8	0.68	0.62	0.91	0.75	0.46
Authorized dealers	0.6	(0.58)	(0.25)	0.18	0.48	0.2
Finance companies	1.5	1.3	0.93	1.17	1.22	1.4
Building societies		0.42	0.34	0.27	0.58	0.68
Credit unions					0.87	1.07

Source: R. Ackland and I.R. Harper, 'Financial deregulation in Australia: boon or bane?', paper presented to the *Economists Conference*, University of New South Wales, Sydney, 1990.

Table 10.2 Net returns to assets (%), 1984/5–88/9. Banking groups in Australia

	1984/5	*1985/6*	*1986/7*	*1987/8*	*1988/9*
Major	0.83	0.74	0.63	0.79	0.86
State banks	0.5	0.47	0.36	0.41	0.14
Other established	0.15	0.33	0.53	0.68	1.28
New domestic		1.74	1.53	1.21	1.02
New foreign	0.4	0.19	0.51	0.43	(0.23)

Source: R. Ackland and I.R. Harper, 'Financial deregulation in Australia: boon or bane?', paper presented to the *Economists Conference*, University of New South Wales, Sydney, 1990.

between 1980 and 1988, and real wages per real deposits per bank worker declined from 0.7 in 1981 to 0.5 in 1988.[21] Some of this drop, however, probably reflects the changing composition of bank business with a larger wholesale component, which entails a lower labour input per dollar of the larger sums transacted.

Another measure of cost efficiency is provided by the ratio of operating costs to operating expenses.[22] This measure includes off-balance-sheet exposure, which the other indexes omit. On this basis the evidence for increased efficiency is far from overwhelming. For while the index shows an upward trend for 1979/80 to 1988/89 this result hinges on the 'outlaying' values of 1988/89 (Table 10.3).

What of efficiency gains through reduced branching and scale economies? Following deregulation the major banks somewhat rationalized their branch networks and staffing. Many of the new banks have specialized in wholesaling commercial loans, rather than retailing services through branches. Both these things have reduced branch proliferation. As to the question of scale economies, there are some difficulties in defining a financial firm's output and of measuring it. The usual way out is to estimate an equation which makes average operating cost a function of some measure of output (deposits, advances, assets) but which also includes variables reflecting banks' activities (for example, transactions *per* deposits). Davis and Lewis surveyed the literature on scale economies in financial institutions for the Campbell Committee, including statistical analyses of

Table 10.3 Bank operating costs, and efficiency index, in Australia

	Bank operating costs (% of average assets)		*Hogan's bank efficiency index (Ratio of operating profit to operating expenses)*	
	Major banks[a]	*Major private banks*[b]	*Major banks*[a]	*Major private banks*[b]
1978–79	–	4.4	–	0.21
1979–80	–	4.5	–	0.21
1980–81	–	4.3	–	0.24
1981–82	–	4.8	–	0.19
1982–83	4.2	4.2	0.17	0.18
1983–84	4.1	4.1	0.22	0.22
1984–85	3.8	3.8	0.22	0.23
1985–86	3.7	3.7	0.19	0.19
1986–87	3.7	3.7	0.17	0.18
1987–88	3.9	3.9	0.2	0.21
1988–89	3.6	3.5	0.26	0.27

Notes: [a]ANZ Bank, National Australia Bank, Commonwealth Bank, Westpac Banking Corporation.
[b]ANZ Bank, National Australia Bank, Westpac Banking Corporation.
Source: R. Ackland and I.R. Harper, 'Financial deregulation in Australia: boon or bane?', paper presented to the *Economists Conference*, University of New South Wales, Sydney, 1990.

Australian banks.[23] These studies suggest the existence of scale economies, although it is possible that they arise in the administration of the payments system and not in other functions that the banks perform.[24] The view that economies exist is reinforced by the fact that there has been continuing consolidation in the banking industry. The large banks are getting larger. This is Stigler's 'survivor principle' test of economies of scale. Crude as the test might be, the larger private banks of yesteryear – the Anglos and the major colonials – are today the ANZ, Westpac, and the National.

Stability of the financial system in an age of extravagance

Stability of the financial system, especially the integrity of the payments system, is necessary for the efficient operation of the macro economy. Bank failures or potential closures disrupt transactions and can also impose costs upon depositors and bank shareholders – customer doubts about one institution can create a snowball effect, rolling onto other banks and financial institutions. Deregulation created a more risky environment for financial intermediaries. Depositors with banks are protected by the statutory obligations upon the Reserve Bank to supply cash to satisfy their demands. In turn liquidity requirements like the banks' LGS ratio, and to a lesser extent the current PAR rating, discourage them from getting into difficulties, as does the recent implementation of the Bank for International Settlements (BIS) capital requirements – at least in terms of credit risk.[25] Nevertheless, the recent financial disasters in Victoria and Western Australia clearly show that the risk of failure (in the case of the Victorian State Bank, the probability of needing to be rescued) is not negligible. On the other hand, government intervention promotes the inefficient pricing of risk, as the 'protected' do not pay the full cost of the risks they take.[26]

Deregulation in the 1980s precipitated a fight for market share between the individual banks and between banks and NBFIs. This was against a backdrop of five things. First, depositor protection was assured through the Reserve Bank. Secondly, initially easy monetary conditions provided a fine conservatory for questionable lending policies. Thirdly, and perhaps most importantly, financial players have short memories;[27] few could, or cared to, remember history and history is replete with episodes of easy credit, bad debts, and financial ruin – in some respects the 1980s was to be a replay of Australian banking of the 1880s. Fourthly, banks changed their assessment procedures of credit risk with deregulation, delegating more responsibility downline than hitherto – something also true of banking in the 1880s. The Australian Bankers' Association reported in 1990:

> There was an increase in the delegation power given to managers to approve loans, and the centralised and layered system of credit control of the 1970s was replaced, in some banks, with a decentralised system. In some banks, there was ... an under-supply of staff sufficiently skilled and experienced in identifying and managing credit risk in a downturn. A trend

for bankers to take advantage of the benefits of early retirement resulted in a drop in the level of experienced staff.[28]

Finally, there was an increase in leverage. The tax laws were important in that interest payments, unlike dividends, were fully tax deductible, including adjustment for inflation. This encouraged loan applications from paper entrepreneurs, whom the banks too readily accommodated.

The banks' post-deregulation scramble for market share in the circumstances just described produced a strong speculative boom, lower quality loans of higher risk and much higher provision for bad and doubtful debts by the banks (see Figure 10.3).

Exchange rate and monetary policy

The floating of the exchange rate and the anticipated growth of the banking sector was expected to give the authorities independent control of monetary aggregates. Yet what was not appreciated at the time was that 'independance' is limited (compromised) in an international economy with major, highly mobile capital flows. There is a growing support for some degree of intervention by the RBA to calm the dollar's wilder movements, even to the directioning of its longer term path. Three considerations appear to be important. First, the volatility in exchange rates has led to unexpected business losses, the most celebrated being associated with offshore foreign currency loans by Australian trading banks to Australian farmers, property developers, and other small businesses. The passage

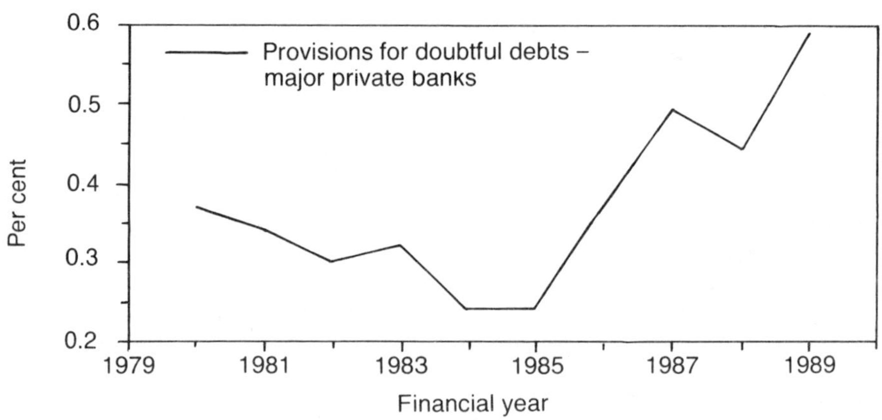

Figure 10.3 Provisions for doubtful debts – major private banks in Australia (per cent of average assets)

Source: R. Ackland and I.R. Harper, 'Financial deregulation in Australia: boon or bane?', paper presented to the *Economists Conference*, University of New South Wales, Sydney, 1990

of time, however, should yield some movement along learning curves as well as new hedging and cover instruments. Secondly, uncertainty about future movements in rates can still damp investment and exports in so far as hedging is costly or information flows are imperfect. Thirdly, currency markets set the dollar's relative value on short-term factors, which do not necessarily accord with longer term considerations: will the Australian dollar fall sufficiently to help correct Australia's current account deficit problem? Can the forex market adjust prices efficiently (or at least more efficiently than policy-makers could) to achieve public policy goals?[29]

The 1880s and early 1890s

Concentration and competition in banking

Notwithstanding the different exchange rate regime, the financial system of a century ago shared many similarities with that of today. In Australia the largest group of financial intermediaries in the nineteenth century, as today, were the commercial trading banks. At first the trading banks took local deposits, discounted commercial paper, made advances, and conducted business in connection with domestic and foreign trade, but distanced themselves from mortgages on real estate. But in the second half of the nineteenth century they expanded their portfolios, as we have seen, to include such mortgages and also, after 1875, actively sought deposits in England and Scotland, thus assisting in the international transfer of capital. The savings banks were set up to encourage thrift and, some hoped, to curb heavy drinking and gambling which threatened to leave convict emancipists 'poor, vicious, unmarried'. Other financial institutions developed in time, the main ones being building societies, which were involved in the funding of residential construction, pastoral companies, insurance offices, and friendly (health insurance) societies.

On the eve of the depression of the 1890s, the trading banks accounted for around 70 per cent of all assets of financial institutions, about double their share today. At this time savings banks accounted for just 6 per cent; pastoral finance companies 12 per cent; building societies 10 per cent; insurance companies 5 per cent.[30] The trading banks grew most rapidly in the 1880s. The annual rate of growth of their real assets averaged 3.2 per cent, 5.9 per cent, and 9.0 per cent in the 1860s, 1870s, and 1880s respectively. Their assets shrank at an average rate of 2.7 per cent per annum in the 1890s. There were never more than about twenty-five trading banks. If we define bank output as the dollar value of banks' advances, deposits, and private bank notes, then between 1850 and 1914 just four banks accounted for around one-half of the total business and eight never controlled less than two-thirds of it. This is not very dissimilar to the position of banking today.

The industrial organization of banking was characterized by extremely high concentration ratios, as we have just noted, and restricted price competition. Most economic models indicate that price competition is relatively unimportant under oligopolistic conditions. Each player is aware of his own market power as well as that of the others, and ways are sought to collude and cooperate with one another. In Australia the banks formed associations and collusive agreements to fix what they called 'terms of business', more explicitly the rates to be charged on deposits, advances, bill discounts, and foreign exchange.[31] Probably as a consequence, the average spread between deposit and loan rates was higher than in other countries, while Australian short rates were poorly correlated with foreign rates and only half as volatile.[32]

However, this is not to suggest that the banks did not compete. The prevalent form of competition was non-price competition. This involved the opening and operation of bank branches. Branching represented an effort to differentiate product quality, namely by location and by advertising. The early banks followed the miners to their diggings, the sheep farmers into the outback, and the dirt farmers to the rainfall-fringe of cultivation. Their offices protected the accounts of existing customers in established centres who might otherwise defect to rivals who set up locally. Similarly, local business could be won from the ranks of customers of rival banks who were slow in providing local facilities. Early occupation also erected a barrier to entry into the industry by unit banks. This is what many new banks discovered in the retail bank market for banking services in the 1980s. Branching was also an explicit type of advertising, akin to the highway bill-board of today.[33]

Counting both branches and agencies, the trading banks operated from over 1000 offices by the early 1880s, double this by 1914. This led to an interesting contrast:

> there are in the present year in England and Wales 121 joint-stock banks, having together 1,617 offices, and 234 private banks, having about 893 branches; and in Ireland, nine joint-stock banks, with 495 branches. There is thus in England and Wales a banking office for every 12,000 persons; in Scotland, one for every 4,000; and in Ireland, one for every 11,000 of the inhabitants. Now, in Victoria ... we have a branch of a bank for every 2,760 colonists.[34]

We can go further with comparisons: in the United States where national banks were not permitted to branch until 1927 and most states prohibited branching until the 1920s, there was one commercial bank per 9,200 Americans in 1880, one per 8,750 in 1900 and one per 5,300 in 1910.[35] Some saw the Australian pattern as wasteful:

> The primitive Australian township consists of a public house [bar], a general store, a smithy, and a butcher's shop. In the second stage of its development it is now an even chance whether the next good allotment finds its way into the possession of a bank, or of a church committee. But

> when two branch managers become rival candidates for the patronage of three or four petty traders, we cannot help considering that branch business is overdone.The spectacle of two or three branch banks in a petty village suggests the same sort of waste capital as the parallel pipes of three rival gas companies.[36]

It is to be remembered that the Campbell Committee anticipated a rationalization of banks' branch networks post-deregulation and viewed such an outcome as beneficial for efficiency.

Profitability and margins

The high concentration ratios, the attempts to collude and cooperate in setting interest rates, and the prevalence of non-price competition in the banking industry, involving as it did product differentiation and advertising through branching, describe elements of oligopolistic behaviour. Did these circumstances make for supernormal bank profits? On an opportunity cost basis profits do not appear to have been excessive. Figures 10.4 and 10.5 suggest that over the period as a whole the banks' profit rate lay in the middle of the league of corporate profit earners. The collapse in profitability in the 1890s is also clearly reflected in share prices (Figure 10.6). Interest margins between the banks' lending (overdraft) rate and the borrowing (deposit) rate fell from extraordinarily high levels attained in the 1860s (see Figure 10.7). Taking the period after 1875, however, there was no pronounced squeeze; margins bounced around 4 per cent. What

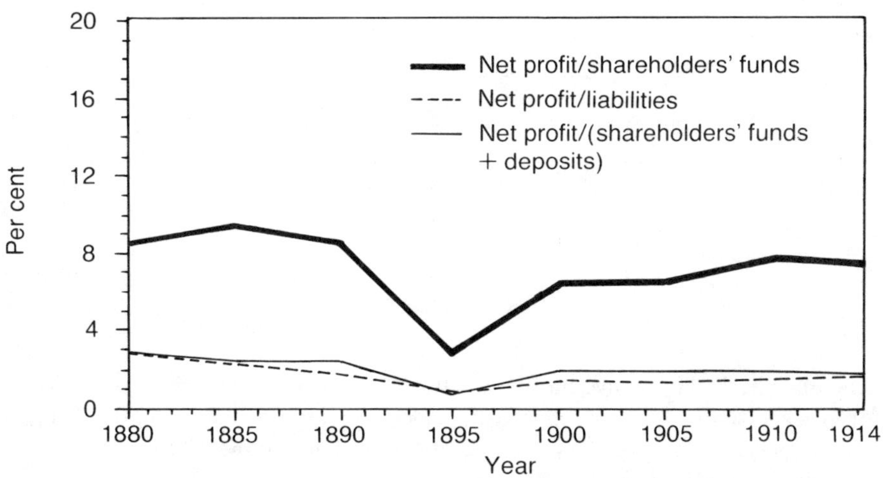

Figure 10.4 Net profit rates of trading banks in Australia, 1880–1914
Source: Butlin-Pope bank database

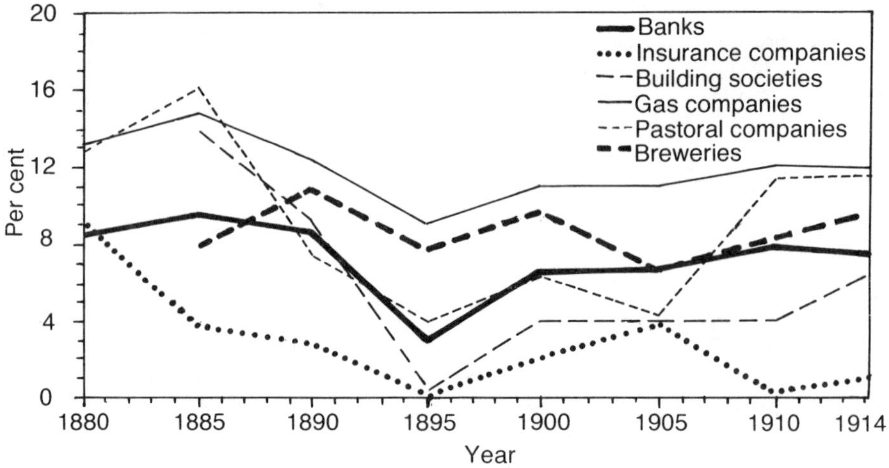

Figure 10.5 Net profits/shareholders' funds in Australia, 1880–1914
Source: Butlin-Pope bank database

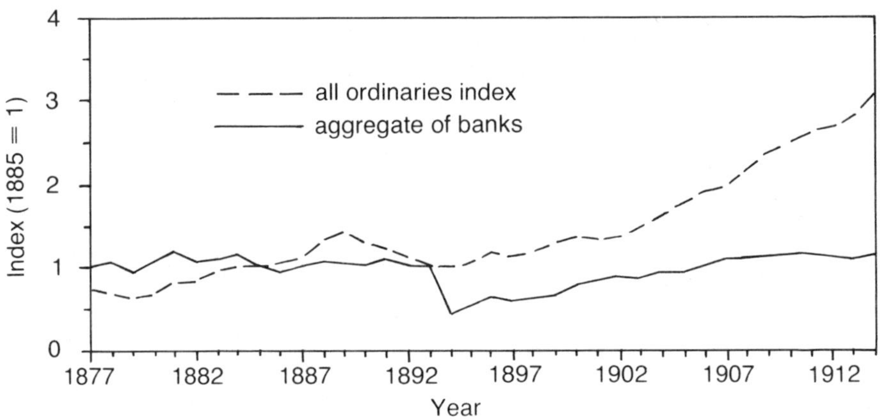

Figure 10.6 Share price index for Australia – all ordinaries and banks, 1877–1914
Source: *AIBR* and Sydney Stock Exchange

generally checked excessive profits was not margins but (non-price) competition for market share, both among rival banks and intermediaries at the fringe. Superimposed on this process was the financial chaos of the 1890s, which was not entirely unrelated to it.

The trend line in Figure 10.8 can be interpreted as a picture of the Australian economy travelling at 'full capacity', with its labour and capital resources fully utilized. The historical values of real output above the line represent excess

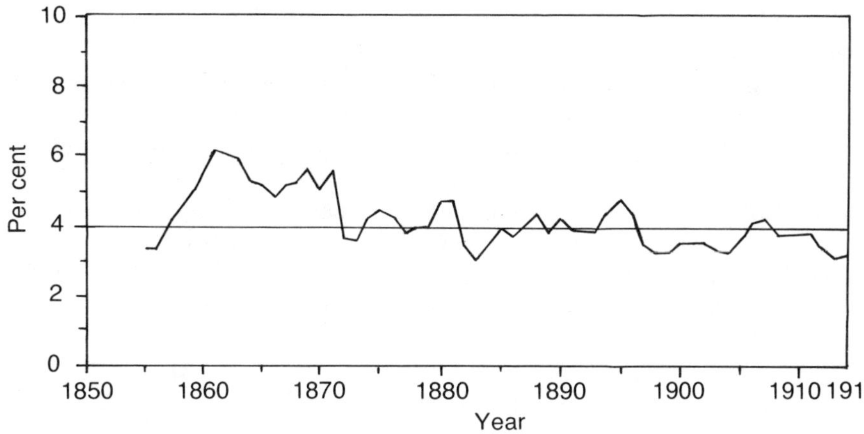

Figure 10.7 Interest margins in Australia, 1850–1914
Source: Butlin-Pope bank database

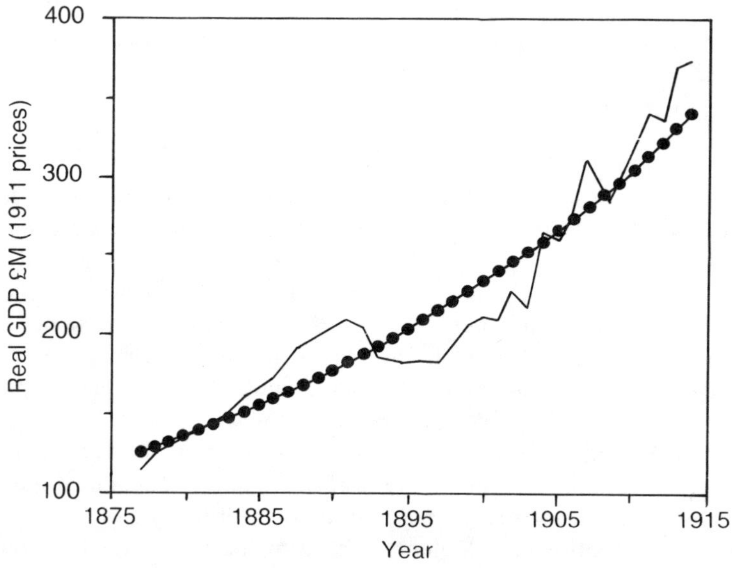

Note Predicted GDP = $1.1822 * 10^{-20} * 10^{0.011733t}$ $\overline{R}^2 = 0.913$

Figure 10.8 Australian economy, 1877–1914
Source: N.G. Butlin, 'Australian national accounts', in Vray Vamplew (ed.), *Australians: Historical Statistics*, Sydney, Fairfax, Syme & Weldon, 1987, pp. 126–44

demand, below it, excess capacity. The second half of the 1880s saw a spending spree, mostly on investment goods and significantly on land and housing. Much of this was financed, one way or another, by Australian financial intermediaries borrowing overseas the savings of Scottish and English depositors, which contributed to Australia's current account deficit. Then the beginning of the 1890s witnessed a contraction and swing to excess capacity. At the height of the speculative mania, in the housing market new houses and office blocks had stood unoccupied. The first signal of the end to the Australian boom was, in fact, the collapse of a major building society at the end of 1889. Other land and mortgage firms soon fell as distrust and loss spread. Deposits of these quasi-banks drained away while land values adjusted downwards. Between the winters of 1891 and 1893, fifty-four deposit-accepting financial intermediaries closed, 60 per cent permanently. The first commercial bank failed in January 1893 and the second in April. From this time until the middle of May no less than twelve banks failed; that is, in five months half of the banks in existence in Australia closed their doors. Nearly all those that suspended payment reopened from one to three months later. But their creditors, the banks' own depositors, lost in that they accepted deferred deposits or other instruments (including stock and debentures) in place of their original deposits; they lost liquidity and choice. That they raised few objections suggests that these arrangements offered more by their calculus of expected utility than risky survival and possible liquidation.

Three historically motivated questions

Three questions arise from this sketch of a century ago which are relevant to banking today. First, in a period of 'free banking', what caused the shift in the riskiness of loans issued? Secondly, was branch networking harmful to bank efficiency? Thirdly, what caused the closures and could it happen again?

The default risk on individual loans arose in the course of the boom and with bankers' retreat from the 'real bills doctrine'. Land and housing prices are subject to strong growth-reversals in the medium run, which increases the default rate on advances. The growth in banking in the 1880s was associated with a strong element of competitive rivalry. As discussed above, rivalry did not mean so much price competition, but the more prevalent form of non-price competition, notably branching. It can now be suggested that another form of non-price competition was the making of more risky loans with a higher than hitherto potential for failure. Non-price rivalry as the norm of competitive behaviour may thus have increased banks' exposure to risk. Moreover, in an environment where credit-worthiness has generally deteriorated, most banks and bankers cannot afford to be choosy. At first the major commercial trading banks shied away from speculative land ventures. But this proved impossible; the question of involvement was one of degree. Through their normal transactions the banks came by deposits built on funds that non-bank intermediaries obtained in Britain; they accepted bills of exchange arising out of land transactions; they acted directly as bankers to the quasi-banks and, in time, approved overdrafts to known speculators secured by land. For not to do so penalized a bank's market share and shareholders' profit. As one banker put it, 'they have now to accept speculative business or to send their money [back] to London and let [others] take their place'. The same writer was later to add that the banker who 'does not run with the multitude gets trodden under foot'.[37] This attitude was prevalent in banking circles a century later. There may have been another factor at work on the side of the debtors, at least in the 1880s. While the requisite data are not available, it is quite likely that wealth was increasingly being concentrated in fewer hands. Now, a side effect of the growing wealth disparity is the rise in speculative investment. This follows from the Arrow–Pratt hypothesis of *decreasing absolute risk aversion.* If the marginal utility of income declines with income growth, the risk premium is smaller at higher levels of income. So, as the distribution of income grows the overall riskiness of investments made by the rich also grows, giving rise to, or encouraging, a speculative fever.

We turn now to our second question. Financial commentators and bankers of the day (and historians since) often portrayed branching as excessive and wasteful. Yet some American commentators today suggest that the repeal of regulations in the United States which restrict branching would, at a minimum, reduce the need for deposit insurance, because of the favourable effects of risk pooling. Certainly, the branch networks in Australia provided room for risk pooling not open to a unit bank. A unit bank in a single district could be ruined by bad debts incurred by random localized disturbances – drought, floods, disease. Returns from a number of *diverse* regions are likely to be imperfectly correlated. Hence returns from a given investment sum spread across diverse regions are likely to exhibit less variability than the returns of a single (constituent) region. Given that Australia's climate, geography, pests, and outputs of farms and factories vary widely, Australian banks had considerable room for risk pooling. Some bankers explicitly acknowledged this. John Sawers, superintendent of one of the biggest banks, reported that he endeavoured 'to pursue a conservative and discriminatory – yet a progressive – policy, avoiding too large risks, and so *widely distributing our business* that depression in any one industry or Colony would not seriously affect the Bank's position'.[38] We also know that, of the three largest banks that did not close their doors in 1893, all had extensive branch networks. While risk pooling provides a logic for branching, pushed beyond a certain limit, however, the practice at the margin causes the marginal cost per pound deposit and loan to rise and expected profits to fall.

Did banks push branching and risk pooling to the point where they were not minimizing marginal cost and maximizing expected profits? For an increase in output, the Australian banks were able to expand their business by increasing output per branch, branch intensity, or by increasing the number of branches. Maximizing expected profit and minimizing the marginal cost of expanding output entails that the marginal costs of these two modes of output expansion be equated. What happened in the past? In a bid to answer this question, a linear in logarithms bank real cost function was estimated on pooled cross-section time-series data of twelve banks. The model posits bank costs as a function of output, Y; the two modes of expanding output – branch intensity, BN, and number of branches, BI; two output compositional variables, X_1, X_2; a time trend; and binary variables representing eleven of the twelve banks,[39] the 1893 financial crisis and the state of the business cycle.[40]

Thus

$$\log\left(\frac{CST}{w}\right)_t = \Omega_1 + \Omega_2 \log Y_t + \Omega_3 \log BI_t + \Omega_4 \log BN_t + \Omega_5 \log X_{1_t} + \Omega_6 \log X_{2_t} + \Omega_7 \, TME_j + \Omega_8 D_{BUSC} + \Omega_9 D_{1893} + \Omega(D_i) + \varepsilon_t \qquad (1)$$

$$i = 10\text{–}20$$

where:

CST	=	operating costs of banks
w	=	index of wage input cost
Y	=	bank output, i.e. total *real* value of accounts in credit (deposits) and debit (advances), the deflator being that of GNE
BI	=	branch intensity, i.e. branches per £'000 of the real £ value of accounts in credit (deposits) and debit (advances), the deflator being that of GNE
BN	=	number of branches
X_{1_t}	=	composition of output: ratio of interest bearing deposits to the bank's total deposits
X_{2_t}	=	composition of output: ratio of advances to the bank's total assets
TME_j	=	time trend (j = 1877, 1878 . . . 1914)
D_i	=	bank binary variables for (n − 1) banks
D_{1893}	=	binary variable for 1893 crisis
D_{BUSC}	=	binary variable for whether economy is above or below trend of capacity
ε	=	disturbance
t	=	year

The econometric estimates are reported in Table 10.4. The third column includes output as a whole, Y, as well as the two modes of increasing output, increasing the number of branches, BN, and increasing output per branch, BI. If the equation is correctly specified, output as a whole, Y, should be redundant and statistically insignificant, as is the case. This equation suggests, as does that reported in column 2 omitting the redundant Y variable, that marginal costs are approximately trebled if output is increased by increasing the number of

Table 10.4 Bank cost functions (linear in logarithms)

Variables	*OLS regression coefficients on variables*		
Constant	−4.42 (−1.69)	7.07 (3.13)**	7.12 (3.15)**
Output (Y)	0.25 (4.74)**		0.03 (0.77)
Output mode: branch intensity (BI)		0.31 (8.97)**	0.29 (7.53)**
Output mode: branch numbers (BN)		0.93 (17.48)**	0.98 (16.06)**
Output homogeneity controls (X_1)	−0.35 (−5.58)**	−1.05 (−1.08)	−0.03 (−0.67)
Output homogeneity controls (X_2)	−0.12 (−0.67)	−0.37 (−2.94)**	−0.39 (−3.00)**
D_1	−0.05 (−0.71)	−0.19 (−3.67)**	0.18 (3.44)**
D_2	0.26 (5.92)**	0.45 (12.65)**	0.45 (12.66)**
D_3	−0.27 (−6.32)**	0.04 (1.05)	0.04 (1.02)
D_4	−0.30 (−5.64)**	−0.19 (−5.10)**	−0.19 (5.04)**
D_5	−0.04 (−1.13)	0.11 (3.85)**	0.11 (3.89)**
D_6	0.11 (−2.61)*	0.18 (6.00)**	0.18 (5.98)**
D_7	−0.11 (−2.64)**	0.30 (7.12)**	0.30 (7.06)**
D_8	0.35 (8.64)**	0.73 (17.22)**	0.73 (17.14)**
D_9	−0.09 (−0.95)	0.47 (6.59)**	0.46 (6.41)**
D_{10}	−0.91 (−12.00)**	0.67 (4.97)**	0.66 (4.81)**
D_{11}	−0.86 (−10.29)**	0.31 (3.00)**	0.31 (2.98)**
Trend (TME)	0.00 (0.60)	−0.00 (−3.61)**	−0.00 (−3.64)**
Financial Crisis (D_{1893})	−0.02 (−0.38)	−0.16 (−4.08)**	−0.14 (−3.78)**
Business Cycle (D_{BUSC})	−0.10 (−4.86)**	−0.01 (−6.02)**	−0.01 (−5.74)**
$\bar{R}^2$	0.96	0.98	0.98

Notes: $\bar{R}^2$ is the coefficient of determination. The figures under the coefficients are t-values. Asterisks indicate degrees of significance. One asterisk indicates significance at the 5% level while two indicates significance at the 1% level. The Durbin–Watson statistic can be calculated, but is meaningless because of discontinuities in the time domain associated with switching *between* banks in the sample.

branches, rather than output per branch. The first column provides a further test of this conclusion by omitting the two separate methods of expanding output, modes *BI* and *BN*, and including output as a whole, *Y*. If there was overbranching, expansions in *Y*, output, should be subject to scale economies because of the excess capacity in place. The results indeed suggest marked scale economies from increasing output: a 10 per cent increase in output raised their costs only of the order of 2.5 per cent.

The excess capacity associated with banks' expanding by increasing the number of branches, when it could have been three times as cheap for them to expand by attracting more business into existing branches, is, other things equal, clearly incompatible with the standard economic theory that banks *should* and *do* minimize costs and maximize expected profits.[41] However, overbranching is compatible with the rival mean-variance model. In the mean-variance model the goal of minimizing marginal cost and maximizing expected profits (*mean* returns) is traded off against another goal, that of reducing the firm's risk of failure by undertaking risk pooling and other methods of reducing the riskiness of profits (the *variance* of returns).[42]

Did risk pooling save some banks from failure, specifically from the closures of 1893? Could, to answer our third question, systemic failure on the scale of 1893 happen again? The question of why banks fail is obviously a complex one. The hypothesis examined here is that the probability of failure arises where banks pursue behaviour which leads to relatively low capital adequacy, liquidity, and profit ratios. To this common ratio analysis the degree of risk pooling has been added. The four panels of Figure 10.9 show these ratios. Core capital roughly corresponds to Tier 1 capital and assets under the BIS Basle capital-adequacy guidelines: capital is shareholders' capital and reserves, assets include cash balances, government securities, and loans (housing loans receiving full weight, not 0.5). The liquidity ratio is the ratio of banks' Australian cash balances to their private notes and total deposit liabilities. The risk-pooling ratio measures the relative branch spread of a bank; specifically, it is the ratio of the square root of the variance of a bank's branch activity across states to the average number of its branches (that is, coefficient of variation). Thus lower values of this ratio imply higher degrees of risk pooling.[43] The profit ratio represents the quotient, recorded net profits divided by earning assets. The time profiles shown in the panels are the unweighted averages of the individual trading banks, grouped in accord with whether or not a bank suspended payments to its customers in the course of 1893. The graphs show the non-failed banks to have had stronger core capital and liquidity ratios, to have risk-pooled their business more, and to have enjoyed a consistently higher return on assets than those that failed. But they also suggest *both* non-failed and failed banks shared common elements: core capital adequacy and profit rates were sliding down, risk pooling was not visibly increasing, nor liquidity ratios much – which were at all-time record lows.

Elsewhere, a logit model using the four ratios has been estimated.[44] The estimated equations provided snapshots of the probability (log odds ratio) of

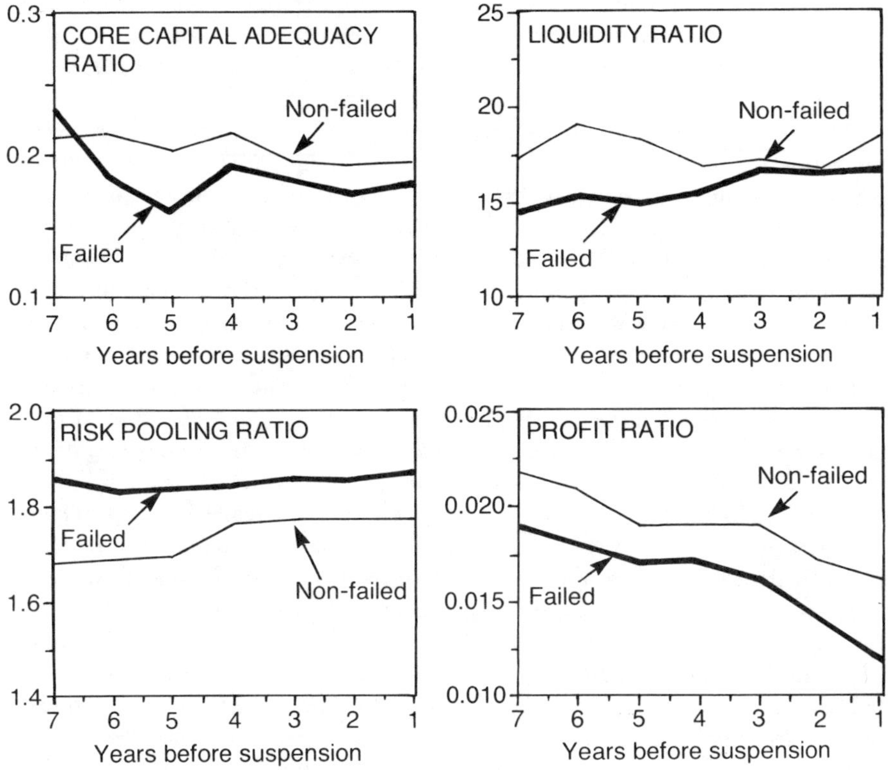

Figure 10.9 Ratios of failed and non-failed banks
Source: Butlin-Pope bank database

failing in 1893, one, three, five, and seven years before the event. The model succeeded in predicting 0.67 to 0.76 of the individual bank failures that occurred. Profit and core capital adequacy ratios were statistically significant in some snapshots and all variables combined met the chi square test for joint significance in one of the four cases. The equations were, however, unsatisfactory in other ways, notably in the low *t*-values and (with the exception of the risk-pooling ratio) switching signs of the estimated coefficients. Relatedly, asymptotic properties underpinning the model were in doubt with so few bank observations – less than twenty-five. Limited degrees of freedom made it difficult to pin down the statistical relations tightly. There were also certain omissions from the estimated model, one being the human capital and decision skills of the management of the different banks. It is thought that at the industry level the rapid expansion of banking in the 1880s may have increased the demand for middle and lower management faster than supply, with some possible dilution of skills.

The role of risk pooling in Australian bank closures is, then, ambiguous. It is known that non-failed banks risk-pooled marginally more and the big bank survivors probably a lot more, but we have been unable to satisfactorily test this statistically for the whole group on the data available.

There is another interpretation of these results. That the difference between the ratios for 'failed' and 'non-failed' banks is comparatively small might be explained by an omitted factor – the banks' choice to close (or at least that of some of them). S.J. Butlin was the first to raise this possibility.[45] The view has also been canvassed by Pope and Dowd.[46] Broadly, reconstruction meant the setting up of a new company using the old name; accession of new capital, a high proportion of which was to be supplied by the creditors of the old bank (the depositors); deferment of payment of deposits. Reconstruction became binding with the approval of three-quarters of the creditors. In the case of the first bank to reconstruct, the Commercial Bank, its depositors accepted one-third of their claims in new shares, the balance being deferred for five years. Some other banks may have followed to seize the vantage ground offered by reconstruction.[47]

Could 1893 happen again? Certainly not on the same scale. The central bank now acts as lender of last resort to trading banks. Had there been a central bank in 1893, then the savings of depositors with the Commercial Bank would have been protected. Moreover, there are now capital adequacy rules in place and the Reserve Bank does take a detailed interest in the affairs of the 'Big Four'. Merchant banks, building societies, and the subsidiaries of the trading banks can fail, though recent history in Victoria shows that governments may even find it prudent to rescue small depositors caught in building society collapses. Tighter supervision of these institutions seems likely in the future. Nor is it likely that depositors accustomed to trading bank deposit security implied by the presence of the Reserve Bank would easily surrender to the sort of terms involved in the bank reconstructions of the last century.

Allais' forgetfulness hypothesis, bank failures, and regulation

None of this means that we live in a riskless world and that bankers and investors will not make wrong decisions. Nobel Laureate Maurice Allais has argued that actions are supremely affected by what he terms the 'psychological' rate of interest, and that forgetfulness progressively erodes conservatism in monetary matters.[48] This seems to be an important but neglected factor in discussions of bank regulation. Did the contraction of the 1890s and the bank closures impose economic discipline on the banks such as to make subsequent regulation really unnecessary? In short, what lessons did Australian bankers and their customers learn from the first episode of regulation-free banking?

For its part the public viewed the banks with considerable suspicion. The public's cash to bank deposits ratio rose sharply (some of the increase reflecting the reconstructions), and suspicion lingered on for many years. Even forty years later when the 1936 Royal Commission came to investigate the need for an

Australian central bank, the experience of bank creditors in the 1893 crisis was not forgotten. As for the banks, the crisis imposed a reassessment of credit risk, reserve, and portfolio management toward more conservative behaviour. Amalgamations ensued in the 1920s and collusive price agreements stuck even tighter than before. Had the banks learned anything useful? In the medium term, certainly yes. One is left to ponder the longrun *sans* central banking. On Allais' hypothesis, conservatism would be eroded.

Such an erosion has taken place in banking circles in recent years. With deregulation the banking industry grew strongly. The growth occurred initially against the background of a strongly growing economy, rather as it had in the 1880s. Profitability increased and, as it did so, expectations of shareholders and bank managements grew, not just for continued but accelerating profit growth. With this went a rise in credit risk, a drop in credit standards. Recently a number of celebrated entrepreneurs have failed; many in delayed reaction to the October 1987 Crash. Today banks' bad and doubtful debts and non-accruing loans are sky-rocketing. Though it is totally improbable that a major bank will fail – and be permitted to do so by the central bank – the recent history of risk behaviour in banking recalls events of a distant past. Old lessons are forgotten.

CONCLUSIONS: LESSONS OF TIME

History, like life, is a continuum of past and present. The passage of time in the historian's sweep of the past provides a vital perspective often missing in the writings of others, including economists and 'econocrats'. Economic history in its study of the longrun can marry that essential perspective with the powerful weaponry of economic analysis. While not all human action is driven by economic considerations alone, the extent to which it is makes such a marriage important. The study of the longrun provides greater degrees of freedom, to use a statistician's term, to reach closer to the 'truths' of economic behaviour. Also, if players in financial markets are notoriously forgetful, as Allais has suggested, then analysis of the longrun may be fruitful in lowering the rate at which players and decision-makers discount the past (and implicitly their, and society's, future income streams).

In this regard, this chapter has suggested that there are many striking similarities between the financial systems and economic behaviour of the 'free-banking' Australia of the late nineteenth century and the post-deregulation Australian banking of today. In both, banks were largely freed of constraints. Yet in retail trade a handful of banks took, and still take, the lion's share of business. Since the recent deregulation, banks have been tardy in 'unbundling' services and competing on the basis of service fees. Evidence of fierce price competition between the main banks in terms of interest rates is scant. In the half century before the First World War there was effectively no price competition; rather there is evidence of intent by the major banks to collude in setting rates. Instead of competing on the basis of price, the banks pursued market share through non-price oligopolistic rivalry, branching and advertising being important ingredients of their strategies.

A number of submissions to the Campbell Committee certainly stressed misgivings with branch proliferation – just as financial commentators had a century before. The modern commentators blamed excessive branching on government intervention in banking, specifically the imposition of ceilings on interest rates. Government control of rates forced banks, so the argument went, into non-price competition. Remove the controls and the nature of competition would change, yielding efficiency gains and lower margins to the benefit of consumers of banking. Those who argued in this way missed a lesson of history. Branching was a key characteristic of the Australian banking *before* the imposition of controls during the Second World War. It was, and is, a feature of oligopolistic behaviour. Given the prohibitive set-up costs, simply issuing licences to new entrants (other than building societies who already had branches) was unlikely to change the face of retailing or bring margins tumbling down.

In this chapter it has been argued that, in the course of the late nineteenth century, Australian commercial banks accepted higher credit risk. This reflected, in part, non-price oligopolistic rivalry over the market share. At the same time the banks' borrowers were subject to decreasing absolute risk aversion (the Arrow–Pratt hypothesis) as incomes rose in the years before the 1890s depression. In short, risk premia fell as incomes advanced. This may have been accentuated by growing wealth disparities, for as the distribution of income grows, so the overall riskiness of investments made by the rich also grows. This implication of the Arrow–Pratt hypothesis takes us some way to explaining the speculative fever of the late 1880s, as it may also do of the mid-1980s. Moreover, the speculative fever and credit expansion which fuelled bank growth in both periods was associated with the increasing delegation of decision-making to middle management. Bank growth outstripped the supply of skilled upper-level management, which partly explains the deterioration in judgement, the rise in credit risk and, in the end, loan losses and doubtful debts.

Finally, it has also been suggested that Allais' hypothesis concerning what he calls the 'psychological' interest rate, from which he derives his notion of forgetfulness in financial affairs, is a useful conjecture capable of illuminating issues of deregulation and reregulation. The fact that forgetfulness seems to have progressively eroded conservatism in monetary matters (in Australia and elsewhere) challenges the almost paradigmatic view of the deregulators that profit maximization and market discipline guarantee the stability of financial systems.

NOTES

1 WHAT CAN HISTORICAL ANALYSIS CONTRIBUTE TO THE SCIENCE OF ECONOMICS?

1 See, for example, B. Higgins, *Economic Development: Principles, Problems and Policies*, London, Constable, 1959; M. Blaug, *Economic Theory in Retrospect*, 3rd edn, Cambridge, Cambridge University Press, 1978; and F.H. Hahn, and R.C.D. Matthews, 'The theory of economic growth: a survey', *Economic Journal*, December 1964, 74, pp. 779–902.

2 See D.J. Harris, 'Classical growth models', in J. Eatwell, M. Milgate and P. Newman (eds), *The New Palgrave: A Dictionary of Economics*, vol. 1, London, Macmillan, 1987, p. 445.

3 The model presented here is largely that of Ricardo which incorporated elements of the theory of both Smith and Malthus.

4 In G.D. Snooks, *Economics Without Time: A Science Blind to the Forces of Historical Change*, London, Macmillan, 1992, chs 6 and 7, it is shown quantitatively that England was subject to competitive forces as early as the eleventh century, that economic agents at the macro and micro levels acted rationally, and that rapid economic growth was achieved during periods when pestilence was absent.

5 E.L. Jones, *Growth Recurring: Economic Change in World History*, Oxford, Clarendon Press, 1988.

6 J.A. Schumpeter, *The Theory of Economic Development: An Inquiry into Profits, Capital, Credit, Interest and the Business Cycle*, Cambridge, Mass., Harvard University Press, 1949, p. 58.

7 Schumpeter, *The Theory of Economic Development*, p. 235.

8 Schumpeter, *The Theory of Economic Development*, p. 236.

9 Schumpeter, *The Theory of Economic Development*, pp. 240–1.

10 Schumpeter, *The Theory of Economic Development*, p. 243.

11 R.F. Harrod, 'An essay in dynamic theory', *Economic Journal*, March 1939, 49, pp. 14–33; and E.D. Domar, 'Capital expansion rate of growth and employment', *Econometrica*, April 1946, 14, pp. 137–47.

12 This was first pointed out by Trevor Swan in 'Economic growth and capital accumulation', *Economic Record*, November 1956, 32, p. 343; but was missed by Solow in 'A contribution to the theory of economic growth', *Quarterly Journal of Economics*, February 1956, 70, pp. 65–94.

13 F.H. Hahn, 'Neoclassical growth theory', in J. Eatwell, M. Milgate and P. Newman (eds), *The New Palgrave: A Dictionary of Economics*, vol. 3, London, Macmillan, 1987, p. 626.

14 The main exception was France, which experienced higher levels of inflation,

possibly as an outcome of their system of indicative planning.

15 See Swan, 'Economic growth and capital accumulation'; and Solow, 'A contribution to the theory of economic growth'.

16 These articles, which represent only a fraction of the research on growth, are included in the Bibliography.

17 Hahn, 1987, 'Neoclassical growth theory', pp. 625–6.

18 The study is N.G. Butlin, *Investment in Australian Economic Development, 1861–1900*, Cambridge, Cambridge University Press, 1964, which is discussed in some detail in Snooks *Economics Without Time*, ch. 4.

19 B.J. Barro and P.M. Romer, 'Economic growth', *NBER Reporter*, Fall 1990, p. 1.

20 P.M. Romer, 'Increasing returns and long-run growth', *Journal of Political Economy*, 1986, 94, pp. 1002–37.

21 G.M. Grossman and E. Helpman, 'Trade, innovation and growth', *American Economic Review*, May 1990, 80, pp. 86 and 90.

22 See Snooks, *Economics Without Time*, ch. 3.

23 This he takes from A. Maddison, 'Per capita output in the long-run', *Kyklos*, 1979, 32, pp. 412–29.

24 A similar dramatic example of what I have called 'historical squeezing' also occurred in the sixteenth century, when growth rates rose to 1.6 per cent per annum between 1492 and 1560, once the vice-like grip of pestilence that had existed for a century was released. See Snooks, *Economics Without Time*, ch. 7.

25 Romer, 'Increasing returns and long-run growth' pp. 1011–2.

26 This evidence is presented (respectively) in G.D. Snooks and J. McDonald, *Domesday Economy: a New Approach to Anglo-Norman History*, Oxford, Clarendon Press, 1986, chs 6 and 10; and Snooks, *Economics Without Time*, ch. 7.

27 An attempt has been made to graphically illustrate these great waves of economic change for England between 1000 and 1990 in Snooks, *Economics Without Time*, p. 257 (Figure 7.3).

28 Grossman and Helpman, 'Trade, innovation and growth', p. 86. See also R.E. Lucas, 'On the mechanics of economic development', *Journal of Monetary Economics*, January 1988, 22, pp. 3–22; and I. Ehrlich, 'The problem of development: introduction', *Journal of Political Economy*, October 1990, 98, pp. S1–S11.

29 Grossman and Helpman, 'Trade, innovation and growth', p. 87.

30 Grossman and Helpman, 'Trade, innovation and growth', p. 86.

31 On the general issue of trade and growth, see A.G. Kenwood and A.L. Lougheed, *The Growth of the International Economy, 1820–1980: An Introductory Text*, London, Allen & Unwin, 1983. The literature on individual open economies is vast; on Australia, for example, see Butlin, *Investment in Australian Economic Development, 1861–1900.*

32 Grossman and Helpman, 'Trade, innovation and growth', p. 86 (my emphasis).

33 For example, see D.C. Colander and A.W. Coats (eds), *The Spread of Economic Ideas*, Cambridge/New York, Cambridge University Press, 1989, pp. 27–8 and 33–4; and W.L. Hansen, 'Educating and training new economics Ph.D.s: how good a job are we doing?' *American Economic Review*, May 1990, 80, p. 437.

34 See the 1992 latest newsletter of the Royal Economics Society.

35 See, for example, G.D. Snooks, *Portrait of the Family within the Total Economy: A study in Longrun Dynamics, Australia 1788–1990*, Cambridge, Cambridge University Press, 1993.

36 See D. North, and R.P. Thomas, *The Rise of the Western World*, Cambridge, Cambridge University Press, 1973; and Snooks, *Portrait of the Family within the Total Economy*, ch. 7.

2 HISTORICAL ECONOMICS IN THE LONGRUN: SOME IMPLICATIONS OF PATH-DEPENDENCE

1 It may be helpful to explain that I am an economist–economic historian. That label, however, does not tell you all you need to know. As Robert Solow remarked some years ago in the *American Economic Review* (May 1985), many of those who described themselves as 'new' economic historians were pretty near indistinguishable from the mass of practitioners of neoclassical economics, except for the fact that they appeared to possess an unusually high tolerance for dust. My case, however, is rather different. Most of my working life has been spent as a member of a small dissenting sect – advocating *historical* economics – within the more-or-less tolerant (albeit largely indifferent) society of academic economists.

2 D.N. McCloskey, *Econometric History*, London, Macmillan Education, 1987, p. 14.

3 And not only that: economists committed to understanding path-dependent phenomena also will accept it as both more natural and more informative to converse with analytically inclined historians who today are finding themselves drawn back toward the narrative mode. In this view I find myself in close agreement with a central theme of Donald McCloskey's Presidential Address to the Social Science Association ('Ancients and moderns', *Social Science History*, Fall 1990, 14, 3, pp. 289–303); but, rather less so with Lawrence Stone's account of the revival of narrative (*The Past and the Present Revisited*, London/New York, Routledge & Kegan Paul, 1987, ch. 3). The term 'narrative' is used here in its fairly conventional sense, to refer to the organization of material in a chronologically sequential order, thereby giving priority to detailed description rather than detached analysis, and emphasis to the coherence of the content when it is arranged in a story-line, however intricate the plot and sub-plots may be.

4 For example, P.A. David, *Technical Choice, Innovation and Economic Growth: Essays on American and British Experience in the Nineteenth Century*, Cambridge, Cambridge University Press, 1975; P.A. David, 'Clio and the economics of QWERTY', *American Economic Review*, May 1985, 75, 2, pp. 332–7; P.A. David, 'Understanding the economics of QWERTY: the necessity of history', in W.N. Parker (ed.), *Economic History and the Modern Economist*, Oxford, Basil Blackwell, 1986, pp. 30–49; P.A. David, 'Some new standards for the economics of standardization in the information age', in P. Dasgupta and P. Stoneman (eds), *Economic Policy and Technological Performance*, Cambridge, Cambridge University Press, 1987, pp. 206–39; P.A. David, 'The hero and the herd in technological history: reflections on Thomas Edison and the "Battle of the Systems"', ch. 2 in P. Higgonet , D.S. Landes, H. Rosovsky (eds), *Favorites of Fortune: Technology, Growth and Economic Development since the Industrial Revolution*, Cambridge, Mass., Harvard University Press, 1991.

5 For example, P.A. David, 'Path-dependence: putting the past into the future of economics', *Institute for Mathematical Studies in the Social Sciences Technical Report*, no. 533, Stanford University, November 1988; P.A. David, 'Path-dependence and predictability in dynamic systems with local network externalities: a paradigm for historical economics', forthcoming in C. Freeman and D. Foray (eds), *Technology and the Wealth of Nations*, London, Pinter Publishers, 1992; P.A. David, 'Why and when does history really matter?', Presidential Address delivered to the Economic History Association, in Washington, D.C., September 1989 (forthcoming in the *Journal of Economic History*).

6 For citations to works illustrative of these new departures, see David, 'path-dependence'; also, the more recent papers by Paul Romer, Kinimori Matsuyama, and others contributed to the Symposium on New Growth Theory in the *Quarterly Journal of Economics*, May 1991; and the papers by Durlauf, Krugman, Heckman,

and Milgrom, Roberts and Qian (from the session 'Path-dependence in economics: the invisible hand in the grip of the past'), in the *Proceedings of the American Economic Association*, May 1991. This is by no means a comprehensive listing.

7 See W.B. Arthur, 'Positive feedbacks in the economy', *Scientific American*, February 1990, 262, 2, pp. 80–5, for a recent non-technical overview of positive feedback mechanisms in economics and their significance. A more technical exposition appears in Arthur's lecture 'The economy and complexity', in D.L. Stein (ed.), *Lectures in the Sciences of Complexity* (Santa Fe Institute Studies in the Sciences of Complexity, Lectures, vol. 1), Menlo Park, CA, Addison-Wesley, 1989, pp. 713–34.

8 As R.G.D. Collingwood, in his review of *Selected Essays of J.B. Bury*, *The English Historical Review*, July 1931, 183, pp. 461–519, pointed out, Bury remained caught in the contradiction between his lingering sympathies for to the positivist view predominant in the later nineteenth century, according to which the business of the 'scientific historian' was to discover the universal laws connecting cause and effects, and the anti-positivist position he enunciated in his Cambridge *Inaugural Lecture* (1903). According to the latter, the unique and contingent had to be acknowledged as the essential elements of history. But, for Bury, lacking the presuppositions of an 'idealist' philosophy, this seemed to imply that history was unintelligible (irrational) in so far as it is essentially a play of 'individualities'. (I am grateful to Stanley Lebergott for referring me to Collingwood's review of Temperley's edition of Bury's essays.)

9 See F.J. Teggart, *Theory of History*, New Haven, Yale University Press, 1925, p. 77.

10 Attention has been drawn to Teggart's work recently by the paleontologist and evolutionary theorist Niles Eldredge, in *Time Frames: The Rethinking of Darwinian Evolution and the Theory of Punctuated Equilibria*, New York, Simon and Schuster, 1985, pp. 22–8.

11 Teggart, *Theory of History*, pp. 74–5.

12 Teggart, *Theory of History*, p. 75.

13 Teggart, *Theory of History*, p. 78.

14 Teggart, *Theory of History*, p. 79.

15 See Teggart, *Theory of History*, pp. 85–7.

16 O.H. Taylor, 'Economics and the idea of natural law', in *Economics and Liberalism: Collected Papers*, Cambridge, Mass., Harvard University Press, 1955, pp. 42–3.

17 Teggart, *Theory of History*, p. 86.

18 Dugald Stewart, *The Collected Works of Dugald Stewart* (edited by Sir William Hamilton), Edinburgh, T. Constable, 1854–60; Farnborough, Gregg International Publishers, 1971, vol. 10, p. 60.

19 A.-A., Cournot, *Researches into the Mathematical Principles of the Theory of Wealth*, first French edition, 1838; English translation by N.T. Bacon, 1897; rev. edn, New York, Macmillan, 1927, p. 36.

20 David, 'path-dependence'.

21 Teggart, *Theory of History*, pp. 124–37; Eldredge, *Time Frames*, pp. 22–8.

22 Jean Baptiste Lamarck, *Hydrogéologie* Paris, 1802, quoted in H.F. Osborn *From the Greeks to Darwin*, New York, Scribner, 2nd edn, 1929, p. 237.

23 See Eldredge, *Times Frames*.

24 See R.A. Cowan and M.J. Rizzo, 'The genetic-causal moment in economic theory', *C.V. Starr Center for Applied Economics, Economic Research Report*, no. 91–13, February 1991, for further discussion.

25 Compare K.J. Arrow and F.H. Hahn, *General Competitive Equilibrium*, Edinburgh, Oliver & Boyd, 1971, and F.M. Fisher, *The Disequilibrium Foundations of Equilibrium Economics*, New York, Cambridge University Press, 1983.

26 Cowan and Rizzo, 'The genetic-causal moment in economic theory', pp. 9–10.

27 See Fisher, *The Disequilibrium Foundations of Equilibrium Economics.*

28 For surveys, see for example, H. Haken, *Synergetics*, 2nd edn, Berlin, Springer-Verlag, 1978; I. Prigogine, *From Being to Becoming: Time and Complexity in the Physical Sciences*, New York, W.H. Freeman, 1980; I. Prigogine and I. Stengers, *Order Out of Chaos*, Boulder, New Science Library, 1984; and D. Stein, (ed.), *Lectures in the Sciences of Complexity* (Santa Fe Institute Studies in the Sciences of Complexity, Lectures Volume 1), Menlo Park, CA, Addison-Wesley, 1989.

29 See P.A. David and W.E. Steinmueller, 'The impact of information technology upon economic science', *Prometheus*, June 1991, 9, 1, pp. 35–61, for further discussion of the implications of the advances in computer and software for research (and teaching) in economics.

30 See, for example, Stein, *Lectures in the Sciences of Complexity.* The term 'complex system' has no standard meaning and is used in many different ways. Some writers use it to signify deterministic systems with chaotic dynamics; others refer to cellular automata, disordered many-body systems, 'neural' networks, adaptive algorithms, pattern-forming systems, and still others. Daniel Stein, p. xiv, observes that complex systems share the property of exhibiting surprising and unexpected behaviour that somehow seems to be a property of the system as a whole. So a common characteristic of 'complexity research' is a synthetic approach, as opposed to reductionism.

31 See J. Haltiwanger and M. Waldman, 'Responders vs. nonresponders: a new perspective on heterogeneity', *UCLA Working Paper*, April 1988.

32 See, for example, W.B. Arthur, 'Competing technologies, increasing returns, and lock-in by historical events', *Economic Journal*, March 1989, 99, 394, pp. 116–31.

33 See David, 'The hero and the herd'.

34 M. Kurz, 'On the impossibility of learning the equilibrium price process in a complex economic environment', *Institute for Mathematical Studies in the Social Sciences Summer Workshop Paper*, Stanford University, August 1988.

35 F. Crick, *What Mad Pursuit: A Personal View of Scientific Discovery* , New York, Basic Books, 1988, pp. 109–11, 138–41.

36 Crick, *What Mad Pursuit*, p. 139.

3 THE LOST DIMENSION: ECONOMICS WITHOUT TIME

This chapter is based upon work undertaken for G.D. Snooks, *Economics Without Time: A Science Blind to the Forces of Historical Change*, London, Macmillan, 1993.

1 I am not concerned here with the various dissenting factions within economics such as the Marxists, neo-Ricardians, post-Keynesians, etc. The word 'historicist' is used simply to refer to those who argue that history provides an important source of economic knowledge that is relevant to current problems. It is not used in the Popperian sense of those who subscribe to the idea of meaning in history.

2 This definition is deliberately general because of the range of different views of past and present economists concerning the essence of their discipline. For a brief survey of these views see P.D. Groenewegen, '"Political economy" and "economics"', in J. Eatwell, M. Milgate and P. Newman (eds), *The New Palgrave: A Dictionary of Economics*, vol. 3, London, Macmillan, 1987, pp. 904–7.

3 On this definition, applied economics (including experimental economics) is a special case of economic history, in that it is concerned only with one point in time, the 'present', whereas economic history is concerned with all points in time.

4 Just as applied economics is a special case of economic history, so too is the comparative approach, as it employs data relating to events that have happened – the domain of economic history.

5 Naturally, the degree to which these problems have affected individual economies in the Western world has varied.

6 There are some, like Paul A. David, who argue that economists and economically literate historians should cooperate to build a new set of models – path-dependent models – that take into account the influence of the past on the present. See Chapter 2, the Bibliography under P.A. David, and the conference session on 'Path dependence in economics: the invisible hand in the grip of the past', *American Economic Review*, May 1991, 81, 2, pp. 70–88.

7 P. Deane, *The State and the Economic System*, Oxford, OPUS, 1989, p. 36.

8 See, for example, C. Colander and A.W. Coats (eds), *The Spread of Economic Ideas*, Cambridge/New York, Cambridge University Press, 1986, pp. 27–8, 33–4.

9 For an illuminating discussion of the English Exchequer in the twelfth century see R.L. Poole, *The Exchequer in the Twelfth Century*, Oxford, Clarendon Press, 1912.

10 Deane, *The State and the Economic System*, discusses the early emergence of political economy largely in terms of changing supply considerations, including the general intellectual culture (i.e. the development of a scientific method in the natural sciences) rather than a response to both demand and supply conditions.

11 The outstanding works in this area are J.A. Schumpeter, *History of Economic Analysis*, London, Allen & Unwin, 1963; M. Blaug, *Economic Theory in Retrospect*, Cambridge, Cambridge University Press, 1983; P. Deane, *Evolution of Economic Ideas*, Cambridge/New York, Cambridge University Press, 1978; and Deane, *The State and the Economic System.*

12 See Deane, *The State and the Economic System*, p. 34; and J.O. Appleby, *Economic Thought and Ideology in Seventeenth Century England*, Princeton, Princeton University Press, 1978.

13 I have been able to trace the physiocratic equation of 'productive' activity with agriculture, and 'unproductive' activities with manufacturing and commerce, back as far as Domesday Book in 1086. See G.D. Snooks and J. McDonald, *Domesday Economy: A New Approach to Anglo-Norman History*, Oxford, Clarendon Press, 1986, p. 19.

14 D.C. Coleman, in *History and the Economic Past*, Oxford, Clarendon Press, 1987, p. 17, sees Smith as part of the 'Scottish enlightenment', which also included David Hume, James Steuart, and John Millar, who, by using history in their discussions of political economy, became the 'progenitors of what we now call economic history'. But, given their rudimentary treatment of history and the fact that there is no clear relationship with the founders of British economic history (Cunningham, Ashley, and Clapham), this argument is questionable.

15 See, for example, G. Becker, *A Treatise on the Family*, Cambridge, Mass., Harvard University Press, 1981.

16 Coleman, *History and the Economic Past*, p. 23.

17 Quoted in Deane, *The State and the Economic System*, p. 88.

18 H.S. Foxwell, 'The economic movement in England', *Quarterly Journal of Economics*, October 1887, 2, pp. 84–103; and J.K. Ingram, *History of Political Economy*, London, Black, 1923, pp. 34–57.

19 Curiously, Jevons first attracted attention with his empirical and statistical work, particularly on cyclical fluctuations. While he claimed that economic theory should be based upon a deductive method employing mathematics, he thought that economic policy should be based upon applied economics that employed a statistical and historical method, and that the laws of social progress should be based upon a study of economic history. But, to his mind, economic theory was the key to the wider profession of economic studies. See G.M. Koot, *English Historical Economics, 1870–1926*, Cambridge, Cambridge University Press, 1987, pp. 26–7.

20 The intellectual climate is discussed in Deane, *The State and the Economic System*, ch. 7. See also S. Collini, D. Winch, and J.W. Burrow, *That Noble Science of Politics: A Study of Nineteenth Century Intellectual History*, Cambridge/New York, Cambridge University Press, 1983.

21 See Koot, *English Historical Economics, 1870–1926*, pp. 27–31. He tends, however, to take Marshall at face value.

22 R.C.O. Matthews and B. Supple, 'Marshall on economic history', unpublished paper, p. 19.

23 Koot, *English Historical Economics, 1870–1926*, p. 147.

24 See Matthew and Supple, 'Marshall on economic history', and Koot, *English Historical Economics, 1870–1926*, pp. 124, 132, 149.

25 Deane, *The State and the Economic System*, p. 135.

26 Matthews and Supple, 'Marshall on economic history', p. 7.

27 See M.S. Morgan, *The History of Econometric Ideas*, Cambridge, Cambridge University Press, 1990, p. 5.

28 The main scholars in this tradition in the first half of the nineteenth century included Roscher, Hildebrand, and Knies, and in the latter part of the century, Wagner and Schmoller.

29 J. Mokyr, 'Evolutionary biology, technological change, and economic history', seminar paper presented to the Economic History Joint Seminar Program, 23 July 1990, Australian National University, Canberra.

30 The changing reputation of these scholars is reflected in the 1896 and 1987 editions of Palgrave. The 1896 entry on Cliffe Leslie, who wore himself out in his militant campaign against deductive economics, ends: 'he will be seen to have taken a leading part in a great work of scientific reform', whereas in 1987 he was seen as a useful critic of neoclassical economics at a time when 'radical criticism of deductive economics was badly needed'. His reputation has changed from 'reformer' to 'critic'. This reflects the changing view of the economics profession regarding historical–empirical studies.

31 Although Mill emphasized the deductive approach, his wide education inevitably led him to using inductive techniques when examining practical issues, such as the land question in Ireland. He also gave considerable support to the historicist Cliffe Leslie. See Koot, *English Historical Economics, 1870–1926*, pp. 44–5.

32 Koot, *English Historical Economics, 1870–1926*, p. 2, goes further when he claims that this school helped the neoclassicists to destroy classical economics. It is clear, however, that the classical school was a century out of date by this time, and was already dead on its feet.

33 A. Kadish, *Historians, Economists, and Economic History*, London, Routledge, 1989.

34 N.S.B. Gras, 'The present condition of economic history', *Quarterly Journal of Economics*, 1920, 34, p. 210.

35 A. Offer, 'Using the past in Britain', *Public Historian*, Fall 1984, 6, 4, pp. 15–34; F.A. Hayek, 'The London School of Economics, 1895–1945', *Economica*, N.S., February 1946, 13, pp. 1–31; Koot, *English Historical Economics, 1870–1926*, ch. 8.

36 The most recent work on this subject appears inconsistent on this issue. Koot, *English Historical Economics, 1870–1926*, argues that, apart from Ashley, the English historical school 'did not aim to construct a systematic historicist economics upon their inductive research' (p. 1), but follows this up with the conflicting statement that they 'were much more successful in their first goal of laying low the old than they were in their second of building a new edifice'.

37 Deane, *The State and the Economic System*, p. 141, quotes a student of Marshall's on the latter point.

38 J.M. Keynes, *The General Theory of Employment, Interest, and Money*, London, Macmillan, 1936, pp. vii–viii.
39 J.M. Keynes, *The Scope and Method of Political Economy*, London, Macmillan, 1891; reprinted New York, A.M. Kelley, 1964.
40 J.M. Keynes, *A Treatise on Probability*, London, Macmillan, 1948.
41 See Morgan, *The History of Econometric Ideas*, ch. 1.
42 G.J. Stigler, 'Palgrave's Dictionary of Economics', *Journal of Economic Literature*, December 1988, 26, p. 1731.
43 The topics include: economic history, cliometrics, industrialization, backwardness, Domesday Book (written by F.W. Maitland in 1894!), Chartism, and open field system. The scholars include: Cunningham, Clapham, Ashley, Gerschenkron, Coghlan (the only Australian economic historian – what of Shann, S.J. Butlin, and N.G. Butlin, who were figures of the first order? No doubt part of the costs of living and working in the antipodes).
44 R.H.I. Palgrave (ed.), *Dictionary of Political Economy*, vol. 2, London, Macmillan, 1896, p. 747.
45 These topics include, among many others: economic history, historical school, historical method, induction method, industrial revolution, domestic system, field systems, early English economic history (eleven pages!), factory acts, famine, and Domesday Book (the same entry as that included in the 1987 edition).
46 For example: gilds, villeins, danegeld, knight's service, and scutage.
47 See G.D. Snooks, 'What should economists be told about the past?', *Australian Economic History Review*, September 1990, 32, 2, pp. 89–94.
48 For example, see B. Higgins, *Economic Development*, London, Constable, 1959, and G.M. Meier, *Leading Issues in Economic Development*, New York, Oxford University Press, 1989.
49 See W.W. Rostow, *The Stages of Economic Growth*, Cambridge, Cambridge University Press, 1963.
50 Deane, *The State and the Economic System*, p. 127.
51 R. M. Solow, 'Faith, hope, and clarity', in D.C. Colander and A.W. Coats (eds), *The Spread of Economic Ideas*, Cambridge/New York, Cambridge University Press, 1989, p. 40.
52 F.H. Hahn, 'Neoclassical growth theory', in J. Eatwell, M. Milgate and P. Newman (eds), *The New Palgrave: A Dictionary of Economics*, vol. 3, London, Macmillan, 1987, p. 625.
53 Morgan, *The History of Econometric Ideas*, p. 263.
54 For a detailed discussion, see M.S. Morgan, 'The stamping out of process analysis in econometrics', unpublished paper, Department of Economic History, London School of Economics.
55 W.L. Hansen, 'Educating and training new economics Ph.D.s: how good a job are we doing?' *American Economic Review*, May 1990, 80, p. 438.
56 For a more detailed discussion, see Snooks, *Economics Without Time*, ch. 2.
57 T.C. Cliffe Leslie, 'The political economy of Adam Smith', in *Essays in Political Economy* , 2nd edn, London, Longmans, Green & Co., 1879, ch. X.
58 Leslie, 'The political economy of Adam Smith', ch. XIV.
59 Leslie, 'The political economy of Adam Smith', p. 231.
60 J.K. Ingram, 'Address of the president of Section F of the British Association, at the forty-eighth meeting, held at Dublin, in August 1878', *Journal of the Royal Statistical Society*, December 1878, 41, 4, p. 626.
61 Ingram, 'Address of the president of Section F of the British Association', p. 614.
62 Ingram, 'Address of the president of Section F of the British Association', pp. 614 and 617.

63 For this exchange, see the *Economic Journal*, 1892.
64 See the *Economic Journal*, 1922.
65 This is discussed in detail in Snooks, 1992, *Economics Without Time*, ch. 2.
66 I am currently investigating these ideas in *The Doomsday Debate: Ecologist Versus Economist*, forthcoming.

4 GETTING YOUR HANDS DIRTY: ECONOMIC HISTORY AND POLICY ADVICE

1 G.R. Hawke, 'Getting your hands dirty? An economic historian and policy', *VUW Working Papers in Economic History 84/5*, June 1984.
2 M. Prebble, *Information, Privacy and the Welfare State*, Wellington, Institute of Policy Studies, 1990.
3 R.M. Solow, *Capital Theory and the Rate of Return*, Amsterdam, North-Holland, 1963, p. 8.
4 P. Callister with G.R. Hawke, A.C. Rayner, M. Tapper and J. Dyall, *Expanding Our Horizons: New Zealand in the Global Economy*, Wellington, New Zealand Planning Council, 1991.
5 Cf. J. Mokyr, 'The Industrial Revolution and the new economic history', in J. Mokyr (ed.), *The Economics of the Industrial Revolution*, Amsterdam, North-Holland, 1985, p. 5.
6 For example, in D.H. Robertson, *Money*, Cambridge Economic Handbook no.2, London, Nisbet, 1992, p. v.
7 M. Blaug, 'John Hicks and the methodology of economics' in N. de Marchi (ed.), *The Popperian Legacy in Economics: Papers Presented at a Symposium in Amsterdam, December 1985*, Cambridge, Cambridge University Press, 1988, pp. 183–95.
8 W.J. Baumol, 'Sir John versus the Hicksians, or theorist malgré lui?', *Journal of Economic Literature*, December 1990, 28, pp. 1708–15.
9 D.W. Hands, 'Ad hocness in economics and the Popperian tradition', in N. de Marchi (ed.), *The Popperian Legacy in Economics: Papers Presented at a Symposium in Amsterdam, December 1985*, Cambridge, Cambridge University Press, 1988, pp. 121–37.
10 For alternative accounts of the Labour Government elected in 1984, see J. Boston and M. Holland (eds), *The Fourth Labour Government*, Auckland, Oxford University Press, 1987, 2nd edn, 1990; M. Wilson, *Labour in Government 1984–1987*, Wellington, Allen & Unwin/Port Nicholson Press, 1989; and R.G. Rabel, 'The world turned upside down? Change and continuity in New Zealand politics in the postwar era', in R.W. Baker (ed.), *Australia, New Zealand, and the United States: Internal Change and Alliance Relations in the ANZUS States*, New York/Westport, Praeger, 1991, pp. 89–108.
11 J. Hicks, *A Theory of Economic History*, Oxford, Clarendon Press, 1969, and E.L. Jones, *The European Miracle: Environments, Economies, and Geopolitics in the History of Europe and Asia*, Cambridge, Cambridge University Press, 1981, provide an introduction to the evidence.
12 M. Friedman, 'Monetary policy in developing countries', in P.A. David and M.W. Reder (eds), *Nations and Households in Economic Growth: Essays in Honor of Moses Abramowitz*, New York/London, Academic Press, 1974, p. 271.
13 B. Galvin, *Policy Co-ordination, Public Sector and Government*, Wellington, Institute of Policy Studies, 1991, p. 50.
14 G. Debreu, 'The mathematization of economic theory', *American Economic Review*, March 1991, 81, pp. 1–7.

5 LABOUR MARKET INTEGRATION AND THE RURAL–URBAN WAGE GAP IN HISTORY

1 See M.P. Todaro, 'A model of labor migration and urban unemployment in less developed countries', *American Economic Review*, March 1969, 59, 1, pp. 138–48; and J.R. Harris and M.P. Todaro, 'Migration, unemployment and development: a two-sector analysis, *American Economic Review*, March 1970, 60, 1, pp. 126–42. Todaro cites the observation of Schultz that in the early 1930s rural–urban migration fell dramatically despite the widening wage gap as urban unemployment mounted (Todaro, 'A model of labor migration', p. 140). Below we offer a formal test of the hypothesis that migration in interwar America was driven by both the wage gap and urban unemployment.

2 E.E. Hagen, 'An economic justification of protection', *Quarterly Journal of Economics*, 1958, 72, p. 503.

3 C. Clark, *The Conditions of Economic Progress*, 2nd edn, London, Macmillan, 1957; S. Kuznets, *Modern Economic Growth*, New Haven, Conn., Yale University Press, 1966.

4 D.J. Ahearn, *The Wages of Farm and Factory Laborers 1914–1944*, New York, Columbia University Press, 1945; L.J. Ducoff, *Wages of Agricultural Labor in the United States* (USDA Technical Bulletin No. 895), Washington, GPO, 1945; G.R. Allen, 'A comparison of real wages in Swedish agriculture and secondary and tertiary industries, 1870–1949', *Scandinavian Economic History Review*, 1955, 3, pp. 85–107.

5 J.R. Bellerby, *Agriculture and Industry Relative Income*, London, Macmillan, 1956, p. 246.

6 G. Bry, *Wages in Germany 1871–1945*, Princeton, Princeton University Press, 1960, p. 470; E.H. Phelps Brown, *A Century of Pay*, London, Macmillan, 1968, pp. 47–8.

7 It has been argued in the development literature that, at least in the first instance, rural migrants find low wage employment in the urban 'informal' sector. Hence the average urban unskilled wage might not be the appropriate one for comparison. A dual labour market of this kind has been identified in the Bombay textile industry by D. Mazumdar in 'Labour supply in early industrialisation: the case of the Bombay textile industry', *Economic History Review*, 1973, 26, pp. 477–96, but he notes that the low wage casual jobs were taken by temporary migrants, while permanent migrants received higher wage rates. Recent studies in the development literature have suggested that, in general, no sharp distinction can be made between the informal and formal sectors (see R. Berry and R.H. Sabot, 'Unemployment and economic development', *Economic Development and Cultural Change*, 1984, 33, pp. 99–116; and S. Kannappan, 'Urban unemployment and the labor market in developing nations', *Economic Development and Cultural Change*, 1984, 33, pp. 699–730.) Evidence cited below for nineteenth-century Britain supports this view.

8 A further question is whether wage gaps should be measured at the regional or the national level. Naturally this depends on the degree of regional labour market integration which itself gives rise to a related set of issues.

9 J.G. Williamson, 'Did English factor markets fail during the Industrial Revolution?' *Oxford Economic Papers*, 1987, 39, p. 645.

10 J.G. Williamson, 'The structure of pay in Britain, 1710–1911', *Research in Economic History*, 1982, 7, p. 48.

11 P. Sicsic, 'City-farm wage gaps in late nineteenth century France', *Journal of Economic History*, 1992, 52, p. 685.

12 J.G. Williamson and P.H. Lindert, *American Inequality: A Macroeconomic History*,

New York, Academic Press, 1980, p. 313.

13 Clark, *The Conditions of Economic Progress*, Table II, pp. 526–31.

14 L. Squire, *Employment Policy in Developing Countries*, New York, Oxford University Press, 1981, Table 30, p. 102.

15 United States, Department of Agriculture, Bureau of Agricultural Economics, *Wage Rates, Farm Employment and Related Data*, Washington, GPO, 1943, p. 3.

16 G.K. Holmes, *Wages of Farm Labor* (USDA, Bureau of Statistics Bulletin no. 99), Washington, GPO, 1912; L.J. Ducoff, *Wages of Agricultural Labor in the United States* (USDA Technical Bulletin no. 895), Washington, GPO, 1945, p. 31.

17 T.J. Hatton and J.G. Williamson, 'Wage gaps between farm and city: Michigan in the 1890s', *Explorations in Economic History*, 1991, 28, pp. 381–408.

18 J.C. Folsom, *Perquisites of Hired Farm Laborers* (USDA Technical Bulletin no. 213), Washington, GPO, 1931.

19 L.J. Alston and T.J. Hatton, 'The earnings gap between agricultural and manufacturing laborers, 1925–1941', *Journal of Economic History*, 1991, 51, p. 86.

20 For an analytical discussion of in-kind payments, see L.J. Alston and J.P. Ferrie, 'A theory of in-kind compensation with an application to agriculture', University of Illinois, unpublished paper, 1990.

21 P. Sanghvi, *Surplus Manpower in Agriculture and Economic Development*, London, Asia Publishing House, 1969, p. 91.

22 A. Wilson Fox, 'Agricultural wages in England and Wales during the last half century', in W.E. Minchinton (ed.), *Essays in Agrarian History*, vol. 2, Newton Abbot, David & Charles, 1968, p. 133; G. Bagge, E. Lundberg, and I. Svenillson, *Wages in Sweden, 1880–1930*, London, P.S. King, 1935.

23 M. Peltonen, 'Agrarian world market and Finnish farm economy', *Scandinavian Economic History Review*, 1988, 36, p. 41; see also D. Warriner, *The Economics of Peasant Farming*, 2nd edn, London, Frank Cass, 1964.

24 Bellerby, *Agriculture and Industry Relative Income*, pp. 211–13.

25 N. Koffsky, 'Farm and urban purchasing power', *Studies in Income and Wealth*, vol. 11, New York, NBER, 1946, pp. 156–78.

26 Alston and Hatton, 'The earnings gap between agricultural and manufacturing laborers, 1925–1941', p. 90.

27 Hatton and Williamson, 'Wage gaps between farm and city', p. 400.

28 Bellerby, *Agriculture and Industry Relative Income*, p. 257; see also M.G. Ried, 'Comment' [on N. Koffsky, 'Farm and urban purchasing power'], *Studies in Income and Wealth*, vol. 11, New York, NBER, 1946, p. 188.

29 G.R. Allen, 'Relative wages in Swedish agriculture and industry, 1930–1950', *Bulletin of the Oxford Institute of Statistics*, 1953, 15, pp. 436–52; and Allen, 'A comparison of real wages in Swedish agriculture'.

30 Allen, 'A comparison of real wages in Swedish agriculture', p. 92; and Allen, 'Relative wages in Swedish agriculture and industry, 1930–1950', p. 445.

31 J.G. Williamson, *Coping with City Growth During the British Industrial Revolution*, Cambridge, Cambridge University Press, 1990, p. 190.

32 The annual wages of unskilled municipal employees can be compared with those of 'statare' (agricultural teamsters) using data from Bagge *et al.*, *Wages in Sweden*, pp. 26, 113–14. Adjusting these (which include the in-kind component of the agricultural wage) by the relative price ratio from Allen, 'A comparison of real wages in Swedish agriculture' (including the farm-gate price adjustment), gives a wage ratio of 1.19 in 1890 and 1.49 in 1913. If the comparison were made between the municipal workers annual wage and the cash wage of farm servants with no adjustment for in-kind payments, the ratios would be 3.34 and 3.86 for 1890 and 1913 respectively.

33 The ratio for Bombay was derived from the figures cited by Mazumdar, 'Labor supply in early industrialisation', for the ratio of all urban wage rates to rural wage rates (p. 495), the ratio of all urban earnings to unskilled earnings (p. 482), and the urban–rural price ratio (p. 479). The ratio for Japan was calculated from Y. Masui, 'The supply price of labor: farm family workers', in K. Ohkawa, B.F. Johnston and H. Kaneda (eds), *Agriculture and Economic Growth: Japan's Experience*, Princeton, Princeton University Press, 1970, p. 230 (series P3) and p. 237 (series W1), and the urban–rural price ratio of 1.224 (p. 225).

34 One type of compensating differential sometimes cited in the literature is that for the loss of earnings for other family members (chiefly women and children) which would be occasioned if a whole family were to move to the city, where employment for women and children was scarce. Both Masui, 'The supply price of labor', for Japan, and Mazumdar, 'Labor supply in early industrialisation', for Bombay, consider the opportunity cost of moving an entire family to the city and find that, in the interwar period, it was considerably higher than for the single unattached (male) worker. We do not consider such adjustments here for two reasons. First, we would have to adjust for the additional leisure gained by family members who gave up working, and secondly, we concentrate on the marginal migrant – typically the young unskilled unattached worker.

35 J.G. Williamson, 'Urban disamenities, dark satanic mills, and the British standard of living debate', *Journal of Economic History*, 1981, 41, pp. 75–83; J.G. Williamson, 'Was the Industrial Revolution worth it? Disamenities and death in 19th century British towns', *Explorations in Economic History*, 1982, 19, pp. 221–45; and Williamson, *Coping with City Growth*.

36 Williamson, 1990, *Coping with City Growth*, pp. 250, 255.

37 Williamson, 1990, *Coping with City Growth*, p. 256.

38 Williamson, 1987, 'Did English factor markets fail during the Industrial Revolution?' p. 656.

39 For analysis of the decline in urban mortality linking this with environmental factors, see D. Friedlander, E. Schellekens, E. Ben-Moshe, and A. Keysar, 'Socioeconomic characteristics and life expectancies in nineteenth century England: a district analysis', *Population Studies*, 1985, 39, pp. 137–51, for England; and S.H. Preston, and E. Van de Walle, 'Urban French mortality in the nineteenth century', *Population Studies*, 1975, 32, pp. 275–97, for France.

40 J.G. Williamson, 'Migrant earnings in Britain's cities in 1951: testing competing views of urban labor market absorption', *Journal of European Economic History*, 1990, 19, pp. 163–90.

41 Similar results have been obtained using microeconomic evidence from Brazil (M.B. Tannen, 'Labor markets in Brazil: does the dual market model apply?', *Economic Development and Cultural Change*, 1991, 39, pp. 567–83).

42 T.J. Hatton and J.G. Williamson, 'Unemployment, employment contracts and compensating wage differentials: Michigan in the 1890s', *Journal of Economic History*, September 1991, 51, 3, pp. 605–32.

43 Hatton and Williamson, 'Unemployment, employment contracts and compensating wage differentials', pp. 621–2.

44 A number of observers have commented, however, on the higher wage rates for casual as compared with permanent workers in agriculture. A notable case is in India where, in 1950–51, casual workers received daily wage rates 42 per cent higher than attached workers, but casual workers had an average of only 200 days of employment during the year compared with 319 for attached workers. Sanghvi comments as follows: 'All agricultural workers have the option of being casual or attached workers; uncertainty of employment is the most important problem in the life of

casual workers. If the monsoon fails, they may not find any employment at all; and even if the rainfall is good, they are not sure of what will be their share in the total employment. The danger of being left without a share in employment is always present in overcrowded agriculture and is an important matter for them, for their level of living has two dimensions, the wage rate and the number of days of employment – the latter being more important. The attached worker has assured employment throughout the year and assured earnings. He is, therefore, willing to accept a lower wage rate in return for assured employment at a security discount' (Sanghvi, *Surplus Manpower*, p. 99).

45 Hatton and Williamson, 'Unemployment, employment contracts and compensating wage differentials' p. 609.

46 S. Engerman and C. Goldin, 'Seasonality in nineteenth century labor markets', Harvard University, unpublished paper, 1990, Table 3.

47 J.L. Rosenbloom, 'One market or many? Labor market integration in the late nineteenth century United States', *Journal of Economic History*, 1990, 50, pp. 85–107.

48 Williamson, 'Urban disamenities, dark satanic mills, and the British standard of living debate', p. 79.

49 These wage ratios are for the agricultural wage relative to the industrial average wage (not the unskilled urban wage). These series were taken largely from B.R. Mitchell, *European Historical Statistics, 1750–1970*, New York, Columbia University Press, 1975, and the sources are discussed in greater detail in T.J. Hatton and J.G. Williamson, 'Integrated and segmented labor markets: thinking in two sectors', *Journal of Economic History*, June 1991, 51, 2, pp. 413–26.

50 For a (largely unsuccessful) attempt to estimate the equilibrium version of the model on data for Ghana, see J.B. Knight, 'Rural urban comparisons and migration in Ghana', *Bulletin of the Oxford Institute of Economics and Statistics*, 1972, 34, pp. 199–228.

51 The migration variable, M, is for the rate of population off-farm migration and is measured April to April, imposing an implicit four-month lag in the model. It was estimated using the Cochrane–Orcutt method to correct for first order serial correlation. The 't' value for rho is 1.99.

52 R.F. Engle and C.W.J. Granger, 'Cointegration and error correction: representation, estimation and testing', *Econometrica*, 1987, 55, pp. 251–76.

53 Hatton and Williamson, 'Integrated and segmented labour markets'.

54 For a detailed analysis of these union effects, see G.R. Boyer and T.J. Hatton, 'Did Joseph Arch raise agricultural wages? Rural trade unions and the labour market in late nineteenth century England', *Centre for Economic Policy Research Discussion Paper* no. 484, 1990.

55 T.J. Hatton and J.G. Williamson, 'What explains wage gaps between farm and city: exploring the Todaro model with American evidence, 1890–1941', *Economic Development and Cultural Change*, 1992, 40, pp. 267–94.

56 A. Newell and J.S.V. Symons, 'The macroeconomics of the interwar years: international comparisons', in B. Eichengreen and T.J. Hatton (eds), *Interwar Unemployment in International Perspective*, Dordrecht, Kluwer, 1988, p. 86.

57 D. Langeweische and F. Lenger, 'Internal migration: persistence and mobility', in K.J. Bade (ed.), *Population, Labour and Migration in 19th- and 20th-Century Germany*, Leamington Spa, Berg, 1987, p. 90.

58 Macroeconomic forces in Japan during the Depression are described in Y. Yasuba, 'The Japanese economy and economic policy in the 1930s', in R.G. Gregory and N.G. Butlin (eds), *Recovery from the Depression: Australia and the World Economy in the 1930s*, Cambridge, Cambridge University Press, 1988, pp. 136–47. For out-

migration rates, see R. Minami, 'The supply of farm labor and the "turning point" in the Japanese economy', in K. Ohkawa, B.F. Johnson and H. Kaneda (eds), *Agriculture and Economic Growth: Japan's Experience*, Princeton, Princeton University Press, 1970, p. 285.

59 B.J. Eichengreen and J. Sachs, 'Exchange rates and economic recovery in the 1930s', *Journal of Economic History*, 1985, 45, pp. 925–46.

60 See M. Tracy, *Government and Agriculture in Western Europe*, 3rd edn, London, Harvester Wheatsheaf, 1989, ch. 6.

61 Sicsic, 'City-farm wage gaps in late nineteenth century France'; Williamson, 'Did English factor markets fail during the Industrial Revolution?'

62 Masui, 'The supply price of labor'.

63 For example, A.C. Kelley, 'International migration and economic growth, 1865–1935', *Journal of Economic History*, September 1965, 25, 3, pp. 333–54.

64 Williamson, *Coping with City Growth*, ch. 6.

65 B. Thomas, *Migration and Urban Development*, London, Methuen, 1972, ch. 5.

66 Williamson, *Coping with City Growth*, ch. 1.

67 J.G. Williamson, 'The evolution of global labor markets in the First and Second World since 1830: background evidence and hypotheses', Harvard University, unpublished paper, 1991.

6 CITIES AND ECONOMIC DEVELOPMENT: SOME LESSONS FROM THE ECONOMIC HISTORY OF THE PACIFIC RIM

I am grateful to Harry Clarke, Eric Jones, and Glenn Withers for comments on an earlier draft of this chapter.

1 See C. McEvedy and R. Jones, *Atlas of World Population History*, Harmondsworth, Penguin Books, 1978, pp. 342–51.

2 United Nations, *Estimates and Projections of Urban, Rural and City Populations, 1950–2025: The 1982 Assessment*, New York, United Nations, 1985, Table A–7.

3 United Nations, *Estimates and Projections*, Tables A–3, A–13.

4 See B.F. Hoselitz, *Sociological Aspects of Economic Growth*, Glencoe, Ill., The Free Press, 1960; J. Gugler, 'Overurbanization reconsidered', in J. Gugler (ed.), *The Urbanization of the Third World*, Oxford, Oxford University Press, 1988, pp. 74–92.

5 T.G. McGee, *The Southeast Asian City: A Social Geography of the Primate Cities of Southeast Asia*, New York, Frederick A. Praeger, 1967, p. 17.

6 M. Lipton, *Why Poor People Stay Poor: Urban Bias in World Development*, Cambridge, Mass., Harvard University Press, 1977.

7 See especially M.P. Todaro, *Internal Migration in Developing Countries: A Review of Theory, Evidence, Methodology and Research Priorities*, Geneva, International Labour Office, 1976, pp. 36–45.

8 Natural increase accounted for an average of 60.7 per cent of urban growth in 29 Latin American and Asian countries (except China) from 1950 to 1978. S.H. Preston, 'Urban growth in developing countries: a demographic reappraisal', in J. Gugler (ed.), *The Urbanization of the Third World*, Oxford, Oxford University Press, 1988, pp. 14–15.

9 See W.A. Lewis, *The Evolution of the International Economic Order*, Princeton, Princeton University Press, 1978, pp. 39–40.

10 See, for example, L. Williams, 'Asian alert: on the economic road to environmental ruin', *The Age*, 12 May 1990.

11 A.C. Kelley and J.G. Williamson, 'The limits to urban growth: suggestions for macromodeling Third World economies', *Economic Development and Cultural Change*, 1982, 30, pp. 595–623.

12 A.C. Kelley and J.G. Williamson, *What Drives Third World City Growth? A Dynamic*

General Equilibrium Approach, Princeton, Princeton University Press, 1984, pp. 178–9. The pessimists' assumption that city growth squanders scarce resources because the per capita cost of infrastructure rises as cities grow large has also been challenged, with some economists arguing that rapid urban growth creates economies (rather than diseconomies) of scale, which make 'lumpy' investment in needed infrastructure more feasible. See W. Alonso, 'Urban and regional imbalances in economic development', *Economic Development and Cultural Change*, 1968, 17, pp. 1–14; J.F. Linn, 'The costs of urbanization in developing countries', *Economic Development and Cultural Change*, 1982, 30, pp. 625–48.

13 Kelley and Williamson, *What Drives Third World City Growth?*, pp. 179.

14 J.G. Williamson, *Coping with City Growth during the British Industrial Revolution*, Cambridge, Cambridge University Press, 1990.

15 R.L. Schiffer, *The Exploding City*, New York, St Martin's Press, 1989, p. 9.

16 The following two paragraphs are drawn from data in United States censuses; also V. Showers, *World Facts and Figures*, New York, John Wiley & Sons, 1979; T. Chandler, *Four Thousand Years of Urban Growth: An Historical Census,* Lewiston/Queenston, St David's University Press, 1987.

17 Calculated from data in United Nations, Estimates and Projections of Urban, Rural and City Populations, 1950–2025, Table A–13; Showers, *World Facts and Figures.*

18 See L. Frost, 'The physical fabric of cities: a long and broad view', *La Trobe University Economics Discussion Paper*, 17/89, 1989.

19 K. Starr, *Material Dreams: Southern California Through the 1920s*, New York, Oxford University Press, 1990, p. 84.

20 W.G. Hoskins, *The Making of the English Landscape*, London, Hodder & Stoughton, 1955, pp. 224–9.

21 Williamson, *Coping with City Growth*, p. 280.

22 See E.G. Pryor, *Housing in Hong Kong*, 2nd edn, Hong Kong, Oxford University Press, 1983, pp. 4–5.

23 Pryor, *Housing in Hong Kong*, p. 270.

24 This theme is developed more fully in P.W.G. Newman and J.R. Kenworthy, *Cities and Automobile Dependence: A Sourcebook*, Aldershot, Gower, 1989.

25 On the effectiveness of Singapore's urban resource pricing policies, see 'The city, the commuter and the car', *The Economist*, 18 February 1989, pp. 19–22; 'More people, bigger cities, greater wealth, worse filth', *The Economist*, 6 October 1990, p. 28.

26 See L. Frost, *The New Urban Frontier: Urbanisation and City-Building in Australasia and the American West*, Sydney, New South Wales University Press, 1991, pp. 77–83.

27 C.P. Ramos, 'Manila's metropolitan problem', *Philippine Journal of Public Administration*, 1961, 5, p. 90.

28 A. Portes, 'Latin American urbanization during the years of the crisis', *Latin American Research Review*, 1989, 24, pp. 16–19; A. Gilbert, 'The provision of public services and the debt crisis in Latin America: the case of Bogota', *Economic Geography*, 1990, 66, pp. 349–61.

7 OLDER WORKERS AND THE BRITISH LABOUR MARKET: ANALYSING LONGRUN TRENDS

1 For a review of the historical literature on Britain, see J. Lewis, *Women in England, 1870–1950: Sexual Division and Social Change*, Brighton, Harvester Press, 1984.

2 The only major exception is the pioneering study of the development of occupational pension schemes by L. Hannah, *Inventing Retirement: The Development of Occupational Pensions in Britain*, Cambridge, Cambridge University Press, 1986.

There is a brief account of work and retirement in the latter part of the nineteenth century in J.S. Quadagno, *Aging in Early Industrial Society: Work, Family, and Social Policy in Nineteenth-century England*, New York, Academic Press, 1982, pp. 139–69.

3 P. Johnson and J. Falkingham, 'Intergenerational transfers and public expenditure on the elderly in modern Britain', *Ageing and Society*, 1988, 8, p. 141.

4 Organisation for Economic Co-operation and Development, *Ageing Populations: The Social Policy Implications*, Paris, OECD, 1988, p. 70.

5 R.L. Clark and R. Anker, 'Labour force participation rates of older persons: an international comparison', *International Labour Review*, 1990, 129, p. 270.

6 For a survey of UK research, see F. Laczko and C. Phillipson, *Changing Work and Retirement: Social Policy and the Other Worker*, Milton Keynes, Open University Press, 1991; for US studies, see J. Quinn and R. Burkhauser, 'Work and retirement', in R.H. Binstock and L.K. George (eds), *Handbook of Aging and the Social Sciences*, 3rd edn, New York, Academic Press, 1990, pp. 318–30.

7 P. Johnson, 'Labour force participation of older men in Britain, 1951–81', *Work, Employment and Society*, 1989, 3, pp. 353–7.

8 As found, for instance, in the 1977 retirement survey. See S. Parker, *Older Workers and Retirement: An Enquiry Carried Out on Behalf of the Department of Health and Social Security*, London, HMSO, 1980.

9 For details, see J. Riley, 'Working health time: a comparison of preindustrial, industrial and postindustrial experience in life and health', *Explorations in Economic History*, 1991, 28, pp. 169–91; J.C. Riley, *Sickness, Recovery and Death*, London, Macmillan 1989, pp. 128–200. For the more recent experience, see D. Piachaud, 'Disability, retirement and unemployment of older men', *Journal of Social Policy*, 1986, 15, pp. 145–62.

10 Hannah, *Inventing Retirement*, p. 124.

11 R. Ransom and R. Sutch, 'Labor of older Americans: retirement of men on and off the job, 1870–1937', *Journal of Economic History*, 1986, 46, pp. 1–30; R. Ransom and R. Sutch, 'Two strategies for a more secure old age: life-cycle saving by late-nineteenth century American workers', University of California, History of Saving Project Working Paper, March 1989.

12 For modern evidence on the complex process of labour force withdrawal, see Quinn and Burkhauser, 'Work and retirement'; P. Johnson and J. Falkingham, *Ageing and Economic Welfare*, London, Sage, 1992, pp. 84–7.

13 C.H. Lee, *British Regional Employment Statistics, 1841–1971*, Cambridge, Cambridge University Press, 1979, p. 10.

14 J.R. Fogerty, 'Growing old in England, 1878 to 1948', PhD thesis, Australian National University, 1992, ch. 1.

15 For example, E. Richards, 'Women in the British economy since about 1700: an interpretation', *History*, 1974, 59, p. 346; L.A. Tilly and J.W. Scott, *Women, Work and Family*, New York, Holt, Rinehart & Winston, 1978, p. 125.

16 E. Jordan, 'Female unemployment in England and Wales, 1851–1911: an examination of the census figures for 15–19 year olds', *Social History*, 1988, 13, pp. 175–90, *passim*.

17 For an historical discussion of these issues, see M. Kohli, 'The world we forgot: an historical review of the life course', in V.E. Marshall (ed.), *Later Life: The Social Psychology of Aging*, Beverly Hills, Sage, 1986, pp. 271–303.

18 Ransom and Sutch, 'Labor of older Americans', pp. 17–19.

19 C. Conrad, 'La naissance de la retraite moderne: l'Allemagne dans une comparaison internationale (1850–1960)', *Population*, 1990, 45, pp. 531–62.

20 R. Floud, K. Wachter, and A. Gregory, *Height, Health and History: Nutritional*

Status in the United Kingdom, 1750–1980, Cambridge, Cambridge University Press, 1990, pp. 287–320.

21 D.K. Sheppard, *Growth and Role of UK Financial Institutions, 1880–1962*, London, Methuen, 1971, pp. 18–19; C.H. Feinstein, *Statistical Tables of National Income, Expenditure and Output of the UK, 1855–1965*, Cambridge, Cambridge University Press, 1972, Table 1. Household encashable assets are defined by Sheppard as: currency + bank deposits + savings banks deposits + building societies deposits and shares + life and annuity funds + national savings certificates, defence bonds, premium bonds and other bonds recorded on the Post Office Register.

22 M. Boddy, *The Building Societies*, London, Macmillan, 1980, p. 154; J. Burnett, *A Social History of Housing, 1815–1970*, Newton Abbot, David & Charles, 1978, p. 145.

23 Hannah, *Inventing Retirement*, pp. 40, 125.

24 D.W. Thomson, 'Provision for the elderly in England, 1830–1908', PhD thesis, University of Cambridge, October 1980, p. 284.

25 P. Johnson, *Saving and Spending: the Working-class Economy in Britain, 1870–1939*, Oxford, Clarendon Press, 1985, p. 205.

26 Great Britain, Treasury, *Economic Progress Report*, 200, February 1989.

27 P. Laslett, *A Fresh Map of Life: The Emergence of the Third Age*, London, Weidenfeld & Nicolson, 1989, p. 127.

28 C. Booth, *The Aged Poor in England and Wales: Condition*, London, Macmillan, 1894, p. 14.

29 Any overlap would have been restricted to outdoor paupers, since indoor paupers over 60 years of age were explicitly excluded from the enumerated occupied population after 1881. Indoor relief was much more prevalent in towns; Booth estimated that of the male population over 65 years of age in 1891, 30 per cent were indoor paupers in London, 15 per cent in urban and suburban areas, and 6–8 per cent in rural and semi-rural areas.

30 For a detailed account, see Thomson, 'Provision for the elderly in England, 1830–1908'.

31 *Old Age Pensions and Aged Pauperism* (Parliamentary Paper LV), 1913; A.T. Wilson and G.S. Mackay, *Old Age Pensions: An Historical and Critical Study*, London, Oxford University Press, 1941, p. 55.

32 Between 1921 and 1931 participation rates for men 65–69 years of age fell from 79.4 to 64.9 per cent, for men aged 70 years and over from 40.5 to 33.0 per cent, in both cases a proportionate decline of 18 per cent.

33 *Social Insurance and Allied Services* (Beveridge Report), London, HMSO, 1942, p. 197.

34 A.B. Atkinson, 'A national minimum? A history of ambiguity in the determination of benefit scales in Britain', *STICERD Welfare State Programme Discussion Paper* no. 47, London School of Economics, March 1990, pp. 5–8.

35 A.W. Dilnot, J.A. Kay and C.N. Morris, *Reform of Social Security*, Oxford, Clarendon Press, 1984, p. 22.

36 G.C. Fiegehen, P.S. Lansley and A.D. Smith, with N.C. Garganas, *Poverty and Progress in Britain, 1953–73: A Statistical Study of Low Income Households, Their Members, Types, and Expenditure Patterns*, Cambridge, Cambridge University Press, 1977, p. 69.

37 Hannah, *Inventing Retirement*, pp. 40, 145.

38 A. Dawson and G. Evans, 'Pensioners' incomes and expenditure, 1970–1985', *Employment Gazette*, May 1987, pp. 243–52.

39 For example, J.A. Spender, *The State and Pensions in Old Age*, London, Swan Sonnenschein, 1894, pp. 23–46.

40 *Royal Commission on the Aged Poor* (Parliamentary Paper XIV), 1895, qq. 5843–4; (Parliamentary Paper XV), 1895, qq. 10869–10884, 13335–13351, 14571–14586, 17559–17560.
41 *Royal Commission on the Aged Poor* (Parliamentary Paper XV), q. 14571.

8 THE NEW BUSINESS HISTORY: THEORY, QUANTIFICATION, AND INSTITUTIONAL CHANGE

1 A.D. Chandler, *Strategy and Structure*, Cambridge, Mass., MIT Press, 1964; L. Hannah, *The Rise of the Corporate Economy*, London, Methuen, 1976; A.D. Chandler, *The Visible Hand*, Cambridge, Mass., Harvard University Press, 1977.
2 O. Williamson, *Markets and Hierarchies: Analysis and Antitrust Implications*, New York, Free Press, 1975.
3 R. Coase, 'The nature of the firm', *Economica*, November 1937, p. 395.
4 D. North, 'Institutions', *Journal of Economic Perspectives*, Winter 1991, 5, 1, pp. 97–112.
5 A.A. Alchian and H. Demsetz, 'Production, information costs, and economic organization', *American Economic Review*, December 1972, 62, 5, pp. 777–95; C.J. Dahlman, 'The problem of externality', *Journal of Law and Economics*, 1979, 22, pp. 141–62.
6 O. Williamson, 'The modern corporation: origins, evolutions, attributes', *Journal of Economic Literature*, 1981, 19, p. 1546.
7 G.B. Richardson, 'The organisation of industry', *Economic Journal*, 1972, 82, pp. 883–96; Williamson, *Markets and Hierarchies*; and O. Williamson, *The Economic Institutions of Capitalism*, New York, Free Press, 1985; M. Casson, *Alternatives to the Multinational Enterprise*, London, Macmillan, 1979.
8 See B.R. Holmstron and J. Tirole, 'The theory of the firm', in R. Schmalensee and R.D. Willig (eds), *Handbook of Industrial Organization*, vol. 1, Amsterdam/New York, North-Holland, 1989.
9 Alchian and Demsetz, 'Production, information costs, and economic organization'.
10 The agent–principal problem is symmetric. Williamson, *Markets and Hierarchies.*
11 Appropriable quasi-rents are the difference between the value of the asset in its primary use and its value in its second-best use. B. Klein, R. Crawford and A. Alchian, 'Vertical integration, appropriable rents and the competitive contracting process', *Journal of Law and Economics*, 1978, pp. 297–326.
12 Holmstrom and Tirole, 'The theory of the firm', p. 68.
13 Williamson, *The Economic Institutions of Capitalism.*
14 S. Macaulay, 'Non-contractual relations in business', *American Sociological Review*, 1963, 28, pp. 55–70.
15 Macauley, 'Non-contractual relations in business', p. 62.
16 Macauley, 'Non-contractual relations in business', p. 61.
17 B. Asanuma, 'Manufacturer-supplier relationships in Japan and the concept of relation-specific skill', *Journal of the Japanese and International Economies*, 1989, 3, pp. 1–31.
18 A.M. Carlos and S. Nicholas, 'Agency problems in the early chartered companies: the case of the Hudson's Bay Company', *Journal of Economic History*, 1990, 50, 4, pp. 853–75; and A.M Carlos and S. Nicholas, 'Managing the manager: an application of the principal–agent problem in the Hudson's Bay Company', *Oxford Economic Papers* (forthcoming July 1993).
19 S. Nicholas, 'Agency contracts, institutional modes, and the transition to foreign direct investment by British manufacturing multinationals before 1939', *Journal of Economic History*, September 1983, 43, 3, pp. 675–86.

20 Williamson, *Markets and Hierarchies.*
21 S. Nicholas, 'Locational choice, performance and the growth of British multinational firms', *Business History*, July 1989, 31, 3, pp. 122–41; S. Nicholas, 'The expansion of British multinational companies: testing for managerial failure', in J. Foreman-Peck (ed.), *New Perspectives on the Late Victorian Economy: Essays in Quantitative Economic History*, Cambridge, Cambridge University Press, 1991, pp. 125–45; and S. Nicholas, 'Debating business history: location, performance and the growth of British MNEs', *Business History*, January 1991, 33, 1, pp. 116–20.
22 J. Atack, 'Industrial structure and the emergence of industrial capitalism', *Explorations in Economic History*, 1985, 22, pp. 29–52.
23 R. Caves, *Multinational Enterprise and Economic Analysis*, New York, Cambridge University Press, 1982, pp. 72–80.
24 D.J. Teece, 'Technology transfer by multinational firms: the resource cost of transferring technological know-how', *Economic Journal*, June 1977, 87, pp. 242–61.
25 Teece, 'Technology transfer by multinational firms'; R.D. Willig, 'Multiproduct technology and market structure', *American Economic Review*, May 1979, 69, 2, pp. 346–51.
26 See T.B. Formby, R.C. Hill and S.R. Johnson, *Advanced Econometric Methods*, New York, Springer-Velag, 1984; G. Judge, W.E. Griffiths, R.C. Hill, H. Lutkepohl and T.C. Lee, *The Theory and Practice of Econometrics*, New York, John Wiley, 1980.
27 Diversification and conglomerate growth are other forms of institutional arrangements and change.
28 Carlos and Nicholas, 'Agency problems in the early chartered companies'; and Carlos and Nicholas, 'Managing the manager'.

9 CULTURAL DETERMINANTS OF ECONOMIC PERFORMANCE: AN EXPERIMENT IN MEASURING HUMAN CAPITAL FLOWS

1 M.J. Wiener, *English Culture and the Decline of the Industrial Spirit, 1850–1980,* Cambridge, Cambridge University Press, 1981.
2 Wiener, *English Culture*, p. 166.
3 For example, Sir James Goldsmith, *Counter-Culture*, privately published, 1985.
4 Critics of this business reaction were quick to point out that it looked like those responsible for business failure shrugging off the blame onto others.
5 For example, R. Jowell, S. Witherspoon and L. Brook (eds), *British Social Attitudes: The Fifth Report*, Aldershot, SCPR/Gower, 1987; I. Crewe, 'Values: the crusade that failed', in D. Kavanagh and A. Seldon (eds), *The Thatcher Effect*, Oxford, Clarendon Press, 1989, pp. 239–50.
6 For example, various essays in N. McKendrick and R.B. Outhwaite (eds), *Businessmen and Public Policy: Essays in Honour of D.C. Coleman*, Cambridge, Cambridge University Press, 1986; W.D. Rubinstein, 'Social class, social attitudes and British business life', *Oxford Review of Economic Policy*, Spring 1988, 4, 1, pp. 51–8.
7 For example, Acton Society Trust, *Management Succession: The Recruitment, Selection, Training and Promotion of Managers*, London, Acton Society Trust, 1956, pp. 28–9; S.P. Keeble 'University education and business management from the 1890s to the 1950s: a reluctant relationship', PhD thesis, University of London, 1984.
8 For example, W. Lazonick, 'Strategy, structure, and management development in the United States and Britain', in K. Kobayishi and H. Morikawa (eds), *Development of Managerial Enterprise: Proceedings of the Fuji Conference* (International Conference

on Business History 12), Tokyo, University of Tokyo Press, 1986, pp. 101–46; G.H. Copeman, *Leaders of British Industry: A Study of the Careers of more than a Thousand Public Company Directors*, London, Gee, 1955; W.L. Warner and J.C. Abegglen, *Occupational Mobility in American Business and Industry, 1928–1952*, Minneapolis, University of Minnesota Press, 1955; H. Kaelble, *Social Mobility in the 19th and 20th Centuries: Europe and America in Comparative Perspective*, Leamington Spa, Berg, 1985, ch. 3; H. Mannari, *The Japanese Business Leaders*, Tokyo, University of Tokyo Press, 1974.

9 *The Making of Modern Managers: A Report on Management Education, Training and Development in the USA, West Germany, France, Japan and the UK* ('The Handy Report'), London, National Economic Development Office, 1987; D. Hall, H.-Cl. de Bettignies, and G. Amado-Fischgrund, 'The European business elite', *European Business*, October 1969, 23, pp. 45–55.

10 For example, W.D. Rubinstein, 'Education and the social origins of British élites, 1880–1970', *Past and Present*, August 1986, 112, pp. 163–207.

11 M. Olson, *The Rise and Decline of Nations: Economic Growth, Stagflation, and Social Rigidities*, New Haven, Yale University Press, 1982.

12 P. Stanworth and A. Giddens, 'An economic elite: a demographic profile of company chairmen', in P. Stanworth and A. Giddens (eds), *Elites and Power in British Society*, Cambridge, Cambridge University Press, 1974, pp. 81–101.

13 H. Young, *One of Us: A Biography of Margaret Thatcher*, London, Macmillan, 1989, p. 331.

14 *Business*, May 1989, pp. 52, 59.

15 Only 8 per cent of all secondary school pupils were in comprehensives in 1965 when Crosland accelerated the pace of comprehensivization.

16 W. Goldsmith and B. Ritchie, *The New Elite: Britain's Top Executives*, London, Weidenfeld & Nicolson, 1987, p. 152.

17 The worldwide turnover of these fifty companies was equivalent to about half of the UK GNP: their influence on British fortunes was, therefore, not trivial.

18 One possibility is the City: banks and other financial institutions are omitted from *The Times 1000* list and so are not reflected in the top 50 in Tables 9.1 and 9.2. Yet the public school elite were already too heavily concentrated there for there to be much increase in their numbers, and today it seems unlikely to have offered them a safe refuge from competition.

19 In 1951, 62 per cent of pupils aged 16+ were in maintained schools, 9 per cent in direct grant schools, and 30 per cent in independent schools (A.H. Halsey, A.F. Heath and J.M. Ridge, 'The political arithmetic of public schools', in G. Walford (ed.), *British Public Schools: Policy and Practice*, Lewes, Falmer Press, 1984, p. 12). This mirrors the proportions in Table 9.1. Of independent school boys, 40 per cent then stayed on in the sixth form, but of course only a small portion in the state sector did. This is compatible with the view that those with education had an equal chance of reaching the top, but fee-paying education still conferred a better chance of sixth form education, which was a virtual prerequisite for top jobs.

20 The precipitous decline of Cambridge merits further investigation.

21 Quoted in *Business*, May 1989, p. 52.

22 See the various statistics in M. Sanderson, *The Universities and British Industry 1850–1970*, London, Routledge & Kegan Paul, 1972; and Political and Economic Planning, *Graduate Employment: A Sample Survey*, London, Allen & Unwin, 1956, p. 59.

23 See Great Britain, University Grants Committee, *University Statistics*, vol. 2: *Details of First Destinations of University Graduates*, Cheltenham, Universities' Statistical Record for the University Grants Committee, for 1981–88.

24 Universities Central Council on Admissions, *Annual Reports*, 1968/9–87/8, *Statistical Supplements*, passim.

25 Wiener, British Culture, p. 136.

10 BANK DEREGULATION IN AUSTRALIA, YESTERDAY AND TODAY: LESSONS OF HISTORY

I thank Bob Jackson and participants of the Longrun Analysis in Economics Conference for their thoughtful comments, and Raha Roggero and Barry Howarth for their excellent research assistance.

1 Royal Commission Appointed to Inquire into the Monetary and Banking Systems at Present in Operation in Australia, *Report*, Canberra, Government Printer, 1937; the Royal Commission was appointed in November 1935, but took its evidence throughout 1936. See also C.B. Schedvin, 'The growth of bank regulation in Australia', paper presented to Joint Universities Conference, *Regulating Commercial Banks: Australian Experience in Perspective*, Canberra, Australian National University, 1989.

2 T.J. Valentine, 'Why the Australian banking system was deregulated', paper presented to Joint Universities Conference, *Regulating Commercial Banks: Australian Experience in Perspective*, Canberra, Australian National University, 1989.

3 Valentine, 'Why The Australian banking system was deregulated'.

4 Australian Bankers Association, *Submission to the Committee of Inquiry into the Australian Financial System*, n.p., S.L., 1979.

5 More recent expression of the 'over-branching' hypothesis has come with the opening moves in the battle for the Commonwealth Bank, which prompted a columnist of the *Australian Financial Review*, 22 April 1988, to proffer the view that: 'mergers ... would lead in the long run to great economies ... [certainly] the spreading of overheads and the rationalisation of branches would eventually strengthen the merged bank's cash position'.

6 For example, merchant banks and cash management trusts.

7 At the microeconomic level, if larger financial intermediaries enjoy scale economies as appears to be the case, then by encouraging fragmentation of the financial system the regulations wasted resources.

8 R. Ackland and I.R. Harper, 'Financial deregulation in Australia: boon or bane?', paper presented to the *Economists Conference*, University of New South Wales, Sydney, 1990; republished in P. Forsyth (ed.), *Microeconomic Reform in Australia*, North Sydney, Allen & Unwin, 1992, pp. 45–71.

9 With one exception, owner-occupied housing loans under $100,000.

10 G. Chalmers, *A History of Currency in the British Colonies*, London, HMSO, 1893, reprinted, 1972.

11 S.J. Butlin, *The Australian Monetary System 1851–1914*, Sydney, Reserve Bank of Australia, 1986, p. 92.

12 The only exception to the prohibition on dealing with land was where it was necessary to dispose of land taken for *unpaid* debts.

13 G. Blainey, *Gold and Paper: A History of National Bank of Australasia*, Melbourne, Georgian House, 1958, p. 84.

14 *Australasian Insurance and Banking Record*, hereafter *AIBR*, 8 December 1880.

15 *AIBR*, 8 December 1880.

16 *AIBR*, 9 December 1878.

17 W.P. Hogan, 'New banks in Australia', Department of Economics, University of Sydney, 1990, mimeo; Ackland and Harper, 'Financial deregulation in Australia'.

18 J.R.S. Revell, *Costs and Margins in Banking: An International Survey*, Paris, OECD, 1980.

19 R. Milbourne and M. Cumberworth, 'Australian banking performance in an era of de-regulation: an untold story?' School of Economics, University of New South Wales, 1990, mimeo.

20 Ackland and Harper, 'Financial deregulation in Australia'.

21 Milbourne and Cumberworth, 'Australian banking performance'.

22 Hogan, 'New banks in Australia'.

23 K. Davis and M. Lewis, 'Economies of scale in financial institutions', in Committee of Inquiry into the Australian Financial System, *Commissioned Studies and Selected Papers*, part 1, Canberra, AGPS, 1982, pp. 645–701. See also R. Edgar, J.H. Hatch, and M.K. Lewis, 'Economies of scale in Australian banking 1947–68', *Economic Record*, March 1971, 47, pp. 17–37; J.H. Hatch and M.K. Lewis, 'Economies of scale in Australian banking: a reply', *Economic Record*, September 1973, 49, pp. 481–4; T.J. Valentine and P.J. Williamson, 'A note on economies of scale in Australian banking', in Committee of Inquiry into the Australian Financial System, *Commissioned Studies and Selected Papers*, part 1, Canberra, AGPS, 1982, pp. 703–9.

24 G.S. Lim and T.J. Valentine, 'Trading banks', in M.K. Lewis and R.H. Wallace (eds), *Australia's Financial Institutions and Markets*, South Melbourne, Longman Cheshire, 1985, pp. 15–63.

25 Under the BIS capital-adequacy guidelines, international banks must hold specified levels of equity and other forms of capital against assets weighted by risk. However, the BIS standards ignore foreign exchange and interest rate risk.

26 Indeed, they are encouraged to take more risky options. Some regulators suggest that higher capital adequacy standards are the best way of dealing with this. Higher capital standards implicitly lower overall bank risk and at the same time increase the cost of risk-taking to management and shareholders (G.J. Benston, 'International bank capital standards', paper presented to Joint Universities Conference, *Regulating Commercial Banks: Australian Experience in Perspective*, Canberra, Australian National University, 1989; and P. Cooke, 'Recent developments in the prudential regulation of banks and the evolution of international supervisory regulation', paper presented to Joint Universities Conference, *Regulating Commercial Banks: Australian Experience in Perspective*, Canberra, Australian National University, 1989). Another regulation, the prohibition of branch banking (in the United States) has been thought to increase the risk of bank failures by reducing banks' ability to risk-pool. It might be argued that the removal of this control would remove, or at least reduce, the need for deposit insurance.

27 M. Allais, 'The psychological rate of interest', *Journal of Money, Credit and Banking*, August 1974, pp. 285–333; M. Allais, 'A new empirical approach of the hereditary and relativistic theory of the demand for money', *Rivista Internazionale di Scienze Economiche e Commerciali*, October–November 1985, 32, 10–11, pp. 905–48.

28 Ackland and Harper, 'Financial deregulation in Australia', p. 12.

29 P. Krugman, *Exchange Rate Instability*, Boston, MIT Press, 1989; R. Dornbush, 'International payments imbalances in the 1980s', *Federal Reserve Bank of Boston Conference Series* 32, 1989; Office of EPAC, *Exchange Rate Policy* (Background Paper no. 9), Canberra, AGPS, 1991.

30 In 1910, two decades later, the corresponding figure for the trading banks was 52 per cent; savings banks then accounted for 22 per cent; building societies, which had lost out most in the financial turmoil of the early 1890s, less than 2 per cent; pastoral companies, 9 per cent, and insurance companies, around 14 per cent.

31 Of course, this is not to say that there was no price competition, but rather that it was

limited. Wrote one banker, 'I do not think it has ever been believed that a strict adherence to the spirit and conditions of the [price] agreements has at any time prevailed and there is no Bank that hasn't . . . at some time or another transgressed the strict letter of it' (S.J. Butlin Collection, ANU ABL, Z199/106/U4).

32 D. Pope, 'Free banking in Australia before World War I', *Working Papers in Economic History* no. 129, Canberra, Australian National University, December 1989.

33 Usually oligopolists differentiate their products, the use of brand names and advertising being common. In banking, branching reflected a conscious effort to differentiate product by quality, that is, by location and by advertising. The corinthian and gothic facades and other elegant configurations of bricks and stone of Australian bank premises were expressions of non-price rivalry.

34 *AIBR*, 8 December 1880.

35 R. Sylla, 'The United States, 1863–1913', in R. Cameron (ed.), *Banking and Economic Development*, New York, Oxford University Press, 1972, p. 238.

36 *AIBR*, 7 July 1877.

37 Quoted in Pope, 'Free banking in Australia before World War 1'.

38 Superintendent Letters, cited in D. Merrett, 'The 1893 bank crashes: a reconsideration', seminar paper, Department of Economic History, RSSS, ANU, 1987 (emphasis added).

39 The twelfth bank's coefficient is captured in the constant to avoid singularity.

40 As the CST series essentially consists of staff salaries, I have chosen to deflate these costs by a labour cost deflator, not by the GNE deflator. The bank output variable in the model is the real value (nominal GNE deflator) of accounts in credit and debit times the rate of account turnover. The two ratios, X_1, X_2, are included in the equation to obtain output homogeneity, first discussed by E. Baltensperger, 'Economies of scale, firm size and concentration in banking', *Journal of Money, Credit and Banking*, IV, 1972, pp. 467–88. The idea is that the composition of a bank's output can affect the basic relation between its output and costs. In the case of X_1, the expectation is that $\partial(CST/w)/\ X_1 < 0$; and for X_2, $\partial(CST/w)/\ \partial X_2 > 0$. I do not view interest on deposits as a direct cost of production of banks' output. Current accounts were typically more costly in terms of bank staff time than term accounts (which were normally serviced at three, six, and twelve months intervals, depending on terms undertaken). Hence a rise in the ratio of term to current deposits would negatively impact on bank costs. With respect to X_2, advances were probably more labour intensive to service than other earnings assets, hence a rise in the ratio of advances to other assets would tend to drive bank costs upwards.

41 See, for example, M. Rothschild and J.E. Stiglitz, 'Increasing risk I: a definition', *Journal of Economic Theory*, September 1970, 2, 3, pp. 225–43; and M. Rothschild and J.C Stiglitz, 'Increasing risk II: its economic consequences', *Journal of Economic Theory*, 1971, 3, 1, pp. 66–84.

42 See for example J. Tobin, 'Comment on Borch and Feldstein', *Review of Economics Studies*, January 1969, 36, pp. 13–14; M. Feldstein, 'Mean-variance analysis in the theory of liquidity preference and portfolio selection', *Review of Economic Studies*, January 1969, 36, pp. 5–12; and K. Borch, 'A note on uncertainty and indifference curves', *Review of Economic Studies*, January 1969, 36, pp. 1–4. See also E. Baltensperger, 'Economies of scale, firm size and concentration in banking', *Journal of Money, Credit and Banking*, 1972, 4, pp. 467–88, for a chance-constrained model in which risk pooling, even where it involves higher marginal costs, can be implemented to reduce the risk of firm failure to an acceptable level.

43 I also calculated by the same method a ratio using the bank's total real advances plus deposits across states (instead of branch numbers). The shape of these profiles

plotted against time are virtually identical to those shown in Figure 10.9.

44 Pope, 'Free banking in Australia before World War 1'.

45 S.J. Butlin, *Australia and New Zealand Bank: The Bank of Australasia and the Union Bank of Australia Limited, 1828–951*, London, Longmans, 1961.

46 Pope, 'Free banking in Australia before World War 1'; K. Dowd, 'Free banking in Australia', Department of Economics, University of Nottingham, 1991, mimeo.

47 They saved themselves but not without damaging their image in the wider community. S.J. Butlin (*Australia and New Zealand Bank*, p. 302) suggested that 'a tradition of unscrupulous motives and maleficent policy as the normal characteristics of "the banks", which was to be a major strand in twentieth century Australian politics, owes much to this apparently obvious deduction: in the nineties the banks' escape by reconstruction was made at the expense of their customers'.

48 Allais, 'The psychological rate of interest'; and Allais, 'A new empirical approach of the hereditary and relativistic theory of the demand for money'.

BIBLIOGRAPHY

Ackland, R. and Harper, I.R., 'Financial deregulation in Australia: boon or bane?', paper presented to the Economists Conference, University of New South Wales, Sydney, 1990; republished in P. Forsyth (ed.), *Microeconomic Reform in Australia*, North Sydney, Allen & Unwin, 1992, pp. 45–71.

Acton Society Trust, *Management Succession: the Recruitment, Selection, Training and Promotion of Managers*, London, Acton Society Trust, 1956.

Ahearn, D.J., *The Wages of Farm and Factory Laborers 1914–1944*, New York, Columbia University Press, 1945.

Alchian, A.A. and Demsetz, H., 'Production, information costs, and economic organization', *American Economic Review*, December 1972, 62, 5, pp. 777–95.

Allais, M., 'The psychological rate of interest', *Journal of Money, Credit and Banking*, August 1974, pp. 285–333.

——, 'A new empirical approach of the hereditary and relativistic theory of the demand for money', *Rivista Internazionale di Scienze Economiche e Commerciali*, October–November 1985, 32, 10–11, pp. 905–48.

Allen, G.R., 'Relative wages in Swedish agriculture and industry, 1930–1950', *Bulletin of the Oxford Institute of Statistics*, 1953, 15, pp. 436–52.

——, 'A comparison of real wages in Swedish agriculture and secondary and tertiary industries, 1870–1949', *Scandinavian Economic History Review*, 1955, 3, pp. 85–107.

Alonso, W., 'Urban and regional imbalances in economic development', *Economic Development and Cultural Change*, October 1968, 17, 1, pp. 1–14.

Alston, L.J. and Ferrie, J.P., 'A theory of in-kind compensation with an application to agriculture', University of Illinois, unpublished paper, 1990.

——and Hatton, T.J., 'The earnings gap between agricultural and manufacturing laborers,1925–1941', *Journal of Economic History*, 1991, 51, pp. 83–99.

anon., 'The city, the commuter and the car', *The Economist*, 18 February 1989, pp. 19–22.

anon., 'More people, bigger cities, greater wealth, worse filth', *The Economist*, 6 October 1990, pp. 25–8.

Appleby, J.O., *Economic Thought and Ideology in Seventeenth Century England*, Princeton, Princeton University Press, 1978.

Arrow, K.J., 'The economic implications of learning by doing', *Review of Economic Studies*, June 1962, 29, pp.155–73.

—— and Hahn, F.H., *General Competitive Equilibrium*, Edinburgh, Oliver & Boyd, 1971.

Arthur, W.B., 'Competing technologies, increasing returns, and lock-in by historical events', *Economic Journal*, March 1989, 99, 394, pp. 116–31.

——, 'The economy and complexity', in D.L. Stein (ed.), *Lectures in the Sciences of Complexity* (Santa Fe Institute Studies in the Sciences of Complexity, Lectures, vol. 1), Menlo Park, Calif., Addison-Wesley, 1989, pp. 713–34.

——, 'Positive feedbacks in the economy', *Scientific American*, February 1990, 262, 2, pp. 80–5.

Asanuma, B., 'Manufacturer-supplier relationships in Japan and the concept of relation-specific skill', *Journal of the Japanese and International Economies*, 1989, 3, pp. 1–31.

Atack, J., 'Industrial structure and the emergence of industrial capitalism', *Explorations in Economic History*, 1985, 22, pp. 29–52.

Atkinson, A.B., 'A national minimum? A history of ambiguity in the determination of benefit scales in Britain', *STICERD Welfare State Programme Discussion Paper* no. 47, London School of Economics, March 1990.

Australasian Insurance and Banking Record, 1877–1914.

Australia, Australian Financial System Review, *Australian Financial System: Report of the Review Group* [Martin Review Group, Chairman: V.E. Martin], Canberra, Australian Government Publishing Service, 1984.

——, Committee of Inquiry into the Financial System, *Australian Financial System: Final Report* [Campbell Committee, Chairman: J.K. Campbell], Canberra, Australian Government Publishing Service, 1981.

——, Royal Commission Appointed to Inquire into the Monetary and Banking Systems at Present in Operation in Australia, *Report*, Canberra, Government Printer, 1937.

Australian Bankers Association, *Submission to the Committee of Inquiry into the Australian Financial System*, n.p., S.L., 1979.

Bagge, G., Lundberg, E. and Svenillson, I., *Wages in Sweden, 1880–1930* (University of Stockholm, Institute for Social Socieces, *Wages, Cost of Living and National Income in Sweden 1860-1930*, vol. 2), London, P.S. King, 1935.

Baltensperger, E., 'Economies of scale, firm size and concentration in banking', *Journal of Money, Credit and Banking*, 1972, 4, pp. 467–88.

Barro, B.J. and Romer, P.M., 'Economic growth', *NBER Reporter* , Fall 1990, pp. 1–5.

Baumol, W. J., 'Sir John versus the Hicksians, or theorist malgré lui?', *Journal of Economic Literature* , December 1990, 28, pp.1708–15.

Becker, G., *A Treatise on the Family*, Cambridge, Mass., Harvard University Press, 1981.

Bellerby, J.R., *Agriculture and Industry Relative Income*, London, Macmillan, 1956.

Benston, G.J., 'International bank capital standards', paper presented to Joint Universities Conference, *Regulating Commercial Banks: Australian Experience in Perspective*, Australian National University, Canberra, 1989.

Berry, R. and Sabot, R.H., 'Unemployment and economic development', *Economic Development and Cultural Change*, 1984, 33, pp. 99–116.

Blainey, G., *Gold and Paper: a History of the National Bank of Australasia*, Melbourne, Georgian House, 1958.

Blaug, M., *Economic Theory in Retrospect*, Cambridge, Cambridge University Press, 1983.

——, 'John Hicks and the methodology of economics' in N. de Marchi (ed.), *The Popperian Legacy in Economics: Papers Presented at a Symposium in Amsterdam, December 1985*, Cambridge, Cambridge University Press, 1988, pp. 183–95.

Boddy, M., *The Building Societies*, London, Macmillan, 1980.

Booth, C., *The Aged Poor in England and Wales: Condition*, London, Macmillan, 1894.

Borch, K., 'A note on uncertainty and indifference curves', *Review of Economic Studies*, January 1969, 36, pp. 1–4.

Boston, J. and Holland, M. (eds), *The Fourth Labour Government*, Auckland, Oxford University Press, 1987, 2nd edn, 1990.

Boyer, G.R. and Hatton,T.J., 'Did Joseph Arch raise agricultural wages? Rural trade unions and the labour market in late nineteenth century England', *Centre for Economic Policy Research Discussion Paper* no. 484, 1990.

Bry, G., *Wages in Germany 1871–1945*, Princeton, Princeton University Press, 1960.

Burnett, J., *A Social History of Housing, 1815–1970*, Newton Abbot, David & Charles, 1978.

Business, May 1989.

Butlin, N.G., *Investment in Australian Economic Development, 1861–1900*, Cambridge, Cambridge University Press, 1964.

——, 'Australian national accounts', in Vray Vamplew (ed.), *Australians: Historical Statistics*, Sydney, Fairfax, Syme & Weldon, 1987, pp. 126–44.

Butlin, S.J., *Australia and New Zealand Bank: The Bank of Australasia and the Union Bank of Australia Limited, 1828–1951*, London, Longmans, 1961.

——, *The Australian Monetary System 1851–1914*, Sydney, Reserve Bank of Australia, 1986.

Butlin, S.J. Collection (Z199), Archives of Business and Labour, Australian National University, Canberra.

Callister, P., with Hawke, G.R., Rayner, A.C., Tapper, M. and Dyall, J., *Expanding Our Horizons: New Zealand in the Global Economy*, Wellington, New Zealand Planning Council, 1991.

Cantillon, R., *Essai sur la nature du commerce en général* (edited with English translation and other material by H. Higgs; London, Macmillan, 1931; first published 1755.

Carlos, A.M. and Nicholas, S., 'Managing the manager: An application of the principal-agent problem in the Hudson's Bay Company', *Oxford Economic Papers* (forthcoming July 1993).

—— and Nicholas, S., 'Agency problems in the early chartered companies: the case of the Hudson's Bay Company', *Journal of Economic History*, December 1990, 50, 4, pp. 853–75.

Casson, M., *Alternatives to the Multinational Enterprise*, London, Macmillan, 1979.

Caves, R., *Multinational Enterprise and Economic Analysis*, New York, Cambridge University Press, 1982.

Chalmers, G., *A History of Currency in the British Colonies*, London, HMSO, 1893; reprinted, 1972.

Chandler, A.D., *Strategy and Structure*, Cambridge, Mass., MIT Press, 1964.

——, *The Visible Hand*, Cambridge, Mass., Harvard University Press, 1977.

Chandler, T., *Four Thousand Years of Urban Growth: An Historical Census*, Lewiston/Queenston, St David's University Press, 1987.

Clapham, J.H., 'Of empty economic boxes', *Economic Journal*, September 1922, 32, pp. 305–14.

——, 'The economic boxes: a rejoinder', *Economic Journal*, December 1922, 32, pp. 560–3.

Clark, C., *The Conditions of Economic Progress*, 2nd edn, London, Macmillan, 1957.

Clark, R.L. and Anker, R., 'Labour force participation rates of older persons: an international comparison', *International Labour Review*, 1990, 129, pp. 255–71.

Coase, R., 'The nature of the firm', *Economica*, November 1937, pp. 386–405

Colander, D.C. and Coats, A.W. (eds), *The Spread of Economic Ideas*, Cambridge/New York, Cambridge University Press, 1989.

Coleman, D.C., *History and the Economic Past*, Oxford, Clarendon Press, 1987.

Colander, D. and Kramer, A., 'The making of an economist', *Journal of Economic Perspectives*, Fall 1987, 1, 2, pp. 95–111.

Collingwood, R.G.D., 'Review of Selected Essays of J.B. Bury', *The English Historical Review*, July 1931, 183, pp. 461–5.

Collini, S., Winch, D. and Burrow, J.W., *That Noble Science of Politics: a Study of Nine-*

teenth Century Intellectual History, Cambridge/New York, Cambridge University Press, 1983.

Conrad, C., 'La naissance de la retraite moderne: l'Allemagne dans une comparaison internationale (1850–1960)', *Population*, 1990, 45, pp. 531–62.

Cooke, P., 'Recent developments in the prudential regulation of banks and the evolution of international supervisory regulation', paper presented to Joint Universities Conference, *Regulating Commercial Banks: Australian Experience in Perspective*, Canberra, Australian National University, 1989.

Copeman, G.H., *Leaders of British Industry: A Study of the Careers of More Than a Thousand Public Company Directors*, London, Gee, 1955.

Cournot, A.-A., *Researches into the Mathematical Principles of the Theory of Wealth*, first French edition, 1838; English translation by N.T. Bacon, 1897; rev. edn, New York, Macmillan, 1927.

Cowan, R.A. and Rizzo, M.J., 'The genetic-causal moment in economic theory', *C.V. Starr Center for Applied Economics, Economic Research Report, a* no. 91–13, February 1991.

Crewe, I., 'Values: the crusade that failed', in D. Kavanagh and A. Seldon (eds), *The Thatcher Effect*, Oxford, Clarendon Press, 1989, pp. 239–50.

Crick, F., *What Mad Pursuit: A Personal View of Scientific Discovery*, New York, Basic Books, 1988.

Cunningham, W., 'The perversion of economic history', *Economic Journal*, 1892, 2, pp. 491–506.

Dahlman, C.J., 'The problem of externality', *Journal of Law and Economics*, 1979, 22, pp. 141–62.

David, P.A., *Technical Choice, Innovation and Economic Growth: Essays on American and British Experience in the Nineteenth Century*, Cambridge, Cambridge University Press, 1975.

——, 'Clio and the economics of QWERTY', *American Economic Review*, May 1985, 75, 2, pp. 332–7.

——, 'Understanding the economics of QWERTY: the necessity of history', in W.N. Parker (ed.), *Economic History and the Modern Economist*, Oxford, Basil Blackwell, 1986, pp. 30–49.

——, 'Some new standards for the economics of standardization in the information age', in P. Dasgupta and P. Stoneman (eds), *Economic Policy and Technological Performance*, Cambridge, Cambridge University Press, 1987, pp. 206–39.

——, 'The hero and the herd in technological history: reflections on Thomas Edison and the "Battle of the Systems"', in P. Higgonet , D.S. Landes and H. Rosovsky (eds), *Favorites of fortune: Technology, Growth and Economic Development since the Industrial Revolution*, Cambridge, Mass., Harvard University Press, 1991.

——, 'Path-dependence: putting the past into the future of economics', *Institute for Mathematical Studies in the Social Sciences Technical Report* 533, Stanford University, November 1988.

——, 'Path-dependence and predictability in dynamic systems with local network externalities: a paradigm for historical economics' forthcoming in C. Freeman and D. Foray (eds), *Technology and the Wealth of Nations*, London, Pinter Publishers, 1992.

——, 'Why and when does history really matter?', Presidential Address delivered to the Economic History Association, in Washington, DC, September 1989; forthcoming in the *Journal of Economic History*.

——, 'Path-dependence in economics: the invisible hand in the grip of the past', *American Economic Review*, May 1991, pp. 70–88.

—— and Steinmueller, W.E., 'The impact of information technology upon economic science', *Prometheus*, June 1991, 9, 1, pp. 35–61.

Davis, K, and Lewis, M., 'Economies of scale in financial institutions', in Committee of Inquiry into the Australian Financial System, *Commissioned Studies and Selected Papers*, part 1, Canberra, AGPS, 1982, pp. 645–701.

Dawson, A. and Evans, G., 'Pensioners' incomes and expenditure, 1970–1985', *Employment Gazette*, May 1987, pp. 243–52.

Deane, P., *Evolution of Economic Ideas*, Cambridge/New York, Cambridge University Press, 1978.

——, *The State and the Economic System*, Oxford, OPUS, 1989.

Debreu, G., 'The mathematization of economic theory', *American Economic Review*, March 1991, 81, pp. 1–7.

Dilnot, A.W., Kay, J.A. and Morris, C.N., *Reform of Social Security*, Oxford, Clarendon Press, 1984.

Domar, E.D., 'Capital expansion rate of growth and employment', *Econometrica*, April 1946, 14, pp. 137–47.

Dornbush, R., 'International payments imbalances in the 1980s', *Federal Reserve Bank of Boston Conference Series* 32, 1989.

Dowd, K., 'Free banking in Australia', Department of Economics, University of Nottingham, 1991, mimeo.

Ducoff, L.J., *Wages of Agricultural Labor in the United States* (USDA Technical Bulletin no. 895), Washington, GPO, 1945.

Eatwell, J., Milgate, M. and Newman, P. (eds), *The New Palgrave: A Dictionary of Economics*, London, Macmillan, 1987.

Edgar, R., Hatch, J.H. and Lewis, M.K., 'Economies of scale in Australian banking 1947–68', *Economic Record*, March 1971, 47, pp. 17–37.

Ehrlich, I., 'The problem of development: introduction', *Journal of Political Economy*, October 1990, 98, pp. S1–S11.

Eichengreen, B.J. and Sachs, J., 'Exchange rates and economic recovery in the 1930s', *Journal of Economic History*, 1985, 45, pp. 925–46.

Eldredge, N., *Time Frames: The Rethinking of Darwinian Evolution and the Theory of Punctuated Equilibria*, New York, Simon and Schuster, 1985.

Engerman, S. and Goldin C., 'Seasonality in nineteenth century labor markets', Harvard University, unpublished paper, 1990.

Engle, R.F. and Granger, C.W.J., 'Cointegration and error correction: representation, estimation and testing', *Econometrica*, 1987, 55, pp. 251–76.

Feinstein, C.H., *Statistical Tables of National Income, Expenditure and Output of the UK, 1855–1965*, Cambridge, Cambridge University Press, 1972.

Feldstein, M., 'Mean-variance analysis in the theory of liquidity preference and portfolio selection', *Review of Economic Studies*, January 1969, 36, pp. 5–12.

Fiegehen, G.C., Lansley, P.S. and Smith, A.D., with Garganas, N.C., *Poverty and Progress in Britain, 1953–73: A Statistical Study of Low Income Households, Their Members, Types, and Expenditure Patterns*, Cambridge, Cambridge University Press, 1977.

Fisher, F.M., *The Disequilibrium Foundations of Equilibrium Economics*, New York, Cambridge University Press, 1983.

Floud, R., Wachter, K. and Gregory, A., *Height, Health and History: Nutritional Status in the United Kingdom, 1750–1980*, Cambridge, Cambridge University Press, 1990.

Fogerty, J.R., 'Growing old in England, 1878 to 1948', PhD thesis, Australian National University, 1992.

Folsom, J.C., *Perquisites of Hired Farm Laborers* (USDA Technical Bulletin no. 213), Washington, GPO, 1931.

Formby, T.B., Hill, R.C. and Johnson, S.R., *Advanced Econometric Methods*, New York, Springer-Velag, 1984.

Fox, A.Wilson, 'Agricultural wages in England and Wales during the last half century', in

W.E. Minchinton (ed.), *Essays in Agrarian History: Reprints Edited for the British Agricultural History Society*, vol. 2, Newton Abbot, David & Charles/New York, A.M. Kelly, 1968, pp. 121–98; reprinted from *Journal of the Royal Statistical Society*, 1903, 66, pp. 273–348.

Foxwell, H.S., 'The economic movement in England', *Quarterly Journal of Economics*, October 1887, 2, pp. 84–103.

Friedlander, D., Schellekens, E., Ben-Moshe, E. and Keysar, A., 'Socioeconomic characteristics and life expectancies in nineteenth century England: a district analysis', *Population Studies*, 1985, 39, pp. 137–51.

Friedman, M., 'Monetary policy in developing countries', in P.A. David and M.W. Reder (eds), *Nations and Households in Economic Growth: Essays in Honor of Moses Abramowitz*, New York/London, Academic Press, 1974, pp. 265–78.

Frost, L., 'The physical fabric of cities: a long and broad view', *La Trobe University Economics Discussion Paper*, 17/89, 1989.

—— *The New Urban Frontier: Urbanisation and City-Building in Australasia and the American West*, Sydney, University of New South Wales Press, 1991.

Galvin, B., *Policy Co-ordination, Public Sector and Government*, Wellington, Institute of Policy Studies, 1991.

Gilbert, A., 'The provision of public services and the debt crisis in Latin America: the case of Bogota', *Economic Geography*, 1990, 66, 4, pp. 349–61.

Goldsmith, Sir James, *Counter-Culture*, privately published, 1985.

Goldsmith, W. and Ritchie, B., *The New Elite: Britain's Top Executives*, London, Weidenfeld & Nicolson, 1987.

Gras, N.S.B., 'The present condition of economic history', *Quarterly Journal of Economics*, 1920, 34, pp. 209–24.

Great Britain, *1921 Census, England and Wales, Occupation Tables*, London, HMSO, 1925.

——, *1931 Census, England and Wales, Occupation Tables*, London, HMSO, 1934.

——, *1951 Census, England and Wales, Occupation Tables*, London, HMSO, 1956.

——, *1961 Census, England and Wales, Occupation Tables*, London, HMSO, 1966.

——, *1971 Census, Great Britain, Economic Activity (10% Sample)*, London, HMSO, 1975.

——, *1981 Census, Great Britain, National Report*, Part I, London, HMSO, 1983.

——, *Social Insurance and Allied Services* (Beveridge Report), London, HMSO, 1942.

——, National Economic Development Office, *The Making of Modern Managers: A Report on Management Education, Training and Development in the USA, West Germany, France, Japan and the U.K.* (Handy Report), London, National Economic Development Office, 1987.

——, Parliament, *1881 Census, England and Wales, Ages, Condition as to Marriage, Occupations and Birthplaces of the People*, Parliamentary Paper LXXX, 1883 .

——, Parliament, *1891 Census, England and Wales*, Vol. III: *Ages, Condition as to Marriage, Occupations, Birth-places and Infirmities*, Parliamentary Paper CVI, 1893–4.

——, Parliament, *1901 Census, England and Wales, Summary Tables*, Parliamentary Paper LXXXIV, 1903.

——, Parliament, *1911 Census, England and Wales, Occupations and Industries*, Parliamentary Papers LXXXVIII, LXXIX, 1913.

——, Parliament, *Old Age Pensions and Aged Pauperism*, Parliamentary Paper LV, 1913.

——, Parliament, *Royal Commission on the Aged Poor*, Parliamentary Papers XIV, XV, 1895.

——, Treasury, *Economic Progress Report*, 200, February, 1989.

——, University Grants Committee, *University Statistics*, Vol. 2: *Details of First*

Destinations of University Graduates, Cheltenham, Universities' Statistical Record for the University Grants Committee, 1961/62– [title varies].

Groenewegen, P.D., '"Political economy" and "economics"', in J. Eatwell, M. Milgate and P. Newman (eds), *The New Palgrave: A Dictionary of Economics*, vol. 3, London, Macmillan, 1987, pp. 904–07.

Grossman, G.M. and Helpman, E., 'Trade, innovation and growth', *American Economic Review*, May 1990, 80, pp. 86–91.

Gugler, J., 'Overurbanization reconsidered', in J. Gugler (ed.), *The Urbanization of the Third World*, Oxford, Oxford University Press, 1988, pp. 74–92.

Hagen, E.E., 'An economic justification of protection', *Quarterly Journal of Economics*, 1958, 72, pp. 496–514.

Hahn, F.H., 'Neoclassical growth theory', in J. Eatwell, M. Milgate and P. Newman (eds), *The New Palgrave: A Dictionary of Economics*, vol. 3, London, Macmillan, 1987, pp. 625–34.

—— and Matthews, R.C.O., 'The theory of economic growth: a survey', *Economic Journal*, December 1964, 74, pp. 779–902.

Haken, H., *Synergetics*, 2nd edn, Berlin, Springer-Verlag, 1978.

Hall, David, de Bettignies, H.-Cl. and Amado-Fischgrund, G., 'The European business elite', *European Business*, October 1969, 23, pp. 45–55.

Halsey, A.H., Heath, A.F. and Ridge, J.M., 'The political arithmetic of public schools', in G. Walford (ed.), *British Public Schools: Policy and Practice*, Lewes, Falmer Press, 1984.

Haltiwanger, J. and Waldman, M., 'Responders vs. nonresponders: a new perspective on heterogeneity', *UCLA Working Paper*, April 1988.

Hands, D.W., 'Ad hocness in economics and the Popperian tradition', in N. de Marchi (ed.), *The Popperian Legacy in Economics: Papers Presented at a Symposium in Amsterdam, December 1985*, Cambridge, Cambridge University Press, 1988, pp. 121–37.

Hannah, L., *The Rise of the Corporate Economy*, London, Methuen, 1976.

——, *Inventing Retirement: The Development of Occupational Pensions in Britain*, Cambridge, Cambridge University Press, 1986.

Hansen, W.L., 'Educating and training new economics PhDs: how good a job are we doing?' *American Economic Review*, May 1990, 80, pp. 437–44.

Harris, D.J., 'Classical growth models', in J. Eatwell, M. Milgate and P. Newman (eds), *The New Palgrave: A Dictionary of Economics*, vol. 1, London, Macmillan, 1987, pp. 445–9.

Harris, J.R. and Todaro, M.P., 'Migration, unemployment and development: a two-sector analysis', *American Economic Review*, March 1970, 60, 1, pp. 126–42.

Harrod, R.F., 'An essay in dynamic theory', *Economic Journal*, March 1939, 49, pp. 14–33.

Hatch, J.H. and Lewis, M.K., 'Economies of scale in Australian banking: a reply', *Economic Record*, September 1973, 49, pp. 481–4.

Hatton, T.J. and Williamson, J.G., 'Wage gaps between farm and city: Michigan in the 1890s', *Explorations in Economic History*, 1991, 28, pp. 381–408.

——, 'Integrated and segmented labor markets: thinking in two sectors', *Journal of Economic History*, June 1991, 51, 2, pp. 413–26.

——, 'Unemployment, employment contracts and compensating wage differentials: Michigan in the 1890s', *Journal of Economic History*, September 1991, 51, 3, pp. 605–32.

——, 'What explains wage gaps between farm and city: exploring the Todaro model with American evidence, 1890–1941', *Economic Development and Cultural Change*, 1992, 40, pp. 267–94.

Hawke, G.R., 'Getting your hands dirty? An economic historian and policy', *VUW Working Papers in Economic History*, 84/5 , June 1984.

Hayek, F.A., 'The London School of Economics, 1895–1945', *Economica*, N.S., February 1946, 13, pp. 1–31.

Hicks, J., *A Theory of Economic History*, Oxford, Clarendon Press, 1969.

Higgins, B., *Economic Development: Principles, Problems and Policies*, London, Constable, 1959.

Hogan, W.P., 'New banks in Australia', Department of Economics, University of Sydney, 1990, mimeo.

Holmes, G.K., *Wages of Farm Labor* (USDA, Bureau of Statistics Bulletin no. 99), Washington, GPO, 1912.

Holmstrom, B.R. and Tirole, J., 'The theory of the firm', in R. Schmalensee and R.D. Willig (eds), *Handbook of Industrial Organization*, vol. 1, Amsterdam/New York, North-Holland, 1989, pp. 61–133.

Hoselitz, B.F., *Sociological Aspects of Economic Growth*, Glencoe, Ill., The Free Press, 1960.

Hoskins, W.G., *The Making of the English Landscape*, London, Hodder & Stoughton, 1955.

Inada, K., 'On a two-sector model of economic growth: comments and a generalisation', *Review of Economic Studies*, 1963, 30, pp. 119–27.

Ingram, J.K., 'Address of the president of Section F of the British Association, at the forty-eighth meeting, held at Dublin, in August 1878', *Journal of the Royal Statistical Society*, December 1878, 41, 4, pp. 602–29.

——, *History of Political Economy*, London, Black, 1923.

Johnson, P., *Saving and Spending: The Working-class Economy in Britain, 1870–1939*, Oxford, Clarendon Press, 1985.

——, 'Labour force participation of older men in Britain, 1951–81', *Work, Employment and Society*, 1989, 3, pp. 351–68.

Johnson, P. and Falkingham, J., 'Intergenerational transfers and public expenditure on the elderly in modern Britain', *Ageing and Society*, 1988, 8, pp. 129–46.

——, *Ageing and Economic Welfare*, London, Sage, 1992.

Jones, E.L., *The European Miracle: Environments, Economies, and Geopolitics in the History of Europe and Asia*, Cambridge, Cambridge University Press, 1981.

——, *Growth Recurring: Economic Change in World History*, Oxford, Clarendon Press, 1988.

Jordan, E., 'Female unemployment in England and Wales, 1851–1911: an examination of the census figures for 15–19 year olds', *Social History*, 1988, 13, pp. 175–90.

Jowell, R., Witherspoon, S. and Brook, L. (eds), *British Social Attitudes: The Fifth Report*, Aldershot, SCPR/Gower, 1987.

Judge, G., Griffiths, W.E., Hill, R.C., Lutkepohl, H. and Lee, T.C., *The Theory and Practice of Econometrics*, New York, John Wiley, 1980.

Kadish, A., *Historians, Economists, and Economic History*, London, Routledge, 1989.

Kaelble, H., *Social Mobility in the 19th and 20th Centuries: Europe and America in Comparative Perspective*, Leamington Spa, Berg, 1985.

Kaldor, N., 'Alternative theories of distribution', *Economic Journal*, 1955, 23, pp. 83–100.

Kannappan, S., 'Urban unemployment and the labor market in developing nations', *Economic Development and Cultural Change*, 1984, 33, pp. 699–730.

Keeble, S.P., 'University education and business management from the 1890s to the 1950s: A reluctant relationship', PhD thesis, University of London , 1984.

Kelley, A.C., 'International migration and economic growth, 1865–1935', *Journal of Economic History*, September 1965, 25, 3, pp. 333–54.

—— and Williamson, J.G., 'The limits to urban growth: suggestions for macromodeling Third World economies', *Economic Development and Cultural Change*, 1982, 30, pp. 595–623.

——— and Williamson, J.G., *What Drives Third World City Growth? A Dynamic General Equilibrium Approach*, Princeton, Princeton University Press, 1984.

Kenwood, A.G. and Lougheed, A.L., *The Growth of the International Economy, 1820–1980: An Introductory Text*, London, Allen & Unwin, 1983.

Keynes, J.M., *The General Theory of Employment, Interest, and Money*, London, Macmillan, 1936.

———, *A Treatise on Probability*, London, MacMillan, 1948.

Keynes, J.M., *The Scope and Method of Political Economy*, London, Macmillan, 1891; reprinted New York, A.M. Kelley, 1964.

Klein, B., Crawford, R. and Alchian, A., 'Vertical integration, appropriable rents and the competitive contracting process', *Journal of Law and Economics*, 1978, 11, pp. 297–326.

Knight, J.B., 'Rural urban comparisons and migration in Ghana', *Bulletin of the Oxford Institute of Economics and Statistics*, 1972, 34, pp. 199–228.

Koffsky, N., 'Farm and urban purchasing power', *Studies in Income and Wealth*, vol. 11, New York, NBER, 1946, pp. 156–78.

Kohli, M., 'The world we forgot: an historical review of the life course', in V.E. Marshall (ed.), *Later Life: The Social Psychology of Aging*, Beverly Hills, Sage, 1986, pp. 271–303.

Koot, G.M., *English Historical Economics, 1870–1926*, Cambridge, Cambridge University Press, 1987.

Krugman, P., *Exchange Rate Instability*, Boston, MIT Press, 1989.

Kurz, M., 'On the impossibility of learning the equilibrium price process in a complex economic environment', *Institute for Mathematical Studies in the Social Sciences Summer Workshop Paper*, Stanford University, August 1988.

Kuznets, S., *Modern Economic Growth*, New Haven, Conn., Yale University Press, 1966.

Laczko, F. and Phillipson, C., *Changing Work and Retirement: Social Policy and the Other Worker*, Milton Keynes, Open University Press, 1991.

Lamarck, Jean Baptiste, *Hydrogéologie*, Paris, the author, 1802.

Langeweische, D. and Lenger, F., 'Internal migration: persistence and mobility', in K.J. Bade (ed.), *Population, Labour and Migration in 19th- and 20th-Century Germany*, Leamington Spa, Berg, 1987, pp. 87–100.

Laslett, P., *A Fresh Map of Life: The Emergence of the Third Age*, London, Weidenfeld & Nicolson, 1989.

Law, J., *Money and Trade Considered: With a Proposal for Supplying the Nation with Money*, New York: Augustus Kelley, 1966; first published 1705.

Lazear, E., 'Why is there mandatory retirement?', *Journal of Political Economy*, 1979, 87, pp. 1261–84.

Lazonick, W., 'Strategy, structure, and management development in the United States and Britain', in K. Kobayishi and H. Morikawa (eds), *Development of Managerial Enterprise: Proceedings of the Fuji Conference* (International Conference on Business History 12), Tokyo, University of Tokyo Press, 1986, pp. 101–46.

Lee, C.H., *British Regional Employment Statistics, 1841–1971*, Cambridge, Cambridge University Press, 1979.

Leslie, T.C. Cliffe, *Essays in Political Economy* , 2nd edn, London, Longmans, Green & Co., 1879.

Lewis, J., *Women in England, 1870–1950: Sexual Division and Social Change*, Brighton, Harvester Press, 1984.

Lewis, W.A., *The Evolution of the International Economic Order*, Princeton, Princeton University Press, 1978.

Lim, G.S. and Valentine, T.J., 'Trading banks', in M.K. Lewis and R.H. Wallace (eds), *Australia's Financial Institutions and Markets*, South Melbourne, Longman Cheshire, 1985, pp. 15–63.

Linn, J.F., 'The costs of urbanization in developing countries', *Economic Development and Cultural Change*, 1982, 30, pp. 625–48.

Lipton, M., *Why Poor People Stay Poor: Urban Bias in World Development*, Cambridge, Mass., Harvard University Press, 1977.

Lucas, R.E. Jr., 'On the mechanics of economic development', *Journal of Monetary Economics*, January 1988, 22, pp. 3–22.

Macauley, S., 'Non-contractual relations in business', *American Sociological Review*, 1963, 28, pp. 55–70.

McCloskey, D.N, *Econometric History*, London, Macmillan Education, 1987.

——, 'Ancients and moderns', *Social Science History*, Fall 1990, 14, 3, pp. 289–303.

McEvedy, C. and Jones, R., *Atlas of World Population History*, Harmondsworth, Penguin Books, 1978.

McGee, T.G., *The Southeast Asian City: A Social Geography of the Primate Cities of Southeast Asia*, New York, Frederick A. Praeger, 1967.

McKendrick, N. and Outhwaite, R.B. (eds), *Businessmen and Public Policy: Essays in Honour of D.C. Coleman*, Cambridge, Cambridge University Press, 1986.

Maddison, A., 'Per capita output in the long-run', *Kyklos*, 1979, 32, pp. 412–29.

Mannari, H., *The Japanese Business Leaders*, Tokyo, University of Tokyo Press, 1974.

Marshall, A., 'A reply', *Economic Journal*, 1892, 2, pp. 507–19.

Marshall, A., *Principles of Economics*, London, Macmillan, 1890; 4th edn, 1898.

Masui, Y., 'The supply price of labor: farm family workers', in K. Ohkawa, B.F. Johnston and H. Kaneda (eds), *Agriculture and Economic Growth: Japan's Experience*, Princeton, Princeton University Press, 1970, pp. 222–49.

Matthews, R.C.O. and Supple, B., 'Marshall on economic history', unpublished paper.

Mazumdar, D., 'Labour supply in early industrialisation: the case of the Bombay textile industry', *Economic History Review*, 1973, 26, pp. 477–96.

Meade, J.E. and Hahn, F.H., 'The rate of profit in a growing economy', *Economic Journal*, June 1966, 75, pp. 445–48.

Meier, G.M., *Leading Issues in Economic Development*, New York, Oxford University Press, 1989.

Merrett, D., 'The 1893 bank crashes: a reconsideration', seminar paper, Department of Economic History, RSSS, ANU, 1987.

Milbourne, R. and Cumberworth, M., 'Australian banking performance in an era of deregulation: an untold story?' School of Economics, University of New South Wales, 1990, mimeo.

Minami, R., 'The supply of farm labor and the "turning point" in the Japanese economy', in K. Ohkawa, B.F. Johnson and H. Kaneda (eds), *Agriculture and Economic Growth: Japan's Experience*, Princeton, Princeton University Press, 1970, pp. 270–99.

Mitchell, B.R., *European Historical Statistics, 1750–1970*, New York, Columbia University Press, 1975.

Modigliani, F. and Samuelson, P.A., 'The Pasinetti Paradox in neo-classical and more general models', *Review of Economic Studies*, 1966, 33, pp. 269–301.

Mokyr, J., 'The Industrial Revolution and the new economic history', in J. Mokyr (ed,), *The Economics of the Industrial Revolution*, Amsterdam, North-Holland, 1985, pp. 1–51.

——, 'Evolutionary biology, technological change, and economic history', seminar paper presented to the Economic History Joint Seminar Program, 23 July 1990, Australian National University, Canberra.

Morgan, M.S., 'The stamping out of process analysis in econometrics', unpublished paper, Department of Economic History, London School of Economics, n.d.

——, *The History of Econometric Ideas* , Cambridge: Cambridge University Press, 1990.

Morishima, M., *Equilibrium Stability and Growth*, Oxford, Clarendon Press, 1964.

Newell, A. and Symons, J.S.V., 'The macroeconomics of the interwar years: international comparisons', in B. Eichengreen and T.J. Hatton (eds), *Interwar Unemployment in International Perspective*, Dordrecht, Kluwer, 1988, pp. 61–96.

Newman, P.W.G. and Kenworthy, J.R., *Cities and Automobile Dependence: A Sourcebook*, Aldershot, Gower, 1989.

Nicholas, S., 'Agency contracts, institutional modes, and the transition to foreign direct investment by British manufacturing multinationals before 1939', *Journal of Economic History*, September 1983, 43, 3, pp. 675–86.

——, 'Locational choice, performance and the growth of British multinational firms', *Business History*, July 1989, 31, 3, pp. 122–41.

——, 'Debating business history: location, performance and the growth of British MNEs', *Business History*, January 1991, 33, 1, pp. 116–20.

——, 'The expansion of British multinational companies: testing for managerial failure', in J. Foreman-Peck (ed.), *New Perspectives on the Late Victorian Economy: Essays in Quantitative Economic History*, Cambridge, Cambridge University Press, 1991, pp. 125–45.

North, D., 'Institutions', *Journal of Economic Perspectives*, Winter 1991, 5, 1, pp. 97–112.

—— and Thomas, R.P., *The Rise of the Western World*, Cambridge, Cambridge University Press, 1973.

Offer, A., 'Using the past in Britain: Retrospect and prospect', *The Public Historian*, Fall 1984, 6, 4, pp. 15–34.

Office of EPAC, *Exchange Rate Policy* (Background Paper no. 9), Canberra, AGPS, 1991.

Olson, M., *The Rise and Decline of Nations: Economic Growth, Stagflation, and Social Rigidities*, New Haven, Yale University Press, 1982.

Organisation for Economic Co-operation and Development, *Ageing Populations: The Social Policy Implications*, Paris, OECD, 1988.

Osborn, H.F., *From the Greeks to Darwin*, 2nd edn, New York, Scribner, 1929.

Palgrave, R.H.I. (ed.), *Dictionary of Political Economy*, 3 vols, London, Macmillan, 1894, 1896 and 1899.

Parker, S., *Older Workers and Retirement: An Enquiry Carried Out on Behalf of the Department of Health and Social Security*, London, HMSO, 1980.

Pasinetti, L.L., 'Rate of profit and income distribution in relation to the rate of economic growth', *Review of Economic Studies*, 1962, 29, pp. 267–79.

Peltonen, M., 'Agrarian world market and Finnish farm economy', *Scandinavian Economic History Review*, 1988, 36, pp. 26–45.

Phelps Brown, E.H., *A Century of Pay*, London, Macmillan, 1968.

Piachaud, D., 'Disability, retirement and unemployment of older men', *Journal of Social Policy*, 1986, 15, pp. 145–62.

Pigou, A.C., 'Empty economic boxes: a reply', *Economic Journal*, December 1922, 32, pp. 458–65.

Political and Economic Planning, *Graduate Employment: A Sample Survey September, 1956*, London, Allen & Unwin, 1956.

Poole, R.L., *The Exchequer in the Twelfth Century*, Oxford, Clarendon Press, 1912.

Pope, D., 'Free banking in Australia before World War I', *Working Papers in Economic History* no. 129, Canberra, Australian National University, December 1989.

Portes, A., 'Latin American urbanization during the years of the crisis', *Latin American Research Review*, 1989, 24, 3, pp. 7–44.

Prebble, M., *Information, Privacy and the Welfare State*, Wellington, Institute of Policy Studies, 1990.

Preston, S.H., 'Urban growth in developing countries: a demographic reappraisal', in J. Gugler (ed.), *The Urbanization of the Third World*, Oxford, Oxford University Press, 1988, pp. 11–31.

—— and Van de Walle, E., 'Urban French mortality in the nineteenth century', *Population Studies*, 1975, 32, pp. 275–97.

Prigogine, I., *From Being to Becoming: Time and Complexity in the Physical Sciences*, New York, W.H. Freeman, 1980.

—— and Stengers, I., *Order Out of Chaos*, Boulder, New Science Library, 1984.

Pryor, E.G., *Housing in Hong Kong*, 2nd edn, Hong Kong, Oxford University Press, 1983.

Quadagno, J.S., *Aging in Early Industrial Society: Work, Family, and Social Policy in Nineteenth-century England*, New York, Academic Press, 1982.

Quinn, J. and Burkhauser, R., 'Work and retirement', in R.H. Binstock and L.K. George (eds), *Handbook of Aging and the Social Sciences*, 3rd edn, New York, Academic Press, 1990, pp. 318–30.

Rabel, R.G., 'The world turned upside down? Change and continuity in New Zealand politics in the postwar era', in R.W. Baker (ed.), *Australia, New Zealand, and the United States: Internal Change and Alliance Relations in the ANZUS States*, New York/Westport, Praeger, 1991, pp. 89–108.

Ramos, C.P., 'Manila's metropolitan problem', *Philippine Journal of Public Administration*, April 1961, 5, 2, pp. 89–117.

Ransom, R. and Sutch, R., 'Labor of older Americans: retirement of men on and off the job, 1870–1937', *Journal of Economic History*, 1986, 46, pp. 1–30.

—— and Sutch, R., 'Two strategies for a more secure old age: life-cycle saving by late-nineteenth century American workers', *University of California, History of Saving Project Working Paper*, March 1989.

Reid, M.G., 'Comment' [on N. Koffsky, 'Farm and urban purchasing power', q.v.], *Studies in Income and Wealth*, vol. 11, New York, NBER, 1946, pp. 179–206.

Revell, J.R.S., *Costs and Margins in Banking: An International Survey*, Paris, OECD, 1980.

Richards, E., 'Women in the British economy since about 1700: an interpretation', *History*, 1974, 59, pp. 337–57.

Richardson, G.B., 'The organisation of industry', *Economic Journal*, 1972, 82, pp. 883–96.

Riley, J.C., *Sickness, Recovery and Death*, London, Macmillan, 1989.

——, 'Working health time: a comparison of preindustrial, industrial and postindustrial experience in life and health', *Explorations in Economic History*, 1991, 28, pp. 169–91.

Robinson, J.V., *Collected Economic Papers*, Oxford, Basil Blackwell, 1965.

Romer, P.M., 'Increasing returns and long-run growth', *Journal of Political Economy*, 1986, 94, pp. 1002–37.

Rosenbloom, J.L., 'One market or many? Labor market integration in the late nineteenth century United States', *Journal of Economic History*, 1990, 50, pp. 85–107.

Rostow, W.W., *The Stages of Economic Growth*, Cambridge, Cambridge University Press, 1963.

Rothschild, M. and Stiglitz, J.E., 'Increasing risk I: a definition', *Journal of Economic Theory*, September 1970, 2, 3, pp. 225–43.

——, 'Increasing risk II: its economic consequences', *Journal of Economic Theory*, 1971, 3, 1, pp. 66–84.

Rubinstein, W.D., 'Education and the social origins of British élites, 1880–1970', *Past and Present*, August 1986, 112, pp. 163–207.

——, 'Social class, social attitudes and British business life', *Oxford Review of Economic Policy*, Spring 1988, 4, 1, pp. 51–8.

Sanderson, M., *The Universities and British Industry, 1850–1970*, London, Routledge & Kegan Paul, 1972.
Sanghvi, P., *Surplus Manpower in Agriculture and Economic Development*, London, Asia Publishing House, 1969.
Schedvin, C.B., 'The growth of bank regulation in Australia', paper presented to Joint Universities Conference, *Regulating Commercial Banks: Australian Experience in Perspective*, Canberra, Australian National University, 1989.
Schiffer, R.L., *The Exploding City*, New York, St Martin's Press, 1989.
Schumpeter, J.A., *The Theory of Economic Development: An Inquiry into Profits, Capital, Credit, Interest and the Business Cycle*, Cambridge, Mass., Harvard University Press, 1949.
——, *History of Economic Analysis*, London, Allen & Unwin, 1963.
Sheppard, D.K., *Growth and Role of UK Financial Institutions, 1880–1962*, London, Methuen, 1971.
Showers, V., *World Facts and Figures*, New York, John Wiley & Sons, 1979.
Sicsic, P., 'City-farm wage gaps in late nineteenth century France', Harvard University, unpublished paper, 1990.
Smith, Adam, *An Inquiry into the Nature and Causes of the Wealth of Nations* (edited by R.H. Campbell and A. S. Skinner; textual editor W.B. Todd), 2 vols, Oxford, Clarendon Press, 1976; first published 1776.
Snooks, G.D., 'The growth process of the firm: a case study', *Australian Economic Papers*, 1973, 12, pp. 162–74.
——, 'What should economists be told about the past?', *Australian Economic History Review*, September 1990, 32, 2, pp. 89–94.
——, *Economics Without Time: a Science Blind to the Forces of Historical Change*, London, Macmillan, 1992.
——, *Portrait of the Family within the Total Economy: A Study in Longrun Dynamics in Australia, 1788–1990*. Cambridge, Cambridge University Press, 1993.
——, *The Doomsday Debate: Ecologist Versus Economist*, forthcoming.
—— and McDonald, J., *Domesday Economy: A New Approach to Anglo-Norman History*, Oxford, Clarendon Press, 1986.
Solow, R.M., 'A contribution to the theory of economic growth', *Quarterly Journal of Economics*, February 1956, 70, pp. 65–94.
——, 'Substitution and fixed proportions in the theory of capital', *Review of Economic Studies*, 1962, 29, pp. 207–18.
——, *Capital Theory and the Rate of Return*, Amsterdam, North-Holland, 1963.
——, 'Economics: is something missing?', *American Economic Review*, May 1985, 75, 2, pp. 320–37; reprinted in W.N. Parker (ed.), *Economic History and the Modern Economist*, New York, Basil Blackwell, 1986, pp. 21–9.
——, 'Faith, hope, and clarity', in D.C. Colander and A.W. Coats (eds), *The Spread of Economic Ideas*, Cambridge/New York, Cambridge University Press, 1989, pp. 37–41.
Spender, J.A., *The State and Pensions in Old Age*, London, Swan Sonnenschein, 1894.
Squire, L., *Employment Policy in Developing Countries*, New York, Oxford University Press, 1981.
Stanworth, P. and Giddens, A., 'An economic elite: a demographic profile of company chairmen', in P. Stanworth and A. Giddens (eds), *Elites and Power in British Society*, Cambridge, Cambridge University Press, 1974, pp. 81–101.
Starr, K., *Material Dreams: Southern California through the 1920s*, New York, Oxford University Press, 1990.
Stein, D.L. (ed.), *Lectures in the Sciences of Complexity* (Santa Fe Institute Studies in the Sciences of Complexity, Lectures, vol. 1), Menlo Park, Calif., Addison-Wesley, 1989.

Steuart, J., *An Inquiry into the Principles of Political Economy*, (abbreviated) 2 vols (edited with an introduction by A.S. Skinner; Edinburgh) Oliver & Boyd for the Scottish Economic Society, 1966; first published 1767.

Stewart, Dugald, *The Collected Works of Dugald Stewart* (edited by Sir William Hamilton), 11 vols, Edinburgh, T. Constable, 1854–60; Farnborough, Gregg International Publishers, 1971.

Stigler, G.J., 'Palgrave's Dictionary of Economics', *Journal of Economic Literature*, December 1988, 26, pp. 1729–36.

Stone, L., *The Past and the Present Revisited*, London/New York, Routledge & Kegan Paul, 1987.

Swan, T.W., 'Economic growth and capital accumulation', *Economic Record*, November 1956, 32, pp. 334–61.

Sylla, R., 'The United States, 1863–1913', in R. Cameron (ed.), *Banking and Economic Development*, New York, Oxford University Press, 1972, pp. 232–62.

Takayama, A., 'On a two-sector model of economic growth: AS comparative statics analysis', *Review of Economic Studies*, 1963, 36, pp. 95–104.

Tannen, M.B., 'Labor markets in Brazil: does the dual market model apply?', *Economic Development and Cultural Change*, 1991, 39, pp. 567–83.

Taylor, O.H. 'Economics and the idea of natural law', in *Economics and Liberalism: Collected Papers*, Cambridge, Mass., Harvard University Press, 1955, pp. 37–69.

Teece, D.J., 'Technology transfer by multinational firms: the resource cost of transferring technological know-how', *Economic Journal*, June 1977, 87, pp. 242–61.

Teggart, F.J., *Theory of History*, New Haven, Yale University Press, 1925.

Thomas, B., *Migration and Urban Development*, London, Methuen, 1972.

Thomson, D.W., 'Provision for the elderly in England, 1830–1908', PhD thesis, University of Cambridge, October 1980.

Tilly, L.A. and Scott, J.W., *Women, Work and Family*, New York, Holt, Rinehart & Winston, 1978.

Tobin, J., 'Comment on Borch and Feldstein', *Review of Economic Studies*, January 1969, 36, pp. 13–14.

Todaro, M.P., 'A model of labor migration and urban unemployment in less developed countries', *American Economic Review*, March 1969, 59, 1, pp. 138–48.

——, *Internal Migration in Developing Countries: A Review of Theory, Evidence, Methodology and Research Priorities*, Geneva, International Labour Office, 1976.

Tracy, M., *Government and Agriculture in Western Europe*, 3rd edn, London, Harvester Wheatsheaf, 1989.

United Nations, *Estimates and Projections of Urban, Rural and City Populations, 1950–2025: The 1982 Assessment*, New York, United Nations, 1985.

United States, Department of Agriculture, Bureau of Agricultural Economics, *Wage Rates, Farm Employment and Related Data*, Washington, GPO, 1943.

Universities Central Council on Admissions, *Annual Reports*, 1968/9–87/8, *Statistical Supplements.*

Uzawa, H., 'On a two-sector model of economic growth', *Review of Economic Studies*, 1961, 24, pp. 40–7.

—— 'Optimum technical change in an aggregative model of economic growth', *International Economic Review*, January 1965, 6, pp. 18–33.

Valentine, T.J., 'Why the Australian banking system was deregulated', paper presented to Joint Universities Conference, *Regulating Commercial Banks: Australian Experience in Perspective*, Canberra, Australian National University, 1989.

—— and Williamson, P.J., 'A note on economies of scale in Australian banking', in Committee of Inquiry into the Australian Financial System, *Commissioned Studies and Selected Papers*, part 1, Canberra, AGPS, 1982, pp. 703–9.

Warner, W.L. and Abegglen, J.C., *Occupational Mobility in American Business and Industry, 1928–1952*, Minneapolis, University of Minnesota Press, 1955.
Warriner, D., *The Economics of Peasant Farming*, 2nd edn, London, Frank Cass, 1964.
Wiener, Martin J., *English Culture and the Decline of the Industrial Spirit, 1850–1980*, Cambridge, Cambridge University Press, 1981.
Williams, L., 'Asian alert: on the economic road to environmental ruin', *The Age, Good Weekend*, 12 May 1990, pp. 14–8.
Williamson, J.G., 'Urban disamenities, dark satanic mills, and the British standard of living debate', *Journal of Economic History*, 1981, 41, pp. 75–83.
——, 'The structure of pay in Britain, 1710–1911', *Research in Economic History*, 1982a, 7, pp. 1–54.
——, 'Was the Industrial Revolution worth it? Disamenities and death in 19th century British towns', *Explorations in Economic History*, 1982b, 19, pp. 221–45.
——, 'Did English factor markets fail during the Industrial Revolution?', *Oxford Economic Papers*, 1987, 39, pp. 641–78.
——, *Coping with City Growth during the British Industrial Revolution*, Cambridge, Cambridge University Press, 1990.
——, 'Migrant earnings in Britain's cities in 1951: testing competing views of urban labor market absorption', *Journal of European Economic History*, 1990, 19, pp. 163–90.
——, 'The evolution of global labor markets in the First and Second World since 1830: background evidence and hypotheses', Harvard University, unpublished paper, 1991.
—— and Lindert, P.H., *American Inequality: A Macroeconomic History*, New York, Academic Press, 1980.
Williamson, O., *Markets and Hierarchies: Analysis and Antitrust Implications*, New York, Free Press, 1975.
——, 'The modern corporation: origins, evolution, attributes', *Journal of Economic Literature*, 1981, 19, pp. 1537–68.
——, *The Economic Institutions of Capitalism*, New York, Free Press, 1985.
Willig, R.D., 'Multiproduct technology and market structure', *American Economic Review*, May 1979, 69, 2, pp. 346–51.
Wilson, A.T. and Mackay, G.S., *Old Age Pensions: An Historical and Critical Study*, London, Oxford University Press, 1941.
Wilson, M., *Labour in Government, 1984–1987*, Wellington, Allen & Unwin/Port Nicholson Press, 1989.
Yasuba, Y., 'The Japanese economy and economic policy in the 1930s', in R.G. Gregory and N.G. Butlin (eds), *Recovery from the Depression: Australia and the World Economy in the 1930s*, Cambridge, Cambridge University Press, 1988, pp. 136–47.
Young, H., *One of Us: A Biography of Margaret Thatcher*, London, Macmillan, 1989.

INDEX